MODERATORS
OF
COMPETENCE

The Jean Piaget Symposium Series
Available from LEA

SIGEL I. E., BRODZINSKY, D. M., & GOLINKOFF, R. M. (Eds.) • New Directions in Piagetian Theory and Practice

OVERTON, W. F. (Ed.) • Relationships Between Social and Cognitive Development

LIBEN, L. S. (Ed.) • Piaget and the Foundations of Knowledge

SCHOLNICK, E. K. (Ed.) • New Trends in Conceptual Representation: Challenges to Piaget's Theory?

NEIMARK, E. D., De LISI, R., & NEWMAN, J. L. (Eds.) • Moderators of Competence

MODERATORS
OF
COMPETENCE

Edited by

Edith D. Neimark
Richard De Lisi
Rutgers—The State University of New Jersey

Judith L. Newman
The Pennsylvania State University—Ogontz Campus

LEA LAWRENCE ERLBAUM ASSOCIATES, PUBLISHERS
1985 Hillsdale, New Jersey   London

Lawrence Erlbaum Associates, Inc., Publishers
365 Broadway
Hillsdale, New Jersey 07642

Library of Congress Cataloging in Publication Data
Main entry under title:

Moderators of competence.

(The Jean Piaget Symposium series)
Includes bibliographies and indexes.
1. Ability—Congresses. 2. Performance—Congresses.
3. Cognition and culture—Congresses. 4. Cognitive
styles—Congresses. 5. Piaget, Jean, 1896-
—Congresses. I. Neimark, Edith D. II. De Lisi, Richard,
III. Newman, Judith. IV. Series.
BF431.M559 1985 153 85-1649
ISBN 0-89859-531-2

Printed in the United States of America
10 9 8 7 6 5 4 3 2 1

Contents

Dedicated to the memory of
Charles D. Smock
(1924–1982)

Preface

The initial planning for the Twelfth Annual Symposium of the Jean Piaget Society began, as had its predecessors, with the selection of a theme. As also was true of its predecessors, the theme focused on an aspect of Piagetian theory, in this instance, its applicability to subject samples very different from those serving as the data base of the original theory. Each participant in his or her letter of invitation was directed: Our theme, Moderators of Competence, "has arisen from recognition that Piagetian theory is fundamentally a competence theory that does not address itself to how competence is translated into performance. Thus, the theory provides no direct basis for the prediction of performance by particular individuals in particular settings. The purpose of the symposium is to consider how the expression of competence may be moderated by several broadly defined classes of variables including intelligence, formal education, cultural features, individual differences in cognitive style, and specific cognitive processes and their organization."

Implicit in those instructions is a belief that a comprehensive theory of intellectual development — or of any psychological process — is both attainable and desirable and that levels of abstraction from observables must be distinguished in constructing such a theory. The very choice of the title, *Moderators of Competence,* reflected our belief that Piagetian theory provides the best available approximation to a comprehensive theory of intellectual development but one that applies only at a higher level of abstraction, i.e., with respect to basic competence. Accumulating "disconfirming" evidence seemed to arise largely when Piagetian tasks were administered to subject samples very different from middle-class school children in Western societies. The apparent disconfirmations might, therefore, be interpreted not as evidence that the theory was not universally applicable but, rather, that additional factors were involved in translating competence into performance. Such factors could be viewed as moderators of competence—hence the title. This view leads to a belief that what is needed is not a new theory but a theory at a lower level of abstraction, a theory of performance and its proximal determinants. We expected the invited contributions to provide an advance toward that goal. The rationale for these expectations is elaborated in the first chapter.

As it turned out, the initial expectations were not borne out for a variety of reasons. First, not all participants shared the belief that the competence-performance distinction is useful or even meaningful. Telling arguments against invocation of a competence concept are offered by Goodnow and Cashmore, by Lefebvre-Pinard and Pinard, and by Spitz. To some extent rejection of the differentiation may reflect preferences in choice of a meta-theory, a subject explored in careful detail by Overton. Even where the differentiation of competence from performance is enthusiastically endorsed, as it is by Davidson and Sternberg, their definition of competence is not in full accord with use of the term by other contemporary investigators. Yet a third obstacle to attainment of the initial goal is illustrated in Brodzinsky's chapter: He deals with evidence that cognitive style, a hypothesized moderator of competence, may affect competence as well as performance. Although other interpretations of the evidence are possible, as Kogan notes, it is still the case that the initial goal of this volume has not been realized and, perhaps, is unattainable.

Where does that leave us? It leaves us with an accurate reflection of current ferment in the field of cognitive development. Although the present volume does not single-mindedly focus upon challenges to the universal applicability of Piagetian theory, or neatly resolve those challenges as performance factor moderations of competence, it does raise important issues, and explore interesting alternative frameworks that will direct future research. Perhaps that is a better resolution than the planners of the Symposium had dared hope for.

Edith Neimark

BACKGROUND ISSUES

1 Moderators of Competence: Challenges to the Universality of Piagetian Theory

Edith D. Neimark
Rutgers University

This is not the first annual Symposium of the Jean Piaget Society to be addressed to challenges to Piagetian theory, nor will it be the last. A good theory should draw challenges like a lightning rod and, in the process of meeting them, advance the understanding of behavior. For a long while Piaget's theory offered the only description of cognitive development which attempted a general comprehensive description of the growth of understanding from infancy to adulthood. In elaborating it, Piaget (Bringuier, 1980) was explicit that he sought universal principles accounting for the underlying structure of intellectual development rather than a detailed description of the effects of all possible variables in all possible tasks. To the extent that subsequent investigators did not share this goal, it was inevitable that they should consider different kinds of behavior and classes of variables that had not been considered by Piaget and his collaborators. This process of pushing the boundaries of the theory has led to the discovery that concepts, especially for stage-related aspects of the theory, become fuzzy as one gets further away from focal instances. Although it is too early to foresee the result of challenges to the universality of stage theory, it is already clear that they give rise to serious questions that must be addressed.

This chapter attempts to provide a context for consideration of some current challenges to the universality of Piagetian theory and, especially, for the chapters that follow. It begins by placing challenges to universality in a context of other challenges to the theory. One major device for dealing with challenges to universality was the differentiation of competence from performance. That differentiation is considered before moving on to a consideration of domains of knowledge and of the groups of variables whose effects give rise to the most serious challenges to universality. The chapter concludes with some speculation about the direction of future research.

OVERVIEW OF PREVIOUS CHALLENGES

Piaget's genetic epistemology has been accepted grudgingly, if at all, by American psychologists from the beginning, but the focus of dissatisfaction has shifted over the years along what might be described as a data-theory-metatheory continuum. Although the challenge to universality is most directly related to the theory per se, responses to it have had important effects upon all levels of the continuum.

The earliest focus of criticism was an incredulity about the data. Could it be possible that young children actually believed that by spreading out a row of candies one increased their number relative to a comparison row of equivalent numerosity? Surely there must be some artifact of the clinical method that incited such apparent irrationality. That reaction led to a great many replication studies and procedural variations, initially centered upon conservation tasks, with larger numbers of subjects and more "objective" methodology. It was a worthwhile endeavor. As a result of it there is no longer any reasonable doubt that the data are robust and awesomely replicable. Conservation, seriation, and the object concept, to cite but a few of the more popular mysterious phenomena, are indeed real as well as universal, at least for the early stages of development.

Having established that the data were reliable, the next focus of challenge was addressed to the central tenets of the theory which Piaget was elaborating in more formal fashion. The concept of developmental stages differing with respect to qualitative features of their organizing structure proved especially uncongenial to many investigators. Most preferred to believe that development takes the form of continuous change, heavily influenced by learning from environmentally based experience, rather than saltatory shifts resulting from the child's own assimilatory efforts with respect to those experiences. The challenges arising from this opposing view took a variety of forms. Some attempted to show that the attainments characterizing later stages were present far earlier (e.g., Cohen & Younger, 1983, for classification or Gelman & Gallistel, 1978, for number). Others attempted to show that stage-related constructions were amenable to direct tuition (cf. Beilin, 1977). A third avenue of attack strove to show that purported structures did not have the requisite structural properties (e.g., Brainerd, 1977).

Investigations of the last formulated and least studied final stage of formal operations (cf. Neimark, 1975, 1982) gave rise to a host of questions; even adolescents and adults in Western cultures failed to evidence formal operations on the Genevan tasks. Challenge to the universality of formal operations became even more inescapable with testing of populations differing more widely from the original data base of Genevan adolescents: other cultures (cf. Dasen, 1977; Werner, 1979); extremes of intellectual ability (Webb, 1974; Weisz & Zigler, 1979); and individuals differing in exposure to formal schooling (Rogoff, 1981). These data all showed the final stage of formal operations to be rarely attained. Taken at face value the data appeared to show that the final stage is not universally attained. There are, of course, alternative interpretations. Piaget (1972) suggested three of them: that rate of development may be slowed by other factors; that aptitudes undergo diversification with age; or that the final stage is attained in areas consonant with aptitude and professional specialization. He preferred the third interpretation, which, in effect, proposes the operation of moderating variables. Such explanations, by assigning to some variables the role of general determinants and to others the role of moderators, direct attention to the metatheory, an area of consideration that was quick to emerge.

One attack on the stage concept itself (Brainerd, 1978) brought forth a number of rejoinders noting that one source of denial of the legitimacy of stages derived from adherence to a different canon of theory construction. Two contending positions were identified (Overton & Reese, 1981), the organismic and the mechanistic. Overton's chapter in this volume provides additional clarification of the two metatheoretic approaches and their implications for a theory of cognitive development. Recently a third position that seems to deny that any universal theory is attainable — even in principle — has emerged from the metatheoretic fray (LCHC, 1983; Rogoff, 1982). This view proposes a multiplicity of context-tied theories. It appears to assert that not only observed behaviors but also the explanatory principles invoked to account for them are determined by the specific context of occurrence. In essence, search for a theory of cognitive development is replaced by description of contexts of behavior, which in turn, leads to search for a theory of contexts or, at least, a taxonomy of them.

In the course of a shift from challenges to Piagetian data to challenges to stage theory — its universality, adequacy qua theory, and metatheoretical underpinnings — related issues are emerging with respect to the areas of understanding to be investigated. Before turning to those issues, it should be noted that some theoretical convergence has also emerged. The developing child is no longer viewed by any major investigator, of whatever theoretical persuasion, as the passive product of environmental influences. Piaget's view that the child creates his or her own understanding (through processes of assimilation and accommodation) seems now to be widely accepted, if not explicitly acknowledged, by all developmental theorists.

COMPETENCE AND PERFORMANCE

The preceding discussion introduced a differentiation of competence from performance as one mechanism for dealing with the universality of Piagetian stage theory. Before embarking on a detailed examination of the competence-performance distinction, it is useful to note that psychologists have generally invoked some form of differentiation of levels of accessibility of behavior to direct examination. From a historical standpoint, the early differentiation of levels of accessibility was couched in terms of accessibility of the determinants of behavior (usually thought) *to the behaving individual.* Herbart, Freud, and Wm. James, to name but a few of our eminent ancestors, distinguished levels of consciousness ranging from explicit awareness in the forefront of consciousness to inaccessibility by reason of repression. Interest in levels of conscious awareness of the determinants of behavior appears to be returning to fashion with the current vogue for studies of metacognition. Metacognition, however, is not the old levels of consciousness in a new guise. Motivation is no longer treated as a major determinant of level, and at least two component avenues for the manifestation of awareness are identified. The term *metacognition* refers both to degree of deliberate (executive) control over one's own thought and behavior and to knowledge about one's cognitive processes and their mode of operation (Campione, Brown, & Ferrara, 1982). Current investigators differ in the relative weighting assigned to the two components. Cavanaugh and Perlmutter (1982) in their review of metamemory emphasize the second component; Lefebvre-Pinard and Pinard (this volume) focus upon the first (as does Piaget, 1976, 1978); Sternberg and Davidson (this volume) deal with both.

With the advent of behaviorism, consciousness and other mentalistic concepts were purged from the vocabulary of American psychologists, and levels of accessibility of the deteminants of behavior underwent a shift in application (to the area of learning) as well as a translation of terms. Hull (1952) introduced the concept of habit family hierarchy to identify alternative possible responses differing with respect to their likelihood of occurrence. In predicting which response would occur, Hull differentiated two measures of response probability that differed with respect to their controlling determinants. Habit strength, the measure of major theoretical interest, was a hypothetical condition (a formal quantity of the theory) determined largely by reinforcement history but accessible only through inference from measures of excitatory potential. Excitatory potential was more directly related to performance and influenced by a variety of situational and motivational conditions. To some extent, Hull's differentiation of habit strength from excitatory potential could be viewed as an intellectual forerunner of today's competence performance distinction: Habit strength was a measure of competence (pure learning), whereas excitatory potential was a measure of performance.

The subtle shift from accessible to the behaving individual to accessible to observation and prediction by the psychological theorist is reflected in today's competence-performance differentiation. Today's distinction traces to an important paper by Flavell and Wohlwill (1969) who borrowed from Chomsky the differentiation of competence, the formal rules of grammar characterizing an individual's knowledge of the structure of language, and automation, its translation into use. Their translation was couched in terms of formal and functional aspects: "The competence model gives an abstract, purely logical representation of what the organism knows or could do in a timeless, ideal environment, whereas the automaton model has the job of describing a real device that could plausibly instance that knowledge or skill, and instance it within the constraints (memory limitations, rapid performance, etc.) under which human beings actually operate." (Flavell & Wohlwill, 1969, p. 71). It is instructive to review the fate of the competence/performance distinction since that 1969 paper. There has been, it seems to me, subtle variation in the interpretation of competence.

Despite variations in interpretation of the term *competence* there remains a core of agreement on two central assumptions: (a) that performance is more directly related to observed behavior whereas competence is an inferred determinant; (b) each is the product of a different set of controlling variables and principles describing the effect of those variables, i.e., in the mind of the theorist they are different phenomena. The next logical step in elaboration of the competence/performance distinction should, therefore, be formulation of a performance model and a competence model where each model spells out the controlling variables and the nature of their effects. Surprisingly, there have been relatively few systematic attempts in this direction. A major exception is the Neo-Piagetian modeling of Pascual-Leone (1980) and his students (Case, 1978). The Pascual-Leone model is a performance model counterpart of the competence model proposed by Piaget. It introduces seven "silent operators" responsible for determination of H, the momentary state of habitual schemes (where habitual schemes are of three types: figurative, transformational, and executive). The seven silent operators are:

M, the number of schemes that can be simultaneously activated.
C, specific content knowledge.
L, procedural learning.
F, Field factors and stimulus salience.
A, Affective and motivational factors.
B, Biases and beliefs.
I, Inhibitory factors.

The first three are competence factors, whereas the last four are performance factors. Sternberg and Davidson (this volume) propose a different model, which overlaps Pascual-Leone's in some respects but differs in others. Their model constitutes a serious and valuable attempt to organize existing evidence collected under the aegis of a variety of different theories while, at the same time, preserving the spirit of the information processing analogy favored by most American developmentalists. But, in associating competence with the *availability* of processes, knowledge (both *L* and *C*), representational formats (figurative schemes), and the functional capacity of working memory (*M*), and linking performance to the *utilization*, it changes the interpretation of competence from the formal coloration given by Flavell and Wohlwill (or Piaget).

The formal-functional differentiation of Flavell and Wohlwill (1969) makes competence a purely theoretical idealization or formalization never directly available to investigation per se. Piaget's theory is clearly a competence theory in that sense of the term *competence*. The use of such formalisms has a long and honorable tradition in classical physics as well as in linguistics and in areas of psychology (e.g., Miller & Johnson-Laird, 1976, in the model of concept formation, or borrowings of game theory, artificial intelligence, etc.). Although the formal idealizations cannot be expected to provide a complete description of observed phenomena, they do have an important directing function in identifying central concepts and the variables to be associated with them. To the extent, however, that one is primarily concerned with description of observed phenomena as an end in itself, it is possible to become impatient with indirect, formal means to that end and to adopt a more direct empirical approach. Such reasoning appears to be the meta-theoretical basis for many criticisms of competence models. Stone and Day (1980), for example, propose the use of Vygotsky's (1978) concept of zone of proximal development as a more empirical alternative to a formal notion of competence. By defining competence in terms of availability, Sternberg and Davidson (this volume) seem to me to be shifting the idealization from the head of the theorist to the head of the subject. In so doing they offer a compromise position that preserves the utility of the competence concept while, at the same time, according it a status closer to reality.

Yet a third interpretation of competence, intermediate in level of abstraction between the two just described, is derivable from a statistical analogy. In this interpretation competence would refer to the role of fundamental processes accounting for a significant proportion of performance variance on related tasks for all individuals in all contexts. The more context-tied and state-related variables and processes accounting for residual variance, on the other hand, would be associated with the utilization of competence in performance. For example, all counting tasks, regardless of material, level of difficulty, or conditions of administration, presumably require a counting skill and should be more similar to each other with respect to performance characteristics than to a variety of tasks such as classification and seriation. To the extent that expectation is supported by evidence, one is justified in invoking some underlying common competence. Although I know of no developmental theorist who explicitly espouses this interpretation of competence, it appears to be a tenable interpretation and one that is both theoretically neutral and methodologically useful.

As noted earlier, the use of a competence/performance distinction provides a means for defending the universality of Piagetian theory (Overton & Newman, 1982). Within that general framework, apparently discrepant evidence is attributable to the effect of performance factors militating against manifestation of competence. However, if the use of a competence/performance distinction, whatever interpretation is placed upon competence, is to be more than an explanatory dodge, important changes in experimental procedures are required. It is necessary to use more than one task and a variety of response measures as well as systematic variation of stimulus and motivational conditions in order to differentiate presumed competence from performance variation resulting from procedural variation. At present little research evidence adequately satisfies this requirement. Until it is met, challenges to the universality of Piaget's, or anyone else's, competence theory cannot be satisfactorily resolved. Before going on to consider challenges to the universality of Piagetian stage theory in light of this caveat about invocation of a competence/performance distinction, it is necessary to consider some questions about the choice of an appropriate dependent variable in a bit more detail.

WHAT IS THE BEHAVIOR TO BE EXPLAINED?

Over the course of a long and incredibly productive career Piaget examined many aspects of children's behavior, increasingly focusing upon the growth of understanding in two domains: logico-mathematical knowledge and physical knowledge. Of the two domains, logico-mathematical knowledge posed the more challenging problem because it transcends direct experience and must be constructed through a process of reflective abstraction. The course of construction of logico-mathematical knowledge was described in terms of progressive restructurings, which could be characterized as stages. Each stage had a unique organizing structure and there was an inherent logic to the structures independent of specific details of content. It was reasonable to expect that this theoretical characterization should be universally applicable because the world is the way it is; there is order and regularity in the universe that is independent of the individual's experience of it. Similarly, there is an inescapable quality to logical necessity or to the impossibility of logical contradition. Thus, to describe the evolution of physical knowledge and of logico-mathematical knowledge it is possible to adopt a convenient fiction of the child as independent or, even, ruggedly individualistic investigator. Serious problems would be expected to arise, however, in extrapolating stage theory beyond the knowledge domains upon which, and for which, it was formulated. Those expected difficulties do, in fact, arise when one attempts to apply the principles of physical or logico-mathematical cognition to social cognition (cf. Damon, 1983; Schantz, 1983; Turiel, 1983; or Glick, this volume; Goodnow & Cashmore, this volume).

Two related issues arise in that extrapolative enterprise, one dealing with the social development of cognition and the other with the development of social knowledge. The latter has to do with knowledge as an end product or dependent variable, the former with the conditions of its acquisition. Recent investigators have gone in both directions. That humans are social animals who develop in a world of other people cannot be denied; Vygotsky's (1978) emphasis on the importance of social influences upon cognitive development is increasingly heeded. Similarly, there is increasing awareness that much of the requisite understanding constructed during the course of cognitive development concerns behavior of other people and relations among them. The purpose of this section is not to utter platitudes but reinforce Glick's (this volume) warning that Piaget's theory for relatively limited knowledge domains—central as they may be—to different knowledge domains is not justified. A theory asserting to be universal for a limited domain need not be universally applicable across domains. Social beliefs, values, and conventions are not only context tied but also culture specific (not only for the group as a whole but also for subgroups within a culture). That being the case, it is unreasonable to expect any structural theory to be applicable to a domain so intrinsically related to content. To the extent that one wants to study different phenomena such as understanding of the self or of society and social rules of conduct, it may be more useful in the long run to construct theories for those phenomena and later examine correspondences among theories for different domains.

PERFORMANCE MODERATOR OR DETERMINANT OF COMPETENCE?

We return to the issue raised earlier: challenges to the universality of Piagetian stage theory arising from data on the administration of Piagetian tasks to widely varying subject populations viewed within the framework of a competence-performance distinction. Can one conclude that effects associated with these population differences may be accounted for in terms of moderation of performance or is it necessary to conclude that competence itself is affected, or is it impossible to decide at the present time? Piaget identified four classes of variables determining competence: maturation, experience (both physical and logico-mathematical), social transmission, and equilibration. To the extent that the independent variables considered here belong in none of those classes, they pose legitimate challenges to the universality of stage theory. The factors selected for consideration have been divided into two partially overlapping categories. The first has to do with all the as-yet-unspecified factors making for differences among aggregates of people, cross-cultural factors. The second has to do with those factors contributing to differences among individuals, intelligence, and cognitive style.

Cross-Cultural Comparisons

There is mounting complaint that Piaget conceived his epistemic child as far too much of a rugged individualist and failed to give adequate consideration to the possible role of social factors in cognitive development. But how does one translate "social factors" into meaningful, researchable units? Goodnow and Cashmore (this volume) mount a searching attack upon that issue and, in so doing, identify many current active areas of investigation. They remind us that parents have "theories" about children and their capacities, how those capacities are to be developed, and time-tables for development. Some of those theories and expectations are culturally based. One implication of this framework is that psychologists themselves are members of a culture — the psychological research culture — with its own theories and expectations, and rules for translating them into research procedures. The warning is well taken. It leads to greater caution in interpretation of cross-cultural data. Perhaps it is inappropriate to treat Piagetian tasks as standardized tests of competence simply because a given task developed within culture A may be a different task in culture B. An understanding of the culture in its own terms is needed in order to devise "equivalent" tasks. That, in turn, leads to the quest for a theory of culture and how it may impact upon cognitive development. Many useful steps in that direction are being taken. Among them is a recognition that societal factors can no longer be treated as "address labels" (Bronfenbrenner & Crouter, 1983) but, rather, must be viewed within the context of researchable questions of the sort suggested by Goodnow and Cashmore (this volume) and by Glick (this volume). The result of such efforts is too far in the future for meaningful anticipation of its outcome, but it is likely to be more complicated than a simple performance moderator or competence determinant decision.

The role of formal schooling is another issue that could be raised within the context of cross-cultural comparisons, but it is unfortunately not included in the present volume. To the extent that what is taught in schools and how it is taught reflect institutionalization of a culture's values, expectations, and theories about capacities, it ought to be an especially valuable source of data. There is already much evidence showing differences in performance on cognitive tasks between schooled and unschooled individuals (e.g., Luria, 1976; Rogoff, 1981; Scribner & Cole, 1981) as well as speculation about what factors of schooling operate to produce the differences (Bruner, 1965; Sharp, Cole, & Lave, 1979). Although the magnitude of effects of schooling is reduced when the effect of other correlated factors such as measures of home influences are removed, the proportion of variance accounted for remains statistically significant (Stevenson, 1982). That there are developmental generalities within schooled children across cultures is also suggested by recent evidence (Stevenson et al., 1982). This suggests the possibility of some factor associated with schooling per se.

Individual Differences

If there is one factor that must pose a challenge to the universality of Piagetian stage theory it has to be individual differences, by definition. The problem is to break that huge umbrella term into meaningful components. One very obvious one is intelligence. Inhelder (1968), in her dissertation research with retarded children, concluded that they go through the same stages as normals but at a slower rate, failing ever to attain the final stage. Weisz and Zigler (1979) after reviewing subsequent evidence reach the same conclusion. It is not universally accepted. Spitz (1982) finds grounds for questioning whether the retarded even attain concrete operations. He argues that they continue to reason at a perceptual rather than a conceptual level and in his chapter in this volume presents evidence for a task in which that mode of responding protects them from the error of false conservation to which even bright adults appear prone.

At the other extreme of the intelligence continuum, among the precociously bright, there is less direct evidence and it is more difficult to interpet. Some early evidence (Lovell & Shields, 1967; Webb, 1974) did not find very bright 6- to 11-year-olds to be formal operational but there is other evidence (Case, 1974; Keating, 1975) showing formal operational performance in 8-year-olds, in the first study, and in bright fifth and seventh graders, in the second. Thus, there is no clear consistent evidence of more rapid rate of development through Piagetian stages among the very bright. Rather, what appears in the interpretation of a number of writers (e.g., Case, 1978; de Ribaupierre & Pascual-Leone, 1979) is speculation that something other than the g component of high intelligence makes for the superior performance of bright children. That "something" seems to include aspects of cognitive style and the repertoire of executive schemes. It also appears (Krutetskii, 1976) to have a motivational component: The gifted appear to enjoy intellectual challenge and actively seek to develop their skills.

Cognitive style is another big umbrella rubric for many poorly differentiated aspects of individual differences. Kogan (1983) in his awesomely comprehensive overview of research on cognitive styles concluded that perhaps that enterprise had peaked and was beginning to decline. In his review of Brodzinsky (this volume), however, he has had some second thoughts about his earlier conclusion.

Brodzinsky (this volume), on the basis of his own research and that of other investigators, proposes a model of the relation between cognitive styles and cognitive structures. It is a more complex relation than has heretofore been hypothesized. That there are differences in level and quality of performance by groups differing with respect to cognitive style (however defined) is now fairly well established. For the most part those differences have been interpreted as evidence that groups do not differ with respect to underlying competence but, rather, that the individual's characteristic style influences the activation of competence into performance (Overton & Newman, 1982). Brodzinsky argues that this simple explanation cannot be correct but that style must also affect the development of competence as well. To further complicate the picture, he notes a reciprocal effect: an effect of competence upon style. To the extent that his model derives from statistical analysis of data from a perspective-taking task, it is not clear how generally applicable it may be but it certainly opens new vistas for future research.

Certainly this is a preliminary attempt, and one fraught with conceptual problems outlined by both Kogan and Brodzinsky. One possible conclusion suggested by Kogan is that if structures and styles are so complexly interrelated there may be no need to treat them as identifiably different processes. Another point well taken is that future efforts should be directed toward better formulation of the concept of cognitive style with less reliance upon tests that happen to be available and more emphasis upon style properties that are needed to account for the data.

One likely property of cognitive style for deeper investigation was noted earlier in the discussion of the gifted child: the striving for mastery in the sense of deeper understanding. Pascual-Leone (1980) and Case (1978) deal with it as does Piaget (1976, 1978) in his discussion of how one brings practical knowledge and skill into consciousness for the purpose of formulating explicit "theories" to be applied in directing performance. Lefebvre-Pinard and Pinard (this volume) provide a stimulating discussion of it in their model for taking charge of a cognitive enterprise. Although they modestly call it a preliminary model, it provides a good start in the investigation of an important but neglected topic. Taking charge of the cognitive enterprise is one important dimension of the difference between novice and expert (or nascent expert). It well describes the gifted child and, perhaps, even the cognitively maturing child. That, in the best sense, is what cognitive growth is all about.

SUMMARY AND SPECULATIONS

This book deals with challenges to the universality of Piagetian theory; the present chapter tries to place them in perspective. The focus of challenges to Piagetian theory have changed over time. The challenges considered here arise from extending the theory beyond its original data base and its intended realm of application. When a theory employing a formal model for the structure of physical and logico-mathematical knowledge is applied to social knowledge and the conditions of its acquisition, where content is of greater import than structure, problems should, and do, arise. Similarly, when it is extended to members of other cultures, the unschooled, the extremes of the intelligence continuum, and to groups differing with respect to cognitive style, then universality is challenged. One means of responding to those challenges is to treat the effects associated with different subject populations as moderators of the utilization of competence in performance. The differentiation of competence from performance was considered from the standpoint of alternative interpretations of competence, two models of the relevant variables affecting each, and research procedures needed to make the distinction empirically meaningful. At present there is disagreement about the utility of the competence/performance distinction. Those shades of disagreement are reflected throughout this volume.

Sources of challenge to universality were considered in terms of social (cross-cultural and effects of schooling) and individual difference effects (intelligence and cognitive style). Piaget devoted little attention to the effects of social factors upon cognitive development. Many recent investigators, on the other hand, take them as the focus of primary concern. Although social factors are proving difficult to analyze into their constituent elements or to analyze in terms of effect, they promise to be an important and fruitful area of future research.

Effects of individual difference variations, although simpler to deal with experimentally, pose a more evident and direct challenge to the universality of Piagetian theory. If they are shown to affect the unfolding of competence, as some current evidence suggests, then they can no longer be dismissed simply as sources of performance variation. It is likely that future research, in going beyond the confines of traditional Piagetian theory with respect to both the independent and dependent variables considered, will lead to a proliferation of narrower theories before a new approximation to a comprehensive theory is attained. The future of research in cognitive development promises to be full of disagreements and excitement.

REFERENCES

Beilin, H. (1977). Inducing conservation through training. In G. Steiner (Ed.), *Psychology of the 20th century: Vol. 7. Piaget and beyond.* Zurich: Kinder.

Brainerd, C. J. (1977). Cognitive development and concept learning: An interpretive review. *Psychological Bulletin, 84*, 919–939.

Brainerd, C. J. (1978). The stage question in cognitive-developmental theory. *Behavioral and Brain Sciences, 2*, 173–213.

Bringuier, J. C. (1980). *Conversations with Jean Piaget.* Chicago: University of Chicago Press.

Bronfenbrenner, U., & Crouter, A. C. (1983). The evolution of environmental models in developmental research. In W. Kessen (Ed.), *Handbook of child psychology: Vol. 1. History, theory, and methods* (pp. 357–414). New York: Wiley.

Bruner, J. S. (1965). The growth of mind. *American Psychologist, 20*, 1007–1017.

Campione, J. C., Brown, A. L., & Ferrara, R. A. (1982). Mental retardation and intelligence. In R. J. Sternberg (Ed.), *Handbook of human intelligence* (pp. 392–490). Cambridge: Cambridge University Press.

Case, R. (1974). Structures and strictures: Some functional limitations on the course of cognitive growth. *Cognitive Psychology, 6*, 544–573.

Case, R. (1978). Intellectual development from birth to adulthood: A neo-Piagetian intepretation. In R. S. Siegler (Ed.), *Children's thinking: What develops?* (pp. 37–72). Hillsdale, NJ: Lawrence Erlbaum Associates.

Cavanaugh, J. C., & Perlmutter, M. (1982). Metamemory: A critical examination. *Child Development, 53*, 11–28.

Cohen, L. B., & Younger, B. A. (1983). Perceptual categorization in the infant. In E. K. Scholnick (Ed.), *New trends in conceptual representation: Challenges to Piaget's theory.* Hillsdale, NJ: Lawrence Erlbaum Associates.

Damon, W. (1983). The nature of social-cognitive change in the developing child. In W. F. Overton (Ed.), *The relationship between social and cognitive development* (pp. 103–142). Hillsdale, NJ: Lawrence Erlbaum Associates.

Dasen, P. R. (1977). Are cognitive processes universal? A contribution to cross-cultural Piagetian psychology. In N. Warren (Ed.), *Studies in cross-cultural psychology* (Vol. 1). London: Academic Press.

deRibaupierre, A., & Pascual-Leone, J. (1979). Formal operations and M power: A neo-Piagetian investigation. In D. Kuhn (Ed.), *Intellectual development beyond childhood* (pp. 1–44). San Francisco: Jossey-Bass.

Flavell, J., & Wohlwill, J. F. (1969). Formal and functional aspects of cognitive development. In D. Elkind & J. H. Flavell (Eds.), *Studies in cognitive development: Essays in honor of Jean Piaget.* New York: Oxford University Press.

Gelman, R., & Gallistel, C. R. (1978). *The child's understanding of number.* Cambridge, MA: Harvard University Press.

Hull, C. L. (1952). *Essentials of behavior.* New Haven: Yale University Press.

Inhelder, B. (1968). *The diagnosis of reasoning in the mentally retarded.* New York: Day.

Keating, D. P. (1975). Precocious cognitive development at the level of formal operations. *Child Development, 46*, 276–280.

Kogan, N. (1983). Stylistic variation in childhood and adolescence: Creativity, metaphor, and cognitive style. In J. H. Flavell & E. M. Markman (Eds.), *Handbook of child psychology* (Vol. 3). New York: Wiley.

Krutetskii, V. A. (1976). *The psychology of mathematical abilities in school children.* Chicago: University of Chicago Press.

Laboratory of Comparative Human Cognition (1983). Culture and cognitive development. In W. Kessen (Ed.), *Handbook of child psychology* (Vol. 1). New York: Wiley.

Lovell, K., & Shields, J. B. (1967). Some aspects of a study of the gifted child. *British Journal of Educational Psychology, 37*, 201–208.

Luria, A. R. (1976). *Cognitive development: Its cultural and social foundations.* Cambridge, MA: Harvard University Press.

Miller, G. A., & Johnson-Laird, P. N. (1976). *Language and perception.* Cambridge, MA: Harvard University Press.

Neimark, E. D. (1975). Intellectual development during adolescence. In F. D. Horowitz (Ed.), *Review of child development research* (Vol. 4). Chicago: University of Chicago Press.

Neimark, E. D. (1982). Adolescent thought: Transition to formal operations in B. B. Wollman (Ed.), *Handbook of developmental psychology*. Englewood Cliffs, NJ: Prentice-Hall.

Overton, W. F., & Newman, J. (1982). Cognitive development: A competence-activation/ utilization approach. In T. Field, A. Houston, H. Quay, L. Troll, & G. Finley (Eds.), *Review of human development*. New York: Wiley.

Overton, W. F., & Reese, H. W. (1981). Conceptual prerequisites for an understanding of stability-change and continuity-discontinuity. *International Journal of Behavioral Development, 4,* 99–123.

Pascual-Leone, J. (1980). Constructive problems for constructive theories: The current relevance of Piaget's work and a critique of information processing simulation psychology. In H. Spada & R. Kluwe (Eds.), *Developmental models of thinking*. New York: Academic Press.

Piaget, J. (1972). Intellectual evolution from adolescence to adulthood. *Human Development, 15,* 1–12.

Piaget, J. (1976). *The grasp of consciousness*. Cambridge, MA: Harvard University Press.

Piaget, J. (1978). *Success and understanding*. Cambridge, MA: Harvard University Press.

Rogoff, B. (1981). Schooling and the development of cognitive skills. In H. C. Triandis & A. Heron (Eds.), *Handbook of cross-cultural psychology* (Vol. 4). Rockleigh, NJ: Allyn & Bacon.

Rogoff, B. (1982). Integrating context and cognitive development. In M. E. Lamb & A. L. Brown (Eds.), *Advances in developmental psychology* (Vol. 2). Hillsdale, NJ: Lawrence Erlbaum Associates.

Schantz, C. U. (1983). Social cognition. In J. H. Flavell & E. M. Markman (Eds.), *Handbook of child psychology*. New York: Wiley.

Scribner, S., & Cole, M. (1981). *The consequences of literacy*. Cambridge, MA: Harvard University Press.

Sharp, D. W., Cole, M., & Lave, C. (1979). Education and cognitive development: The evidence from experimental research. *Monographs of the Society for Research in Child Development, 44* (Serial No. 178).

Spitz, H. H. (1982). Intellectual extremes, mental age, and the nature of human intelligence. *Merrill-Palmer Quarterly, 28,* 167–192.

Stevenson, H. W. (1982). Influences of schooling on cognitive development. In D. A. Wagner & H. W. Stevenson (Eds.), *Cultural perspectives on child development*. San Francisco: W. H. Freeman.

Stevenson, H. W., Stigler, J. W., Lucker, G. W., Lee, S-Y, Hsu, C-C., & Kitamura, S. (1982). Reading disabilities: The case of Chinese, Japanese, and English. *Child Development, 53,* 1164–81.

Stone, C. A., & Day, M. C. (1980). Competence and performance models and the characterization of formal operational skills. *Human Development, 23,* 323–353.

Turiel, E. (1983). Domains and categories in social-cognitive development. In W. F. Overton (Ed.), *The relationship between social and cognitive development*. Hillsdale, NJ: Lawrence Erlbaum Associates.

Vygotsky, L. S. (1978). *Mind and society*. Cambridge, MA: Harvard University Press.

Webb, R. A. (1974). Concrete and formal operations in very bright 6- to 11-year olds. *Human Development, 17,* 292–300.

Weisz, J. R., & Zigler, E. (1979). Cognitive development in retarded and nonretarded persons: Piagetian tests of the similar sequence hypothesis. *Psychological Bulletin, 86,* 831–851.

Werner, E. E. (1979). *Cross-cultural child development*. Monterey, CA: Brooks/Cole.

2 Scientific Methodologies and the Competence–Moderator–Performance Issue

Willis F. Overton
Temple University

In a recent paper, Overton and Newman (1982) presented a theoretical, methodological, and empirical elaboration of the competence-performance distinction in cognitive development. This distinction was termed the competence-activation/utilization approach. This approach begins from the assumption that cognitive competence, or the idealized abstract forms of knowing that Piaget termed structure, is a necessary but not sufficient determinant of overt cognitive behavior or performance. From this perspective, competence is moderated by various subprocesses such as attention, motivation, interests, memory, cognitive styles, and learning strategies; and also by various environmental effects such as schooling, task variables, and situational variables. Ultimately then, actual cognitive performance depends on the relationship between competence and its moderators.

COMPETENCE AND MODERATORS

A primary aim of the earlier paper was to argue that what we may now term the competence-moderator-performance distinction provides an important starting point for constructing a bridge between traditional and rival forms of explanation for cognitive developmental phenomena. In the past, there has been continuing rivalry between those who have focused on the constancy and universality of behavior and development, and those who have focused upon the variability and individuality of behavior and development. Each group has tended to take a kind of "nothing but" stance and has tended to trivialize or deny explanations offered by the rival group. Those impressed with constancy and universality have offered formal explanations in terms of the universal structures of knowing, (i.e., competence) and have treated contingent explanations as epiphenomena. Coming from the opposite extreme, those impressed with variability and individuality have proposed that universal structures are at best temporary heuristics, and have suggested that ultimately these, as well as all other phenomena, will be totally explained by contingent rather than formal explanations.

The competence-moderator-performance distinction establishes a middle ground between these two extreme positions and offers the potential of a more adequate explanation of cognitive behavior and development. Within this approach, both formal and contingent explanations are introduced as cooperative partners in the general explanatory effort. Each plays a distinct but mutually supportive role. Formal explanation yields the abstract idealized models of competence and the development of competence. It provides the laws of the universal, the regular, the normal, the necessary. Contingent explanation focuses on moderators and provides answers to questions of how competence and the development of competence is accelerated, retarded, or deflected from its normal course; and how the activation or utilization of competence is facilitated or hindered by specific psychological processes and situational effects.

To concretize this issue somewhat, let me refer to Piaget's theory. Piaget's theory is primarily a theory of competence and the development of such competence. In other words, Piaget's explanations primarily concern the development of the epistemic (i.e., universal) rather than the psychological (i.e., individual) subject.

As often noted, Piaget paid little systematic attention to the role of individual differences or contingent determinants of behavior. This should not be taken as a criticism, for Piaget chose a methodologically distinct strategy from one that requires explanation of behavior in terms of contingent events. Piaget's strategy for understanding the cognitive domain, like Chomsky's for understanding language, requires that the theorist answer the Kantian question of what one must necessarily assume about the nature of the organism in order for it to have the behaviors that it does exhibit. The method for answering this question is that of observing a sufficient subset of behaviors in the domain in question and constructing a competence model that best captures the universal features of the subset. If the model is valid and powerful, it will prove through further empirical demonstrations to be applicable to a much wider array of behaviors in the domain. The particular form of such a competence model is also guided by issues of parsimony, simplicity, internal coherence, and aesthetics (Miller, 1975; Stone & Day, 1980).

For Piaget, the construction of a competence model (and hence a *formal* explanation) of the universal features of cognitive skills was complicated by a developmental perspective which led to the view that there are progressive and qualitative changes in the nature of these skills. This meant that several distinct but interrelated competence models were required. Piaget's solution was to construct four distinct competence models as the "best" representation of seemingly discontinuous cognitive skills that develop between infancy and adolescence. These four models were those described by the structures of the sensori-motor period, the period of intuitions, the concrete operations period, and the formal operations period. These four competence models were, in turn, ordered and integrated by the functional component of the theory. That is, Piaget offered a further formal explanation in terms of the equilibration principle and its subsidiary features of reflective abstraction, regulations, and compensations to explain how and why the structures of competence develop.

The effect of this almost total concentration on formal explanatory principles led to immediate attacks from investigators who favored contingent explanations. The result was a now familiar series of studies which sought to demonstrate that various cognitive skills could be better accounted for or explained by contingent features such as memory, attention, direct experience or training, and task features than by formal explanation. Although positive findings generated by these studies did serve to tarnish the image of Piaget's theory as a complete explanation of cognitive development, they were not successful in providing a satisfactory alternative.

It was then, from this base of the clash between formal and contingent explanations that we were led to suggest the kind of rapprochement provided by the competence-moderator-performance distinction. Formal explanations are relevant to competence and its development. Contingent explanations are relevant to the moderators of competence.

Research Strategies

In developing our argument for the significance of this approach we also described a diversity of independent but interrelated research strategies that the distinction generates. One strategy entails the formulation of the idealized abstract models that constitute competence at each level of cognitive development. This is the problem of representing the form or organization — not the content of knowing — at each level. Here the ambiguities and vagueness of specific task and situational anomalies are subsumed to the interest of providing general representations of necessary fundamental features of thought. This strategy involves a strongly rational component. That is, although the abstract idealized models will be based on empirical intuitions, they are not a product of simple inductive generalizations drawn from the observation of performance. Models of competence are scientific constructions that reflect the hunches, guesses, and creative imagination of the scientist. They are, as Einstein said of the physical concepts of the natural sciences, "free creations of the human mind, and are not, however it may seem, uniquely determined by the external world" (Einstein & Infeld, 1938, p. 31).

The second research strategy involves the validation of the proposed competence. Here the research task is that of conducting studies that control individual psychological processes, task variables, and situational variables in an effort to demonstrate that the proposed cognitive competence has empirical implications as well as rational meaning. Thus, for example, it might be asked whether Piaget's logical grouping, "primary addition of classes," is an adequate representation of the 8- to 10-year-old's understanding of problems involving hierarchical classes. This question must be answered empirically, providing that such processes as memory demand, attention, and emotional state, and such task factors as stimulus saliency, response bias, and task instructions are carefully controlled. It should also be noted that well-controlled studies that fail to validate a particular representation of competence may provide clues for more adequate representations; but they do not, as we see later, falsify the view that competence is a necessary component of a theory of cognitive development.

These first two research strategies focus on cognitive competence and bracket or control moderators. A third strategy accepts competence as represented and focuses on the moderators themselves in an effort to discover how these are related to and determine the application of competence in actual thought or behavior. Here it is explicitly recognized that predictions concerning thought or behavior based on competence are distorted by various moderators. Within this strategy, several research questions may be raised. One question asks how various moderators might enhance or retard the rate of acquisition of competence. A second question asks how moderators might activate the application of recently acquired competence. A third question asks how moderators might facilitate or hinder the utilization of competence given that competence has been fully consolidated and stabilized. Finally, with respect to the general strategy of focusing on the relationship between *accepted* competence and moderators, I should also note that it is reasonable to investigate the manner in which competence itself operates as a moderator of various individual processes. That is, in true Piagetian reciprocal causal fashion, competence both moderates and is moderated. Competence as the moderator is demonstrated in studies that show the influence of cognitive level on seemingly far removed behaviors such as sex role behavior (e.g., Ruble, Balaban, & Cooper, 1981), and other social behaviors (e.g., Overton, 1983a) and learning strategies (Gholson & Beilin, 1978).

THE ROLE OF SCIENTIFIC METHODOLOGIES

Although each of these described strategies has generated a body of research, the literature Overton and Newman (1982) reviewed in their original paper, and the theme of the present volume, all focus upon the third strategy of inquiring into the ways in which competence is moderated by individual processes and variables. Rather than further examining this literature in the present essay, I would like instead to develop a stronger scientific rationale and conceptual foundation for the competence-moderator-performance distinction. *Competence-moderator-performance-like* distinctions have not gone without criticisms. I believe that the most serious criticisms are based upon a failure to appreciate the scientific context within which the distinction is generated. As a consequence I would like to discuss the distinction in the light of some recent advances that have taken place in the philosophy of science.

In this discussion I propose three general arguments. First, I claim that the most defensible, significant, and productive meaning of the competence-moderator-performance distinction is found within the context of a scientific methodology that the philosopher Imre Lakatos (1978) has called "scientific research programs." Such research programs, as we shall see, are broader than any particular theory or set of observations, and I argue that the specific research program that gives scientific legitimacy to the competence-moderator-performance distinction has been called the "organismic approach."

My second claim is that most of the criticisms that have been leveled against the competence-moderator-performance distinction are the result of improper interpretation of this distinction within the context of rival scientific methodologies, including positivism, conventionalism, and a research program called the "mechanistic approach." The claim here is that to the extent that the competence-moderator-performance distinction is interpreted in the context of one of these scientific methodologies, it is indeed a weak and nonproductive distinction.

My third claim is that the competence-moderator-performance distinction is a natural and coherent extension of Piaget's theory rather than a patched-up set of ad hoc hypotheses, and that this is exactly because Piaget's theory is one exemplar of a family of theories that derive from the organismic scientific research program.

To set the stage for this discussion I would first note that in a recent lead article in the *Behavioral and Brain Sciences,* L. Jonathan Cohen (1981) introduced the competence-moderator-performance distinction into the field of adult deductive and probabilistic reasoning. This was done in an effort to provide a general "conceptual framework within which to think coherently about problems of cognitive rationality and the relevant experimental data" (Cohen, 1981, p. 317). Cohen's basic argument was that experimental evidence suggesting the inadequacies of human rationality are best understood as performance factors or moderations operating upon normative valid reasoning criteria (i.e., competence).

Cohen further proposed that the experimental findings can best be described in terms of several classes of situations, or what we would have called moderators, that lead to faulty application of competence. These included (1) situations in which task effects induce cognitive illusions analagous to perceptual illusions; (2) situations in which intelligence or schooling effects limit the generality of applications of competence to novel problems; (3) situations that elicit an inappropriate competence.

Immediately following Cohen's article, 34 peer critiques were also published. This group of replies forms a kind of compendium of competence-moderator-performance criticisms. On reading these I was particularly impressed with the fact that almost all of the negative comments were directed against the nature and status of the concept *competence*. That is, no one seemed to have any trouble with the directly observable performance side of the competence-performance equation but many of the critiques had a great deal of trouble with the not directly observable, or inferred entity status of competence. This has led me to believe that the development of a stronger scientific rationale or conceptual foundation for the competence-moderator-performance distinction must primarily focus on the scientific status and nature of propositions that purport to describe nonobservable entities (e.g., competence) and the relationship of these to the scientific status and nature of propositions that purport to describe the observable entities (e.g., performance).

This issue of the status, nature, and relationship of nonobservable and observable entities has a history as ancient as philosophy itself, and it forms the basic debate between the epistemological position of empiricists who claimed that all knowledge must ultimately derive directly from observation and rationalists who claimed that knowledge is the product of reason or man's imaginative faculty. In the scientific arena the influence of variants of these epistemological positions generated rival methodologies also divided on the observable–nonobservable entity issue.

Two primary scientific methodologies, positivism and conventionalism, emerged from the empiricist position, and these were articulated by contemporary philosophers of science such as Rudolph Carnap, Carl Hemple, Ernest Nagel, Karl Popper, and Dudley Shapere. The common core of each of these methodologies, as we see in some detail shortly, is that in the final analysis, science and its progress are judged on the basis of neutral observations assessed in the crucible of experimental manipulation.

The rationalist influence, on the other hand, has led to the methodology of scientific research programs proposed by Lakatos (1978) and recently extended by Laudan (1977). This methodology owes much of its contemporary origin to the work of N. R. Hanson and his often quoted statement that "All data are theory laden." Hanson denied that there is a fixed neutral observational base and asserted that propositions that describe nonobservable entities enter into scientific activity in an essential and formative fashion. This view was, in turn, elaborated by the contributions of Mary Hesse, Paul Feyerabend, Thomas Kuhn, Stephen Toulmin, Gerald Holton, and Marx Wartofsky. In essence, as developed by Lakatos and Laudan, the methodology of scientific research programs on research traditions (Laudan, 1977) asserts that propositions describing nonobservable entities (e.g., theoretical propositions) such as those about "competence," or metaphysical propositions such as those concerning the structure of the universe, as well as observational propositions (e.g., performance), enter the essential body of science as relatively independent co-equals. Science and its progress, from this perspective, are judged not in terms of uncovering hard observable facts but rather in terms of the success with which both types of propositions promote problem solving in a coherent, systematic, preplanned fashion.

COMPETENCE IN POSITIVISM AND CONVENTIONALISM

I now describe the methodologies of positivism and conventionalism in order to demostrate how, when interpreted in these contexts, the competence-moderator-performance distinction is indeed weak, non-productive, and open to damaging criticisms. I then consider the nature of Lakatos' scientific research programs in order to support my claim that one such program (i.e., the organismic approach) provides the most defensible and productive meaning for the competence-moderator-performance distinction, and also my claim that the competence-moderator-performance distinction is a natural and coherent extension of Piaget's theory.

Positivism

As a scientific methodology the two central characteristics of positivism were its disparagement of interpretation and its strong reliance on inductive inference. For positivists, propositions describing inherently nonobservable entities were not admissible into the body of science. The only admissible propositions were those describing hard facts (i.e., observations) or infallible inductive generalizations drawn from observation. Thus, theoretical propositions were defined as inductive empirical generalizations and were, in principle, reducible to observation. Deductive inference was also employed by the positivists but this was used only to derive from proven empirical generalizations other potentially provable propositions (i.e., other observations).

The effect of positivism on psychology was enormous. Positivism led to systems like Skinner's where theory was held to consist of nothing but functional correlations of data statements. It led to the more common belief that psychology must follow the "hypothetical deductive" method, where the term *hypothetical* merely meant "inductive empirical generalization." It led to the view that inferred entities were the work of the devil "mentalism." This devil could be exorcised only if inferred entities were tied to observable antecedents and consequences and called "intervening variables," of if the scientists were to promise that inferred entities would someday be actually observed and thus could be called "hypothetical constructs." Finally, positivism led to the absolute horror that more general propositions such as metaphysical statements might be in any way considered relevant to science (see Lakatos, 1978, p. 105).

As a general methodology of science, positivism died. Both the friends and foes of positivism came to recognize the impossibility of reducing general theories to observational propositions and, more importantly, they recognized that the laws of science can seldom be adequately described as inductive generalizations (Lakatos, 1978; Pepper, 1942; Wartofsky, 1968). Although positivism died as a general scientific methodology, its ghostly influence continued to be felt in psychology. Guided by this influence, many still distrust an inferred entity approach; many still justify inferred entities as inductive generalizations; and many still believe psychology can advance only on the basis of hard, proven (i.e., observable) fact.

Positivism and Competence-Performance

An implicit commitment to positivism results in a weak and flawed interpretation of the competence-performance distinction. Here performance constitutes the real, the observable, and competence is merely a set of rules induced as empirical generalizations from this reality. If this interpretation is allowed to frame the competence-performance distinction, it is easy to see how valid criticisms can be raised against the viability of the distinction. The most general criticism, when competence-performance is approached from this framework, usually runs as follows: First, it is asserted that all we really have ultimately in psychology is observable behavior (i.e., performance). As a result, it is held, any serious focus on competence (i.e., an abstraction) diverts us from our primary goal, which should be a careful analysis of what the child actually does in performing various tasks and how this behavior is determined by cultural and stimulus effects.

The interpretation of competence as an inductive generalization also leads to the criticism that the competence-performance distinction entails a vicious circularity of reasoning. Indeed, if competence is a direct, inductive empirical generalization from performance and if competence in turn explains performance, then the distinction is a virtual prototype of such circular reasoning. The problem should, in fact, serve as a caution to investigators who have recently embraced what is termed *task analysis*. This approach involves the induction of rule sets or strategies (i.e., a type of competence) that are presumed to underlie specific tasks or concepts (Siegler, 1981). Thus, for example, Gelman and Gallistel (1978) formulate five principles to account for numerical counting, and Siegler (1981) formulates separate rules for several tasks (balance scale, projection of shadows and probability tasks) that derive from the Piagetian formal operations literature. Siegler and Richards (1979) have also produced a rule set for the concept of time. The point here is that if competence is not to some extent formulated independently of specific task behavior, such circularity of reasoning is indeed a valid criticism. Further, tying competence to specific tasks raises the related issue of parsimony of explanation. That is, if we are to have another set of inductive rules (competence) for each new task or concept, all explanatory power is lost and we are left with what we started with, i.e., a wide variety of behavior and an only slightly smaller set of descriptive summary statements of these behaviors.

Conventionalism

The second scientific methodology generated by empiricism is conventionalism. Conventionalism was built upon positivism and incorporates many of its features, including a heavy reliance on inductive inference (Lakatos, 1978, p. 106). Conventionalism, however, recognizes that not all scientific propositions can be reduced to observational statements. As a consequence, conventionalism permits the introduction of nonobservable propositions including propositions describing general models such as the computer model of information processing approaches. Although such propositions are held to be irreducible to observational statements, their primary feature is that they operate *only as convenient and conventional ways of ordering and organizing hard data* (i.e., observations). They do not influence the data base itself. Rather, they operate like pigeonholes to classify, arrange, and organize hard data into coherent units. The framework of encoding, storage, and retrieval arrangement in memory offers a familiar example.

As conventions, theoretical entities or models are lightly held and readily given up when *simpler* ways are found of organizing hard data. As Lakatos pointed out, "For the conventionalist...[theoretical] discoveries are primarily inventions of new and simpler pigeonhole systems" (1978, p. 107). However, the "genuine progress of the science... takes place [still, as with the positivists] on the ground level of proven facts [i.e., hard data] and changes on the theoretical level are merely instrumental" (p. 106).

Conventionalism, then, leads to two distinct and noninteracting levels of scientific activity. These have been termed the context of justification and the context of discovery (Nickles, 1980; Reichenbach, 1938). One level (the context of justification) includes observations, experimental manipulations, and inductive generalizations, and it is at this level that genuine progress and explanation take place. The other level (context of discovery) includes theoretical terms, nonobserved entities, and models. These propositions may themselves be the products of the scientist's hunches, guesses, creative imagination, or metaphysical presuppositions. It matters little, because according to conventionalism this level exerts no real influence on the essential features of science, i.e., those included in the context of justification.

Conventionalism and Competence-Performance

Except for those who are still strongly influenced by positivism, most investigators would agree that "competence" is a nonobservable entity, i.e., a theoretical term that is not reducible to specific observations. Performance, on the other hand, directly entails observations. Therefore, when interpreted within conventionalism, the competence-performance distinction is strengthened somewhat over its interpretation in positivism in that competence is not reducible to observations. However, this is a minor advance in the viability of competence because competence still assumes no vital role in *explanation*. Competence merely arranges the hard facts and inductive laws found in performance.

In a word, positivism finds competence to be neither nice nor necessary; conventionalism finds competence to be nice but not necessary. This interpretation within a conventionalist psychological framework was clearly and forcefully presented by Osgood in his statement, "It is one thing to use notions like 'competence'...as heuristic devices; ...it is quite another thing to use them as explanations of performance — unless, of course, one is ready to give up his behavioristic moorings entirely in exchange for a frankly dualistic mentalism" (Osgood, 1968, p. 505). Similarly, in replying to the article by Cohen mentioned in an earlier section of this chapter, Griggs asserted from a conventionalist position that the main concern of researchers should be to gain an understanding of the cognitive functioning underlying observed behavior in experiments. Formal systems such as competence, Griggs asserted, "may be employed in the design of experimental tasks, but subjects only make responses" (1981, p. 338). The responses may be defined according to the formal systems, but the researcher's job "is to explain why the responses were made" (Griggs, 1981, p. 338).

Conventionalism with Falsification

Before turning to a description of Lakatos' methodology of scientific research programs and hence to a more viable interpretation of the competence-performance distinction that allocates equal explanatory weight to both nonobservable and observable entities, a few words should be said about an important variant of conventionalism. This is Popper's falsification methodology (Popper, 1959). Popper recognized that the acceptance of theories or models based on comparison of intuitive *simplicity,* as suggested by "classical" conventionalism, can only be a matter of subjective taste and hence is a very weak criterion. Popper also recognized that theories or theoretical constructs such as competence can be neither verified — according to the positivists' verification principle — nor confirmed — under pain of the logical fallacy of affirming the consequence. As a result, Popper proposed that in order for a theory or theoretical construct to be accepted into the body of science, it must be shown to be, in principle, falsifiable. That is, the scientist, if his or her theory is to be scientific, must specify results that, if found, would disprove the theory.

This criterion of scientific acceptance, although attaining a good deal of popularity among conventionalists, has also been severely criticized because of the ambiguity over whether falsification of an observational experimental hypothesis can spread to falsification of the theory that generated the hypothesis. This issue is considered again in the next section when we examine Lakatos' methodology of scientific research programs. Two points with respect to conventionalist falsification should be noted. First, falsification methodology has frequently been applied as a major point of criticism against the competence-performance distinction. Thus, Sampson has maintained with respect to the distinction, "by now it is perhaps no longer controversial to suggest that one of its chief functions is to protect... theories from refutation by permitting observations contradicting [falsifying] the theories to be dismissed as 'performance' 'effects', while those that confirm the theories are taken as a true reflection of a ... 'competence' " (1981, p. 350). As we see in the next section, although this criticism has some validity when the competence-performance distinction is interpreted within a conventionalist methodology, it loses force within a methodology of scientific research programs or research traditions.

Falsification and Competence-Performance

The second point about falsification methodology concerns the issue of what it accepts and what it excludes as defining the essential body of science. Unlike that of other conventionalists, Popper's methodology accepts specific theories into the essential body of science. However, more general propositions, such as metaphysical propositions, are explicitly excluded from the essential body of science because these are propositions that have no potential falsifiers. For example, consider metaphysical propositions that make claims that organisms are either inherently organized and active or inherently uniform and stable. Although, from the perspective of falsification methodology, claims of this sort might provide interesting sociological sidelights to science, they would not be considered essential components of scientific understanding. Since such general propositions are excluded from both a "classical" and a "falsification" conventionalist position, these views provide no *rational* scientific explanation for why the theoretical construct "competence" should be either included or excluded from our theories. Thus, neither positivism nor either variant of conventionalism affords a base from which to develop what I originally claimed to be the main aim of this paper, i.e., a stronger scientific rationale and conceptual foundation for the competence-moderator-performance distinction. Such a rationale must await a consideration of Lakatos' methodology of scientific research programs.

To summarize the story to this point: Initially I suggested that the competence-moderator-performance distinction can provide an important starting point for constructing a bridge between those who favor formal explanations in terms of universal structures or competence and those who favor contingent explanation in terms of moderators. However, when the competence-moderator-performance distinction is interpreted within either a positivist or a conventionalist scientific framework, no such bridge is formed. Instead, those methodologies either eliminate or trivialize the potential explanatory power of one side of the equation (i.e., the formal explanation of competence) and rely almost exclusively upon contingent explanation. Thus does the spirit of epistemological empircism exert a strong and continuing influence upon our scientific activity.

COMPETENCE IN THE ORGANISMIC SCIENTIFIC RESEARCH PROGRAM

The establishment of a balance between formal explanation and contingent explanation, between competence and its moderators, between the epistemic subject and the psychological subject, as well as a rationale for this balance is found in the implication of the methodology of scientific research programs described by Lakatos, and particularly in one research program, i.e., the organismic program.

Scientific Research Programs

Lakatos, as mentioned earlier, was influenced by early rationalist philosophers of science, who, following Kant, assert that scientific knowledge is the product of both reason and observation. For Lakatos, the basic unit for the analysis of scientific activity is broader than the observational data base, and broader than any isolated theory or conjunction of theories. This unit is called the "research program." The research program can be thought of as being composed of three levels arranged in a hierarchy. From most to least general these consist of first, a *hard core* and second a *positive heuristic*. These levels define problems and outline the construction of the third level, called the *belt of auxiliary hypotheses* that are embodied in a *family of specific theories*. A general representation of two research programs that are more fully discussed later is presented in Table 2.1.

The hard core and positive heuristic of a scientific research program consist of a set of basic doctrines which gives the program its identity and thus differentiates the program from others. Laudan (1977) described these doctrines as ontological (hard core) and methodological (positive heuristic) assumptions that determine what should or should not be done within the given research program or research tradition.

The hard core itself may consist of various types of propositions, including metaphysical propositions (see Table 2.1). This is particularly important because, in contrast to positivism and conventionalism, the "hard core" of a research program admits into the essential body of science propositions that may have no potential falsifiers. Metaphysical propositions, as they constitute a hard core of a scientific research program, are not simply idle psychological or sociological curiosities, rather they are essential components of scientific activity. They exert a formative influence on lower levels and give meaning to the theoretical concepts of specific theories. For example, Lakatos describes how Cartesian metaphysics (i.e., the mechanistic theory of the universe) operated as a hard core of a scientific research program that discouraged work on scientific theories that were inconsistent with mechanistic theory (e.g., Newton's theory of action at a distance) while encouraging work on auxiliary hypotheses that might have saved mechanistic theory from counter-evidence (Lakatos, 1978, p. 48).

In addition to bringing into the essential body of science that which is an external influence in positivism and conventionalism, another characteristic of the hard core is that it is, by design, not open to falsification. That is, by methodological decision the hard core is irrefutable.

The reason for exempting the hard core from refutation is that it allows for the development of the "positive heuristic" without unnecessary distraction. The positive heuristic of the research program (see Table 2.1) is influenced by the hard core, but it describes the long term research policy of the program. It is more flexible than the hard core and consists of, to quote Lakatos, "a partially articulated set of suggestions or hints on how to change and develop the 'refutable variants' of the research program, how to modify and sophisticate the 'refutable' protective belt of auxiliary hypotheses" (Lakatos, 1978, p. 50).

Taken together, the hard core and positive heuristic of a given program constitute a conceptual framework that generates specific theories that within any given program constitute a family of theories (see Table 2.1). These theories in turn embody the "belt of auxiliary hypotheses" which are sets of observational hypotheses that constitute the falsifiable or refutable

TABLE 2.1
Comparison of Organismic and Mechanistic Scientific Research Programs

LEVEL OF PROGRAM	ORGANISMIC	MECHANISTIC
I. HARD CORE (ontological assumptions)		
A. World Models	1. Organization of nature. 2. Activity. 3. Change (dialectic). 4. Accidental factors *moderate* organization, activity, and change.	1. Uniformity of nature. 2. Stability. 3. Fixity. 4. Accidental factors *cause* organization, activity, and change.
B. Human Models	*Active Organism* 1. Inherent organization of psychological functions. 2. Inherent activity. 3. Organizational changes are qualitative.	*Responsive Organism* 1. Uniformity. Apparent organization reduced to accidental causes. 2. Stability. Apparent activity reduced to accidental causes. 3. Changes are quantitative.
C. Epistemology	*Constructivism – Rationalism.* Knower actively constructs the known.	*Realism – Empiricism.* Knower comes to reflect or acquire a copy of reality (the known).
II. POSITIVE HEURISTIC (methodological assumptions)	1. *Holism.* Understanding in context of the organic whole. 2. *Structure – Function Analysis.*	1. *Elementarism.* Understanding through reduction to elements. 2. *Antecedent – Consequent Analysis.*

a. Establishing the organization of a system explains behavior (formal explanation).
b. Establishing contingent factors explains rate of behavior (contingent explanation).

3. *Necessary Change*
a. Establishing the order of organizational change explains development (formal explanation).
b. Contingent factors explains rate of development (contingent explanation).

4. *Discontinuity—Continuity of Change.* Emergent systematic properties and levels of organization.

a. Establishing contingent factors explains behavior (contingent) explanation).

3. *Accidental Change.*
a. Establishing the contingent factors explains development (contingent explanation).

4. *Strict Continuity of Change.* Strict Additivity.

III. *FAMILY OF THEORIES*

Contemporary Structuralists Piaget, Werner, Chomsky, Kohlberg, Pascual-Leone. *Ego development theories.* Erikson, Sullivan. *Gestalt theories. Humanistic theories. Rychlak. Ecological perspective theories.* Bronfenbrenner, Wapner, and Kaplan.

Behaviorist and neobehavioristic theories. Conditioning Theories. Observational learning theories. Mediational learning theories. Information processing theories. Skinner, Bijou, Baer, Berlyne, Spiker, Bandura, Gewirtz, H. Kendler, J. J. Gibson.

component of the scientific research program. Examples of the hard cores, positive heuristics, and family of theories are presented in later sections.

For Lakatos, falsification constitutes a local and minor criterion of scientific progress. The major criterion of progress of a scientific research program is that it predicts novel or unexpected phenomena with some degree of success. Further, the anticipation of novel events should be guided by a coherent, planned positive heuristic rather than via patched up ad hoc auxiliary hypotheses. Thus, scientific progress is measured ultimately by a pragmatic criterion and not by the realist truth criterion of positivism and conventionalism. For Lakatos and for Laudan (1977), the advance of science is best described in terms of problem solving rather than in terms of making observational discoveries (see Nickles, 1980, p. 47).

With respect to the falsification of observational hypotheses, Lakatos points out that the scientist must note them as they occur "but as long as his research program maintains its momentum, he may freely put them aside.... Only when the driving force of the positive heuristic weakens, may more attention be given to anomalies" (1978, p. 111).

Research Programs and Competence-Performance

From this short sketch of Lakatos' position, it should be clear that if a strong scientific rationale is to be found for the competence-moderator-performance distinction, it will be in the methology of scientific research programs. Specifically, it will be found in the hard core and positive heuristic of a program currently in operation in the field of psychology. The program that generates such a distinction will be one that *requires* a concept like competence, not just as a nice feature but as a necessary feature. As a consequence, essential features of competence (i.e., the concept of "competence" itself) will be irrefutable although other features (i.e., specific descriptions of competence) will be open to falsification. Further, the program will be one that requires both formal and contingent explanation.

The question then is what programs are currently available in psychology, and which program generates a strong scientific rationale for the competence-moderator-performance distinction? Over the past dozen years, my colleague Hayne Reese and I have maintained that the field of psychology has been and continues to be shaped primarily by two rival scientific research programs, those which we (Overton, 1975, 1976, 1983b; Overton & Reese, 1973, 1981; Reese & Overton, 1970) and others (Nagel, 1979; Pepper, 1942; Wartofsky, 1968) have called the "mechanistic" and the "organismic" approaches. In making this assertion that psychology has been and continues to be shaped by these programs, we have not denied that other new programs may emerge or even that other programs may already be in operation. However, if other approaches are to count as rival scientific research programs rather than as positivistic or conventionalist methodologies, it is incumbent upon their practitioners to clearly define both the hard core and positive heuristic of their programs. It may be, for example, that some forms of information processing will one day constitute a scientific research program. However, at present it appears that information processing is framed by a conventionalist scientific methodology in which the computer is treated as merely a conventional model to arrange hard data.

The thrust of the Overton-Reese analyses has been to articulate the hard cores of the mechanistic and organismic rival programs, to describe the positive heuristic that each hard core generates, and to demonstrate how each hard core and positive heuristic have resulted in rival families of theories that embody planned testable auxiliary hypotheses. We have also maintained, following Lakatos, that the hard cores of rival programs are not open to experimental test, i.e., they are irrefutable; that the hard cores represent an essential component of each group's scientific activity; that the hard cores, through their positive heuristics, exert a strong influence on the way the investigator formulates theoretical concepts and tests derived observational auxiliary hypotheses. The following presents some of the basic features of the mechanistic and organismic programs. For a more detailed schematic sketch see Table 2.1.

The Mechanistic Research Program

The mechanistic program, like the methodologies of positivism and conventionalism, does not lead to a strong rationale for the competence-moderator-performance distinction. The *hard core* of the mechanistic program is expressed in a commitment to a Lockean-Humean metaphysics of Being wherein *activity, change* and particularly *organization* are understood as acquisitions and these acquisitions are determined solely by chance or contingent events. The *positive heuristic* of this program — or what Overton and Reese (1973, 1981) have called "corollary model issues" — encourages its practitioners to work within a framework of elementaristic-reductionistic analysis, to explain activity, change, and organization as the product of antecedent determinants, and to represent change as strictly additive or continuous in nature. Within this program then, necessary organization as embodied in theoretical concepts of structure or competence is either trivialized as was the case with conventionalism, or ultimately reduced to antecedent-consequent functional relationships, as was the case with positivism.

For purposes of clarity, it is important to note that the proponents of any psychological approach formulated according to mechanistic principles may, in fact, interpret that approach within the context of a positivist, a conventionalist, or a research program demarcationist strategy. The primary feature that distinguishes which demarcationist strategy is being employed at any given time is whether proponents (a) deny the existence of presuppositions (positivism), (b) accept the existence of presuppositions, but deny they exert a necessary influence on observations (conventionalism), (c) accept presuppositions, and accept that they exert a necessary influence on observations (research program).

It may indeed then be the case that a system such as behaviorism will, either at any given time or at different times, be understood according to each of these strategies. Consider, for example, Skinner's behavioristic approach. In his early works, Skinner (1950) apparently understood his approach according to a positivist strategy. Here, Skinner advocated virtually a totally inductive approach and claimed that a commonsense explanation of the field was sufficient to generate laws. Theory was to consist of summary statements of the functional relationships observed between behavior and environment. Here "conceptual models" (Skinner, 1956, p. 231) were meaningless to science, and theories themselves were the direct product of observation. In later writings, however, Skinner (1971) appears to adopt a conventionalist strategy when he argues against one set of presuppositions, i.e., the view that man is an active agent, and in favor of another set, i.e., the view that causes of behavior reside totally in the environment. As Skinner stated, "environmental contingencies now take over functions once attributed to autonomous [active agent] man" (Skinner, 1971, p. 205). This view represents a conventionalist rather than a research program strategy because the presuppositions are not viewed as having an impact upon the object of study itself, i.e., "no theory changes what it is a theory about" (Skinner, 1971, p. 206). Finally, in a more recent account, Schwartz and Lacey (1982) have interpreted Skinner's presuppositions as a world view, and here we find the research program strategy exemplified. "When we understand the essentials of behavior theory's research program we can understand the reasons behind the particular experiments behavior theorists do" (p. 256). In this account they further argue that "the application of behavior theory can actually transform the phenomena to which it is applied" (p. 258).

The Organismic Research Program and the Competence-Moderator-Performance Distinction

All of the foregoing comments lead to my major claim: It is the organismic scientific research program and only the organismic program that currently yields a strong scientific and productive rationale for the competence-moderator-performance distinction. The *hard core* of the organismic program is expressed in a Leibnizian-Kantean-Hegelian metaphysics of Becoming. Here *activity, change,* and *organization* are understood as natural and necessary features of the universe and not as the simple product of contingent forces. This hard core statement is understood within Aristotle's distinction between the necessary and the accidental. Features of an entity that are accidental are those that are caused by fortuitous or contingent events. Those that are necessary are free of causal determinants and are natural and essential to the entity being considered. For example, a plant has a particular form or organization and it goes through a sequence of changes. These features, the organization and changes of organization, are as necessary to the essence of a plant as are any other intrinsic features. On the other hand, the plant also has a history in the sense that accidental events such as favorable or unfavorable nutrients or good or bad weather may occur. These accidental or contingent events do not explain the necessary features of organization and change, but they are related to the way in which the plant functions and to its rate of growth.

Thus the hard core of the organismic program asserts that universal formal features of organization (i.e., the underlying structures of behavior) and change (i.e., development of structures) are basic, but it admits contingent features as moderators of contemporary functioning and rate of change.

The *positive heuristic* of the organismic program encourages its practitioners to work within a holistic analytic framework; to explain universal necessary behavioral change, activity, and organization in terms of structure-function relationships; to explain individual behavioral variation in terms of contingent events; and to represent change of organization (the structure of behavior) as having both continuous and discontinuous features.

The hard core and positive heuristic of the organismic program influence the generation of sets of testable auxiliary hypotheses embodied in a family of theories. Before turning to these, however, it is appropriate to note how implications of the organismic hard core and positive heuristic constitute the rationale for a general competence-moderator-performance distinction. First, it is within this program that the concept "competence" achieves a defensible scientific status. Regardless of how a particular competence is described, "competence" is a direct reflection of the program's instruction to establish the necessary organization or structures of the events under investigation, i.e., in our case, cognition and cognitive development. Constructing a representation of this necessary organization as a nonobservable inferred entity is not merely acceptable within this program, it is mandatory. Further, the formal system of competence, i.e., the underlying structure of behavior, so constructed, constitutes an essential dimension of the explanation of the events under investigation. That is, this formal explanation provided by the representation of competence is necessary to explanation and not just nice.

As a second point, notice that within the context of the organismic program, the general concept "competence" is not open to falsification, i.e., it is not refutable. Thus, although specific descriptions of competence will be open to experimental test, experimental findings will affect only these descriptions and not the hard core requirement that some kind of competence be generated. Thus, for example, to come to the conclusion through experimental investigations that Piaget's or Chomsky's descriptions of competence are inadequate merely leads to the necessity of finding other descriptions, it does not lead to the abandonment of the concept of "competence."

A third and final point is that within the organismic program, contingent explanation is also necessary. However, contingent explanation plays a distinct role from that played by formal explanation. Specifically, contingent explanation applies to moderators of competence.

To summarize the general argument to this point: Within the organismic program, the competence-moderator-performance distinction establishes a scientifically defensible and viable middle ground between those who would explain cognition and its development either in terms of universal structure or in terms of contingent events. That is, within the organismic interpretation of the competence-moderator-performance distinction both formal and contingent explanations are introduced as equal cooperative partners in the total explanatory effort. Each plays a distinct but mutually supportive role. Formal explanation yields the abstract idealized models of competence and the development of that competence. It provides laws of the universal, the regular, the normal, the necessary. Contingent explanation focuses on moderators and provides answers to questions of how competence and the development of competence is accelerated, retarded, or deflected from its normal course; and how the activation or utilization of competence is facilitated or hindered in specific situations or classes of situations.

Families of Theories

The foregoing discussion leads to my final claim, that the competence-moderator-performance distinction is a natural and coherent extension of Piaget's theory rather than a patched-up set of ad hoc hypotheses. To establish this claim it is first necessary to elaborate upon the concept of "family of theories" that derives from a scientific research program perspective. In his extension of Lakatos' work, Laudan (1977) described a research program or research tradition as an organized set of ontological (hard core) and methodological (positive heuristic) do's and don'ts. Each research program or tradition exhibits metaphysical and methodological commitments that define the nature of the entities and processes in a domain of study and provides general procedures for their examination. The hard core and positive heuristic do not however, in themselves, provide specific detailed answers to particular questions. They do not, for example, tell us what occurs when the child is faced with a spatial problem or a classificatory problem. These detailed answers to particular questions are provided by specific theories. Therefore, it is important to understand the relationship between research traditions and specific theories.

In establishing metaphysical and methodological commitments, a research program or tradition provides a set of guidelines for the construction of specific theories. A given theory is constructed within the context of these guidelines and at the same time it is sensitive to the empirical issues that it confronts. If a theory violates what is forbidden by metaphysical and methodological guidelines of a tradition, it is, in essence, repudiating that particular tradition. On the other hand, those theories that are formulated in a manner consistent with the guidelines constitute a family of theories with respect to that tradition and they entail sets of testable auxiliary hypotheses.

In a critical analysis of recent theories of conceptual development Scholnick (1983) examined several theories that illustrate the relations both within and between families of theories. Rosch's (1978) prototype theory represents a contemporary extension of Hull's (1920) behavioristic theory. The influence of the mechanistic tradition is demonstrated in (a) the use of the equivalence response as a basic definition of "concept," i.e., making a unique response to a diverse set of stimuli, (b) the retention of an associative learning paradigm to account for the acquisition of equivalence responses, (c) the representation of the organism as a pattern recognitive device, and (d) the localization of real categories in the environment. Thus, as Scholnick (1983) pointed out, "Rosch claims there are real categories out there that the subject learns to detect by maximizing cue validity….The process is one of perceptual learning of co-occurrences" (p. 50). Here, as in earlier mechanistic theories, the organism is not endowed with active organized structures or self-regulating systems that operate upon the environment to construct new categories. Instead, the theory, following the ontological commitment of the mechanistic tradition, endows the organism with more peripheral and reactive skills (i.e., pattern recognition) not unlike the traditional behavioristic processes of discrimination and generalization. In addition, the mechanistic positive heuristic is closely adhered to by asserting that the phenomena of interest be reduced to the elementaristic or atomistic features (i.e., the equivalence response) and by insisting that all complexity be understood as the result of an acquisition process (i.e., perceptual learning) derived from a real environment.

Scholnick (1983) has further pointed out that these mechanistic ontological and methodological themes are also carried into the schema theory (e.g., Nelson, 1977, 1979) and information theory (e.g., Trabasso et al., 1978). The main point is that although prototype theory, schema theory, and information theory differ with respect to various specific theoretical constructs and vary with respect to the nature of the empirical phenomena they approach, as a group they are formulated in a manner that is consistent with and does not violate the underlying mechanistic ontological tradition (see Table 2.1). Thus, they constitute a family of theories generated by the guidelines of the mechanistic tradition.

In contrast to prototype theory, schema theory, and information theory, Chomsky's, Piaget's, and Werner's theories, among others, reflect commitments to the organismic tradition and hence represent a family of theories that rival the mechanistic family. If one is to understand conceptual representation from the perspective of the organismically based theories, it must be recognized that these theories do not represent the organism as a detection device that simply recognizes, encodes, and arranges stimuli or patterns. Instead these theories follow the organismic ontological guidelines of necessary organization and activity and consequently represent the organism in terms of central and general patterns of activity that are to some degree imposed upon the environment (see Table 2.1). Concepts are thus constructed, not acquired, and the major methodological commitment is to understand the relationship between function, (the activity of constructing concepts) and structures (the underlying competence that is presupposed by this activity). In similar fashion the definition of a concept itself is not the mechanistically derived elementaristic equivalence response. Organismically, concepts are defined holistically as rules for ordering experience and the primary task for the investigator is to examine the general structures that form the basis for rule generation.

A family of theories, then, is a set of theories, each formulated in a manner that is consistent with and does not violate the ontological and methodological commitments of the parent tradition (see Table 2.1). This does not mean, however, that the theories within any one family must be totally compatible with each other. Indeed, as Laudan (1977) has pointed out, although a research program or tradition provides vital guidelines for theory construction, theories within a given family may be mutually inconsistent rivals with respect to specific theoretical issues. An important example of this rivalry within the organismic family, and one that has a direct bearing upon the competence-moderator-performance distinction, is the relationship between Piaget's and Chomsky's theory.

Consider, first, the evidence suggesting that both Piaget's and Chomsky's theories derive from an organismic research program. Both theories accept and explicitly reflect the hard core ontological assumptions of the integrated relationship of necessary organization and activity. As Piattelli-Palmarini noted, both theories accept the assumptions that "(1) nothing is knowable unless cognitive organization of some kind is there from the start; and (2) nothing is knowable unless the subject acts in one way or another on the surrounding world" (1980, p. 54). In addition, each theory reflects positive heuristic methodological features of holism and structure-function analysis and each theory places primary emphasis on formal explanation. Taken as a whole, this evidence strongly supports the contention that the two theories constitute two members of the organismic family of theories.

The conflicts between Piaget's and Chomsky's theories reside in issues concerning the explanation of language, the nature and extent of the initial organization, and the question of necessary change. The first two of these conflicts are significant theoretical debates (Piattelli-Palmarini, 1980), which establish that the theories are rivals in certain areas despite the fact that they derive from the same basic ontological and methodological commitments.

The issue of necessary change opens a more interesting general problem because it involves significant features of the organismic hard core and the positive heuristic. The question here is whether, given some type of initial organization, later novel structures emerge and whether this development is at least partially independent of formative environmental factors. With respect to this question, the debate between Piaget and Chomsky (Piattelli-Palmarini, 1980) focuses almost exclusively on the problem of the role of the environment. Stated simplistically, Chomsky agues that at least in the domain of language, the environment plays little role beyond a triggering function for innate structure. Piaget, on the other hand, takes his well-known "third way" between nativism and environmentalism and maintains that cognitive structures develop out of the interaction in which the initial organization assimilates and accommodates the environment. Here, as with other issues, Piaget's and Chomsky's theories are engaged in an important theoretical debate, but in terms of the hard core of the organismic tradition, neither is arguing that structures or their development can be accounted for on the basis of contingent environmental events. That is, both accept the organismic research program commitments that if there is change it is to some significant degree necessary rather than contingent.

However, this still leaves the question of whether there are, in fact, structural changes. Or more specifically, is there a progression from less to more advanced structures (competence) in which each successive general structure (level of competence or stage) exhibits some novelty (discontinuity) that is not totally reducible to the initial organization? Piaget answers this question with an explicit and emphatic yes. The theory Piaget constructed attempts to document the developmental progression (the structural and stage components of the theory), to explain the progression (the functional or equilibration component of the theory), and to provide testable auxiliary hypotheses that will support the theoretical representation. Thus, Piaget clearly employs organismic hard core and positive heuristic features regarding change as deep-seated guidelines in theory construction (see Table 2.1).

In contrast to Piaget, Chomsky does not address the question of structural change in any systematic manner. His comments on this topic are usually framed within general discussions that do not directly implicate his theory. Thus, for example, he has asserted, "it is reasonable to suppose that just as intrinsic structures of the mind underlie the development of cognitive structures, so a 'species character' provides the framework for the growth of moral consciousness" (Chomsky, 1975, p. 133). And, in his debate with Piaget he suggested "successive maturation of specialized hardware" as a metaphor that "holds rather well for the embryological development and also for the growth of mental structures....We should next explore the question of what the special mechanisms are that come into operation at various stages of growth" (Chomsky, in Piattelli-Palmarini, 1980, pp. 75–76). Comments of this sort cannot be taken as evidence that Chomsky adopts a commitment to necessary change. They do, however, suggest that he does not repudiate this organismic hard core and positive heuristic feature. Rather, this feature is simply not directly incorporated into the theory designed to explain language.

Chomsky's failure to incorporate necessary change into his theory might be dealt with by simply noting that he is not very interested in development. That is, it might be said that Chomsky's theory, like Gestalt theory, or George Kelly's personality theory, represents a form of truncated organicism. However, such statements, although not incorrect, miss an important point concerning the nature of scientific research programs; empirical problems in a particular domain of study provide the impetus to elaborate various features of a research program's positive heuristic.

Scientific research programs function to provide guidelines for the construction of theories that are directed toward the solution of empirical problems. But the empirical problems differ in nature depending on the domain of investigation and the degree to which earlier research has already provided some solutions. Thus, the elaboration of features of the positive heuristic depends to a significant degree upon the problems or puzzles that confront the investigator *at any particular time* with respect to his or her field of investigation.

From this perspective, Piaget, in considering the intellectual domain, was initially faced with empirical problems concerning seemingly major transformations that occur in thinking between infancy and adulthood. Given his organismic commitments, these empirical problems led to theory formation that incorporated necessary change features as well as holism and structure-function features of the positive heuristic. In contrast, Chomsky, in considering the domain of language, was faced with the relatively early expression of universal components of syntax. This empirical problem fostered an elaboration of the holistic and structure-function features of the organismic program, but it did not require an elaboration of the necessary change features. Both theories are members of the organismic family but they are individuated by the problems they seek to solve.

The fact that within any given research program features of the positive heuristic may be differentially elaborated, depending upon the empirical problems that face the theory at a particular time, both clarifies the concept of a family of theories and suggests how theories may be extended in a natural and coherent fashion. At any given time a specific theory may turn back to the hard core and draw upon the untapped resources of this program to deal with novel problems. This is what Lakatos (1978) meant when he stated that the positive heuristic is theoretically progressive in that it provides a set of suggestions on how to modify and sophisticate theories in a prescribed, coherent fashion. To take Piaget and Chomsky again as examples, at an early point in theory development Chomsky and his colleagues, dealing with language expression, as well as language knowledge, recognized the need to draw on both the contingent and the formal explanation features of the organismic positive heuristic. As a consequence, the competence-performance distinction was proposed and used in linguistic theory (Chomsky, 1965). Piaget, in contrast, was not initially faced with the kind of empirical puzzles that required more than an occasional allusion to contingent effects. Today, as it becomes clear that contingent effects do influence the universal structures of cognition, it is reasonable for Piaget's theory or any other organismic-based cognitive developmental theory to draw upon the positive heuristic and productively employ a competence-moderator-performance distinction. To do so is not to proceed via patched-up ad hoc hypotheses designed to save the theory. To propose the competence-moderator-performance distinction within an organismic research program is to proceed in a theoretically progressive manner by systematically developing the positive heuristic in a fashion that victoriously turns seeming anomalies into examples, all according to a preconceived plan (Lakatos, 1978, p. 111).

CONCLUSIONS

In this essay I have tried to establish a strong scientific rationale and conceptual foundation for the competence-moderator-performance distinction. This rationale is not found if the distinction is interpreted within the scientific methodologies of positivism, conventionalism, or a general research program called the mechanistic approach. Each of these methodologies either eliminates or trivializes formal explanation (i.e., competence) and relies exclusively upon contingent explanation. However, a strong rationale for the competence-moderator-performance distinction is found in the general scientific research program called the organismic approach. This methodology requires a balance between formal and contingent explanation, i.e., between competence explanations and explanations in terms of moderators. Further, this general methodology provides guidelines for the formulation of a family of specific theories — currently including those of Chomsky, Piaget, and

Werner — that may represent the competence-moderator-performance distinction, not as an ad hoc special hypothesis, but as a natural and coherent part of the theory development process.

REFERENCES

Chomsky, N. (1965). *Aspects of the theory of syntax.* Cambridge, MA: M.I.T. Press.

Chomsky, N. (1975). *Reflections on language.* New York: Pantheon Books.

Cohen, L. J. (1981). Can human irrationality be experimentally demonstrated? *The Behavioral and Brain Sciences, 4,* 317–331.

Einstein, A., & Infeld, L. (1938). *The evolution of physics.* New York: Simon & Schuster.

Gelman, R., & Gallistel, C. R. (1978). *The child's understanding of number.* Cambridge, MA: Harvard University Press.

Griggs, R. A. (1981). Human reasoning: Can we judge before we understand? *The Behavioral and Brain Sciences, 4,* 338–339.

Gholson, B. & Beilin, H. (1978). A developmental model of human learning. In H. W. Reese & L. P. Lipsitt (Eds.), *Advances in child development and behavior* (Vol. 13). New York: Academic Press.

Hull, C. L. (1920). Quantitative aspects of the evolution of concepts. *Psychological Monographs, 28,* No. 1 (Whole No. 123).

Lakatos, I. (1978). *The methodology of scientific research programmes: Philosophical papers* (Vol. 1.) Cambridge University Press.

Laudan, L. (1977). *Progress and its problems: Towards a theory of scientific growth.* Berkeley: University of California Press.

Miller, G. A. (1975). Some comments on competence and performance. In D. Aaronson & R. W. Rieber (Eds.), *Developmental psycholinguistics and communication disorders.* New York: New York Academy of Sciences.

Nagel, E. (1979). *The structure of science.* Cambridge, MA: Hackett.

Nelson, K. (1977). Cognitive development and the acquisition of concepts. In R. C. Anderson, R. J. Shapiro, & W. E. Montague (Eds.), *Schooling and the acquisition of knowledge.* Hillsdale, NJ: Lawrence Erlbaum Associates.

Nelson, K. (1979). Explorations in the development of a functional semantic system. In W. A. Collins (Ed.), *Minnesota symposium on child psychology.* (Vol. 12). Hillsdale, NJ: Lawrence Erlbaum Associates.

Nickels, T. (1980). Introductory essay: Scientific discovery and the future of philosophy of science. In T. Nickles (Ed.), *Scientific discovery, logic and rationality.* Boston: D. Reidel.

Osgood, C. E. (1968). Toward a wedding of insufficiencies. In R. R. Dixon & D. L. Horton (Eds.), *Verbal behavior and general behavior theory.* Englewood Cliffs, NJ: Prentice-Hall.

Overton, W. F. (1975). General systems, structure, and development. In K. Riegel & G. Rosenwald (Eds.), *Structure and transformation: Developmental aspects.* New York: Wiley Interscience.

Overton, W. F. (1976). The active organism in structuralism. *Human Development, 19,* 71–86.

Overton, W. F. (Ed.). (1983a). *The relationship between social and cognitive development.* Hillsdale, NJ: Lawrence Erlbaum Associates.

Overton, W. F. (1983b). World views and their influence on psychological theory and research. Kuhn — Lakatos — Laudan. In H. W. Reese (Ed.), *Advances in child development and behavior.* (Vol. 18). New York: Academic Press.

Overton, W. F., & Newman, J. (1982). Cognitive development: A competence-activation/utilization approach. In T. Field, A. Houston, H. Quay, L. Troll, & G. Finley (Eds.), *Review of human development.* New York: Wiley.

Overton, W. F., & Reese, H. W. (1973). Models of development: Methodological implications. In J. R. Nesselroade & H. W. Reese (Eds.), *Life-span developmental psychology: Methodological issues.* New York: Academic Press.

Overton, W. F., & Reese, H. W. (1981). Conceptual prerequisites for an understanding of stability-change and continuity-discontinuity. *International Journal of Behavioral Development, 4,* 99–123.

Pepper, S. (1942). *World hypotheses.* Berkeley: University of California Press.

Piattelli-Palmarini, M. (Ed.). (1980). *Language and learning: The debate between Jean Piaget and Noam Chomsky.* Cambridge, MA: Harvard University Press.

Popper, K. R. (1959). *The logic of scientific discovery.* London: Hutchinson.

Reese, H. W., & Overton, W. F. (1970). Models of development and theories of development. In L. R. Goulet & P. B. Baltes (Eds.), *Life-span developmental psychology: Research and theory.* New York: Academic Press.

Reichenbach, H. (1938). *Experience and prediction.* Chicago: University of Chicago Press.

Rosch, E. (1978). *Principles of categorization.* In E. Rosch & B. B. Lloyd (Eds.)., *Cognition and categorization.* Hillsdale, NJ: Lawrence Erlbaum Associates.

Ruble, D. N., Balaban, T., & Cooper, J. (1981). Gender constancy and the effects of sex-typed television toy commercials. *Child Development, 52,* 667–673.

Sampson, G. (1981). Human rationality: Misleading linguistic analogies. *The Behavioral and Brain Sciences, 4,* 350–351.

Scholnick, E. K. (1983). Why are new trends in conceptual representation a challenge to Piaget's theory? In E. K. Scholnick (Ed.), *New trends in conceptual representation: Challenges to Piaget's theory?* Hillsdale, NJ: Lawrence Erlbaum Associates.

Schwartz, B., & Lacey, H. (1982). *Behaviorism, science, and human nature.* New York: W. W. Norton.

Siegler, R. S. (1981). Developmental sequences within and between concepts. *Monographs of the Society for Research in Child Development, 46,* (Whole No. 189).

Siegler, R. S., & Richards, D. D. (1979). The development of time, speed, and distance concepts. *Developmental Psychology, 15,* 288–298.

Skinner, B. F. (1950). Are theories of learning necessary? *Psychological Review, 57,* 193–216.

Skinner, B. F. (1956). A case history in scientific method. *American Psychologist, 11,* 221–233.

Skinner, B. F. (1971). *Beyond freedom and dignity.* New York: Bantam Books.

Stone, C. A., & Day, M. C. (1980). Competence and performance models and the characterization of formal operational skills. *Human Development, 23,* 323–353.

Trabasso, T., Isen, A. M., Dolecki, P., McLanahan, A. G., Riley, C. A., & Tucker, T. (1978). How do children solve class inclusion problems? In R. S. Siegler (Ed.), *Children's thinking: What develops?* Hillsdale, NJ: Lawrence Erlbaum Associates.

Wartofsky, M. (1968). *Conceptual foundation of scientific thought.* Toronto: Macmillan.

3 Competence and Performance in Intellectual Development

Janet E. Davidson
Robert J. Sternberg
Yale University

Intellectual development has traditionally been studied by the examination of children's performance on a variety of tasks, such as tests of verbal ability, memory, number skills, and problem solving. However, experimental results that purport to show children's intellectual levels often are ambiguous as to whether the observed levels reflect the children's competence or, instead, their ability to use this competence. Attempts to resolve this ambiguity have focused upon the distinction between competence and performance (e.g., Flavell & Wohlwill, 1969). Such attempts specify, at least in some degree of detail, the extent to which observed behavior represents limitations in children's competence and the extent to which it represents limitations in children's ability to apply this competence in specific tasks and situations. Some current theories of cognitive development are treating competence and performance components as co-equals in intellectual development (e.g., Overton & Newman, 1982).

In this chapter, we present a proposed model of intellectual development that includes both competence and performance components. Our presentation is divided into four main parts. First, we briefly describe how we interpret the competence-performance distinction and discuss why we believe the distinction is an important one. Second, we present the competence component of our model, describing those aspects of human competence that we believe play a crucial role in intellectual development. Third, we present the performance component of our model, describing the aspects of human performance that we believe limit the expression of competence in significant ways. Finally, we draw some implications of our model for understanding intellectual development.

THE COMPETENCE-PERFORMANCE DISTINCTION

By competence, we refer to the availability of skills and logical structures such as information processes, knowledge, functional capacity of working memory, and representational formats in which information can be stored. *By performance, we refer to the utilization of competence, as mediated by the accessibility in a given task and situation of factors* including processes, knowledge, working memory, representations, motivation, cognitive styles, and external resources. Performance factors determine the application of competence in a variety of situations. Both competence and performance are essential in cognitive development.

Several benefits accrue from clearly distinguishing between competence and performance components of intellectual development. First, the distinction may provide some resolution of seemingly irresoluble (and endless) debates regarding the age at which particular aspects of intellectual functioning first appear. Such debates are rampant throughout the cognitive-developmental literature (e.g., Bryant & Trabasso, 1971; Gelman & Gallistel, 1978; Inhelder & Piaget, 1958; Lefebvre-Pinard & Pinard, this volume; Piaget, 1972). Although we do not believe the competence-performance distinction provides a resolution to all such debates, we do suspect that at least in some cases, the difference in age between when a competence is first acquired and the range of ages during which that competence becomes successively better expressed accounts for some past disagreements. "Horizontal decalage" may be one way of expressing the distinction, but we believe that the competence-performance perspective may prove more illuminating in the long run.

Second, awareness of the competence-performance distinction may enable us to better design experiments that veridically elucidate what children *can* do and what they *do* do at different ages. In particular, by controlling performance factors, we can better determine (a) the underlying organization of a particular logical structure; (b) the typical developmental course of this structure; and (c) what a child "has," that is, where he or she is developmentally with respect to (a) and (b) (Flavell, 1977). We do not underestimate the difficulty of designing experiments that clearly distinguish between competence and performance: These two components of development undoubtedly interact in subtle ways, and moreover, competence can be inferred only through observed performance. But we believe that sensitivity to the competence-performance distinction can lead us to at least preliminary indications of which component(s) is or are limiting performance as observed at a given age.

Third, sensitive diagnosis of an individual child's strengths and weaknesses requires heeding the difference between what the child shows in a test-like situation and what the child could potentially show in any situation. Vygotsky's (1978) brilliant conceptualization of a "zone of potential development" recognizes how great the difference between competence and performance can be: A child who seems initially not to have a particular skill may display the skill if properly guided by an examiner. (Obviously, the examiner must be aware of whether he or she has elicited the behavior from the child or merely given it to the child.) Feuerstein's (1979) Learning Potential Assessment Device represents the first operationalization of the Vygotskian construct, and in initial tests seems to have proven highly successful in eliciting from children competences that they might otherwise not have displayed. This device involves giving children progressive feedback on cognitive test items, and assessing the extent to which they are able to utilize this feedback.

Fourth, appropriate training procedures for children — both as individuals and in groups — require knowledge of what particular children can do under what circumstances. Availability of a given capacity is necessary (although not sufficient) for the success of a training intervention: If a capacity is simply unavailable, no amount of training will be successful (Gelman, 1978; Inhelder, Sinclair, & Bovet, 1974). Instructional programs based upon the work of Piaget have been extremely popular in recent years (e.g., Furth, 1970). These programs have met with mixed success because, we believe, they have not always given sufficient heed to the performance factors that mediate the competence structures proposed in Piaget's theory of intellectual development.

Finally, we believe that a complete theory of intellectual development (such as has not yet been specified) will need to take fully into account both competence and performance factors, as well as their interactions. The most nearly complete theory so far — that of Piaget (1952, 1972; Inhelder & Piaget, 1958; Piaget & Inhelder, 1964/1970) — is essentially a theory of intellectual competence. Indeed, a major goal of the contributions in this book is to provide a performance interface that will increase the applicability of Piaget's theory to real-world performance. The theory is open to criticism for not including a clear performance component, but should not be criticized for performance claims it never made.

In conclusion, we believe that the competence-performance distinction is an important one, both from theoretical and practical points of view. Our hope, like that of other contributors to this volume, is that our model will contribute to the clarification of the distinction, and will serve the future needs of both theoreticians and practitioners. The model is summarized in Table 3.1 and Fig. 3.1

Table 3.1 simply summarizes the competence and performance variables theorized to influence observed performance. These variables are discussed further in the remainder of the chapter. Figure 3.1 indicates the nature of the relations among competence variables, performance variables, and performance. Competence affects performance through the mediation of the performance variables. Because the effects of competence variables are always

TABLE 3.1
Competence and Performance
Factors in Intellectual Development

Competence Factors

Process availability
  Metastrategic processes
  Strategic processes
  Knowledge acquisition processes
Automatization of component processes
Knowledge availability
Functional capacity of working memory
Representational formats

Performance Factors

Efficacy of process execution
  Accessibility
  Speed
  Accuracy
  Process activation and feedback
Knowledge accessibility
Usable capacity of working memory
Accessibility of representations
Motivation
Selection of goals
Cognitive styles
External resources

mediated by the effects of performance variables, it is never possible to make direct inferences about these competence variables; rather, one must infer their existence and effects indirectly. Such inferences can be made only if one understands the effects of the performance variables. If one does, then one can understand the effects of the competence variables essentially by partialing out from observable performance those effects localized as being due to the performance variables. The less accurate one's understanding of these latter effects, the less accurate will be one's understanding of the former effects, because competence cannot be understood without a thorough understanding of how performance variables affect performance. It is for this reason that most information-processing psychologists have chosen, at least initially, to concentrate their theory and research on issues relating to performance variables, and that many of them have given up in despair even at the thought of separating competence from performance variables. But on the present view, such a separation is possible, so long as one understands performance variables, as well as their interactions with performance, on the one hand, and the competence variables, on the other.

According to the model, the effects of competence on performance are always mediated, but the feedback from performance to the competence variables may be either direct or mediated. Moreover, competence variables provide feedback to each other. This feedback is the source of much of the observed improvements in performance that children show over age. (See Sternberg, 1982, for a fairly detailed discussion of just how these feedback mechanisms work.)

THE COMPETENCE COMPONENT

Our model of the competence component of intellectual development is an attempt to provide an integrated account of the intellectual skills and logical

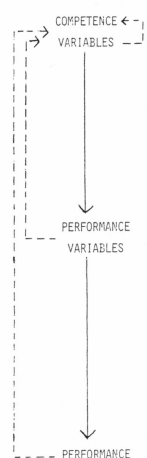

FIG. 3.1   Relations among competence variables, performance variables, and performance. Competence affects performance through the mediation of the performance variables (with effects indicated by solid arrows). Feedback is provided to the competence variables through knowledge gained from performance, performance variables, and competence variables providing feedback to each other (with feedback indicated by broken arrows).

structures that are necessary for intelligent functioning. The account we propose draws heavily upon the work of both Piagetian and information-processing researchers. This account deals with five factors that we believe are critical in and, to a large extent, constitute the development of intellectual competence: availability of information processes, automatization of information processes, availability of knowledge, functional capacity of working memory, and representational capacity (i.e., the capacity to represent knowledge mentally in structured and efficacious ways). We consider each of these five factors of competence in turn.

Process Availability

Process availability refers to the capacity of an individual to plan, coordinate, monitor, and (potentially) bring to bear those mental activities that are needed for successful intellectual functioning. We divide processes into three types: metastrategic processes, strategic processes, and knowledge-acquisition processes.[1]

Metastrategic Processes. Piaget (1976) defined intellectual development as the movement toward greater flexibility and increased intentionality of thought. Using a variety of tasks, such as the colored liquids problem (which requires the child to discover what combination of four liquids produced a specific chemical reaction), Piaget found that with increasing age, the child is better able to plan beforehand how to attack the problem, to carry out this plan systematically, and to monitor the results and evaluate various hypotheses until he or she arrives at the best possible explanation of the phenomenon observed (Inhelder & Piaget, 1958; Lovell, 1961).

Like Piaget, we believe there are sophisticated control strategies (metastrategic processes) that develop with age (see also Brown, 1978; Brown & DeLoache, 1978; Butterfield & Belmont, 1977; Flavell, 1981; Lefebvre-Pinard & Pinard, this volume). We propose seven metaprocesses that we believe are of particular importance (see also Sternberg, 1982).

1. Decision as to Just What the Problem is That Needs to be Solved. Anyone who has done research with young children knows that half the battle is getting the children to understand what is being asked of them. Their difficulty often lies not in actually solving the problem, but in figuring out just what the problem is that needs to be solved (see, e.g., Flavell, 1977). A major feature distinguishing retarded persons from normal ones is the need of the retardates to be instructed explicitly and completely

---

[1]Metastrategic processes are called metacomponents, and strategic processes are called performance components, in some earlier papers, e.g., Sternberg (1980c).

about the nature of the particular task they are performing, and to be instructed about just how to perform it (Butterfield, Wambold, & Belmont, 1973; Campione & Brown, 1977, 1979). The importance of figuring out the nature of the problem is not limited to children and retarded persons. Resnick and Glaser (1976) have argued that intelligence is in large part the ability to learn in the absence of direct or complete instruction.

2. Selection of Lower Order Processes.   An individual must select a set of lower order (strategic or acquisition) processes to use in the performance of a given task. Selecting a nonoptimal set of processes can result in incorrect or inefficient task performance. In some instances, the choice of processes will be partially attributable to differential availability of the processes: Young children may lack certain processes that are necessary or at least desirable for the accomplishment of particular tasks. For example, Sternberg and Rifkin (1979) found that in solving analogies with schematic pictures as content, 7-year-olds were unable to perform second-order mapping of a relation between relations, whereas older children were able to perform such a mapping. The results were quite consistent with Piaget's notion that the ability to perceive second-order relations is a signal for the entrance of a child into the formal-operational period (Inhelder & Piaget, 1958). Sternberg and Downing (1982) carried the earlier research one step further, finding that the ability to perform a third-order mapping apparently did not emerge until middle to late adolescence. Although one could not be certain in either the Sternberg and Rifkin experiment with analogies or the Sternberg and Downing experiment with "higher order" analogies that inability to perform mappings was due to differential availability rather than differential accessibility of processes, the experimental manipulations in each study were such as to create a high probability of the processes being elicited if indeed they were available: Materials were simple (schematic pictures or high-frequency words) and instructions made clear what needed to be done in order for the task constraints to be met.

3. Selection of One or More Representations or Organizations for Information.   A given process can often operate on any one of a number of possible representations or organizations for information. The choice of representation or organization can facilitate or impede the efficacy with which a given process operates. For example, it has commonly been found that younger children tend to organize information about concepts and classes of concepts syntagmatically, whereas older children tend to organize the same information paradigmatically (Anglin, 1970; Nelson, 1977). Without sufficient information about a class of concepts, paradigmatic organization is simply impossible (and thus unavailable). Differences in organization have been used as a basis for scoring items on intelligence tests administered to both children and adults. On the Stanford-Binet, for example (Terman & Merrill, 1973), more highly abstracted and classificatory definitions are given more points on the vocabulary scale than are more concrete or functional definitions. Differences in ways information is encoded can be found in perceptual as well as in conceptual development. For example, Shepp (1978) reported a tendency for children to move from integral to separable perception of attributes with increasing age; Smith and Kemler (1978) elaborated upon this notion by suggesting a shift toward increasing use of dimensional structure with increasing age.

4. Selection of a Strategy for Combining Lower Order Processes.   In itself, a set of processes is insufficient to perform a task. One must also sequence these processes in a way that facilitates task performance, and decide how nearly exhaustively the processes will be executed. For example, it is well known that younger children tend to process with early (and often premature) termination the same stimuli that older children tend to process exhaustively (Brown & DeLoache, 1978; Sternberg & Nigro, 1980; Sternberg & Rifkin, 1979; Vurpillot, 1968). One reason for the differential strategy choice seems clearly to relate to a competence factor: The younger children do not have the functional working memory capacity to hold in working memory the extent of information required by exhaustive processing (Case, 1974; Sternberg & Rifkin, 1979). The processing demands of such a strategy — working memory considerations aside — may also be too great for young children. Along these lines, Brown and Smiley (1977a, 1977b) showed that as they develop, children become better able to predict the essential elements and organizing features of a text. Because of this foreknowledge, older children are better able to make good use of study time on a text-comprehension task.

5. Allocation of Mental Resources.   Problem solvers often encounter various barriers to their efforts. Some of these barriers are external, such as the total time made available for problem solution or the computational or other aids that are allowed to be used; other barriers are internal, such as the amount of processing capacity one is able to bring to bear upon a given problem. The problem solver must decide what resources might ideally be used in solving a problem, and what resources he or she actually can bring to bear. For example, individuals with less expertise in a given area of endeavor seem to spend relatively less time in global, "upfront" planning for solution, and relatively more time in actually attempting to implement a solution. This pattern holds both across age levels and across different levels of expertise within age levels (see, e.g., Chi, Glaser, & Rees, 1982; Larkin, McDermott, Simon, & Simon, 1980; Sternberg, 1981; Sternberg & Rifkin, 1979). We believe that this difference in planning time reflects in large part a competence difference between the more and less skilled problem solvers: The less skilled problem solvers do not have the available knowledge and processing resources that would be required for extended global planning. Not having the wherewithal to plan intelligently, they "muddle through," and often get bogged down in garden path solutions.

6. *Solution Monitoring.* As individuals proceed through a problem, they must keep track of what they have already done, what they are currently doing, and what they still need to do. Indeed, Flavell (1981) has made this and other kinds of "cognitive monitoring" the basis for his theoretical account of human metacognition. Broadly conceived, solution monitoring includes one's control over the mental constructions one has formed and as yet needs to form for understanding text or directions. For example, the failure of Markman's (1977, 1979) children in monitoring their comprehension can be seen as a failure in solution monitoring in which individuals fail to realize the bearing of recently acquired knowledge on knowledge currently being acquired. In this case, the children simply failed to realize contradictions between what they had already learned and what they were currently learning. "Keeping track" of one's knowledge and place in comprehension and problem-solving tasks was once relegated to the role of a minor bookkeeping operation. Work such as Flavell's and Markman's makes it clear that this relegation was inappropriate. That young children are surprisingly resistant to strong manipulations designed to help them monitor their comprehension suggests that competence limitations play at least some role in the children's failures in monitoring. Presumably, the integrative capacity required in the comprehension monitoring experiments exceeds the capacities of the young children who have been involved.

7. *Understanding and Utilization of Feedback.* Early concept-learning research showed the critical importance of feedback in the learning of new information (see, e.g., Bourne, 1966; Bruner, Goodnow, & Austin, 1956). The role of feedback in intellectual development has been recognized to be critical. In Feuerstein's (1979, 1980) theory of mediated learning experience, for example, the keystone of intellectual development is the recursive feedback loop between mother and child that is provided by the mother's interpretation of the events going on in the child's life. Feuerstein's (1979) Learning Potential Assessment Device can be seen as, in part, a measure of a child's ability to use feedback, providing, as it does, an operationalization of Vygotsky's (1978) zone of potential development.

   To summarize, we believe that metastrategic processes play a very important part in the development of intellectual competence. Indeed, these skills may be the central intellectual competences of the human mind through which most, if not all, other competences come to be expressed. It is perhaps for this reason that metastrategic processes have sometimes been called "control" or "executive" processes. In a sense, they seem to run all other aspects of mental functioning.

Strategic Processes. Strategic processes are used in the execution of various kinds of intellectual tasks. Although the number of possible strategic processes is probably quite large, many of these processes probably apply only to small or uninteresting subsets of tasks, and hence are of little interest to the theory of intellectual development. But even the set of interesting processes is quite large (see, e.g., Ford & Keating, 1981; Keating & Bobbitt, 1978; Keating, Keniston, Manis, & Bobbitt, 1980; Pellegrino & Kail, 1982; Sternberg, 1982). We describe here only a small subset of those processes that we believe are particularly central to development.

1. Encoding. In any problem-solving situation, an individual must encode the terms of the problem, storing aspects of them in working memory and retrieving from long-term memory information relevant to the terms. Qualitative and quantitative changes in encoding seem to constitute a major source of intellectual development. For example, Siegler (1978) has found that a key source of improved performance on his balance-scale (and other) tasks in older children can be attributed to more thorough encoding of the stimulus situation on the part of the older children. This finding seems to be one more instance of the previously mentioned tendency for older and more skilled individuals to encode information more nearly completely than do younger and less skilled individuals, as is the finding by Sternberg and Rifkin (1979) that older children spent relatively more time encoding analogy terms than did younger children. The more careful encoding of stimulus terms enabled the children to perform other performance processes more rapidly. The Sternberg and Rifkin finding is a particularly apt one for illustrating the need to distinguish competence from performance. If one were simply to look at performance, one might come to the (nonsensical) conclusion that older children's prolonged encoding time reflects *lesser* ability to encode. Indeed, for the overwhelming majority of performance processes, prolonged process times are associated with reduced ability. But we believe that the prolongation in encoding time reflects the operation of a strategic competence whereby a decision is made to trade off increased encoding time for reduced time to operate upon these encodings, and ultimately, reduced time and increased accuracy in solving the problems as a whole.

2. Inference. In making an inference, a person detects one or more relations between two objects, either or both of which may be concrete or abstract. Inference making is central to various forms of inductive reasoning (Gallagher & Wright, 1979; Sternberg, 1977), including such reasoning as operates in the real world (Collins, Warnock, Aiello, & Miller, 1975), and also to various kinds of memory tasks (see Kail, 1979). For example, studies by Paris and his associates (Paris & Lindauer, 1977; Paris, Lindauer, & Cox, 1977) have shown that children's ability to make inferences increases greatly during the elementary school years. They showed that when presented with sentences such as "His mother baked a cake," older children but not younger children were able to use "oven" as a retrieval cue to remember the sentence. The inference drawn from this result was that only the older children inferred the instrument for baking the cake at the time of sentence storage. This inference may have been facilitated by the richer knowledge base upon which the older children could draw. It appears that the competence to make simple inferences develops quite early (Piaget, 1972). We have relatively little knowledge about the ages at which various kinds of inferences can first be made, although the pursuit of this question is now an active area of research (see Brown, Bransford, & Ferrara, 1982).

3. Mapping.   In mapping, a person relates the structure of a newly encoded situation to a previously encoded one (see Gentner, 1977; Holyoak, 1984; Sternberg, 1977). For example, in a standard analogy, the person seeks a higher order relationship that relates the first half of an analogy to the second half. Mapping appears relatively late in children's repertoires of cognitive skills (Gallagher & Wright, 1979; Lunzer, 1965; Piaget, with Montangero & Billeter, 1977; Sternberg & Rifkin, 1979). Concrete-operational children appear not to select the mapping component in solving analogies because it is unavailable to them. Instead, they may rely on word association in verbal analogies (Achenbach, 1979, 1971) or holistic comparisons in figural analogies and matrices (Hunt, 1974). Case (1978) has suggested that the acquisition of mapping abilities of orders higher than the second may define successive post-formal operational stages. The evidence of Sternberg and Downing (1982) cited earlier for higher order analogies, and also a study by Commons, Richards, and Kuhn (1982), which investigated mappings of systems in individuals assumed at least to have entered the formal-operational period, suggest that higher orders of mapping can be associated at least with advanced subperiods within the formal-operational period. We remain neutral as to whether anything is to be gained by viewing acquisition of these higher order mappings as sufficient evidence for a distinctly different period from the formal-operational. If there are such periods, it is not wholly clear to us at this point on what basis they should be defined. (See Commons & Armon, 1983, for a variety of perspectives on the issue of post-formal-operational development.)

To summarize, strategic processes such as encoding, inference, and mapping can play an important part in the development of intellectual competence. Differential availability of such processes seems to affect performance in a wide range of tasks, from the basic perceptual to the advanced conceptual level.

Knowledge-Acquisition Processes. Knowledge-acquisition processes provide ways of learning about the world. They supply the mechanisms for a steadily increasing knowledge base. Although there is an enormous literature on the development of learning and memory capacities (see, e.g., Kail, 1979; Kail & Hagen, 1977), researchers on learning and memory have arrived at no consensus as to just what the available knowledge-acquisition processes are. Hence, in describing three such processes, we hasten to say that we are probably representing only our own idiosyncratic viewpoint.

1. Selective Encoding. Acquisition of knowledge involves actively, selectively, and sequentially acquiring information from one's environment (e.g., Brown & DeLoache, 1978). By selective encoding, we refer to the sifting process by which an individual decides what information to commit to memory and what information to ignore from the barrage of informational inputs presented to him or her. In classical learning experiments, subjects were (and often still are) presented with lists of words (numbers, nonsense syllables, or whatever) to commit to memory; subjects would then be tested on the lists in various ways (see, e.g., Crowder, 1976). Such experiments have been criticized for ecological invalidity on a number of grounds. We believe such experiments have told us a great deal about learning and memory, but not as it most frequently occurs in real-world situations where there is a large amount of information, only some of it important. We believe that a critical determinant of the extent, organization, and quality of the knowledge base is the quality of one's decisions regarding what information should and should not be remembered.

Note that the selective encoding to which we refer here differs from the encoding we considered under strategic processes both in the operation to which a stimulus input is committed, and in the ultimate fate of that stimulus input. Many stimuli are encoded so that they can be processed in working memory (a strategic process), but we believe that only a small subset of these stimuli are encoded in such a way as to result in a long-term memory trace. The latter kind of encoding requires a greater and, we believe, qualitatively different commitment of resources from the former kind of encoding.

Research on selective encoding has appeared under a number of different guises. Much of the recent research on story memory and memory for texts falls into this class, in that remembering information from a text almost always requires some kind of decision as to what is and is not worth remembering (see, e.g., Bartlett, 1932; Bower, Black, & Turner, 1979). We believe that a particularly interesting example of research on selective encoding can be found in the work of Werner and Kaplan (1952), who studied acquisition of word meanings in context. In their experiments, subjects would be presented with six sentences containing a neologism, and the subjects would have to use the context in the sentences to figure out what the word means. We believe that much of the learning of new vocabulary occurs in this way, rather than through simple rote memorization. One encounters a previously unknown word in context, and then must sift out what in the surrounding context is irrelevant to inferring the word's meaning. One's success in figuring out the word's meaning and, we believe, in retaining the word's meaning in one's memory will be largely dependent upon one's ability to sift out the relevant clues from the morass of useless information (Sternberg, Powell, & Kaye, 1982).

2. Selective Combination. By selective combination, we refer to the process of combining known informational items in a new way so as to acquire knowledge one formerly did not have. Whereas selective encoding operates upon new informational inputs, selective combination operates upon informational inputs that have already been stored in long-term memory. Selectivity is involved in the decision of just which of the many possible combinations of inputs is appropriate for a given purpose. In selective combination, one puts together pieces of information one already has in much the same way that one fits together the pieces of a jigsaw puzzle. We believe that much mathematics learning is of this kind. The difficulty in learning how to solve many simple kinds of arithmetic (e.g., complex multiplication or long division) as well as in learning how to solve more complex kinds of word problems seems to be not so much in learning individual steps, but in knowing how and when to combine them in particular ways (see also Resnick & Ford, 1981). Similarly, learning to play a game such as chess involves learning a relatively small number of possible moves, but an extremely large number of possible combinations of moves (see Chase & Simon, 1973). As a final example, consider learning how to read. The number of things one needs to learn is enormous; but perhaps the greatest difficulty in learning to read is learning how to put together the various skills one has acquired into a meaningful and workable package (see Spiro, Bruce, & Brewer, 1980).

3. Selective Comparison. By selective comparison, we refer to the process of relating new informational inputs to old ones so as to acquire knowledge one formerly did not have. Thus, whereas selective encoding deals with new informational inputs and selective combination with old informational inputs, selective comparison deals with the relating of new informational inputs to old ones in such a way that one learns something distinctively new. Learning by analogy is learning of this kind. For example, when one attempts to learn a second language by relating aspects of it to one's first language, one is using selective comparison. Selectivity is virtually always involved because one first has to decide what old information is analogous, and then decide in what ways the old information is also disanalogous. Because analogies are virtually always partial, learning by analogy can involve negative as well as positive transfer. Skilled selective comparison minimizes the negative transfer by careful recognition of just how far a given analogy extends (Holyoak, 1984; Oppenheimer, 1956; Sternberg, 1977).

To summarize, we believe that acquisition of nontrivial, real-world knowledge involves knowledge-acquisition processes that are a far cry from the fairly mechanical processes used in rote learning. Learning of this kind is a form of problem solving, and the learner must act as a problem solver. His or her competence in applying knowledge-acquisition processes will in large part determine the knowledge base available for subsequent learning and problem solving.

Automatization of Component Processes

Cognitive development results not only from improved availability of component processes, but also from increased automatization of such processes. In particular, the functioning of a given componential subsystem for a particular task domain proceeds from controlled to automatic. *Controlled* processing is of strictly limited capacity, primarily serial, but unlimited in its ability to call upon all of an individual's stored knowledge base. *Automatic* information processing is of almost unlimited capacity, primarily parallel, but strictly limited in the knowledge base stored in long-term memory upon which it can draw. Typically, controlled processing is conscious and automatic processing is preconscious.

In processing information from new domains (and especially non-entrenched ones; see Sternberg, 1981) or domains in which one does not have much expertise, the individual relies primarily upon controlled, global processing. In contrast, in processing information from old domains or domains in which one has acquired considerable expertise, the individual relies primarily upon automatic, local processing. In the latter case, multiple local subsystems for processing information can act in parallel, increasing the mind's ability to get work done. Consider, for example, driving a car. For a novice, driving a car consumes almost all of his or her available resources. Processing of information is primarily controlled. For an expert, however, driving may consume little attention, so that it is possible to carry on a discussion while driving, or to do other things that would overtax the capabilities of a novice. Note that degree of automatization affects what is available but not what is accessible. It is for this reason that we refer to automatization as a competence rather than as a performance factor.

An implication of this view is that the learner who is unable to automatize performance — whether at the level of metaprocesses, performance processes, or knowledge-acquisition processes — will be quite slow to develop expertise in any area for which automatization is impaired. Indeed, specific learning disabilities may result from automatization failure in particular domains of learning. In such cases, processing that has become smooth and automatic in most people remains labored and controlled in the disabled individual. Such an individual will be less able to integrate multiple aspects of a task (such as reading), and thus to perform the task in the effortless way that characterizes the skilled performer.

Knowledge Availability

As a child develops, his or her knowledge base becomes increasingly large and diverse. Increments in the knowledge base take the form both of increased numbers of informational items, and of increased numbers of interconnections among these items. Knowledge is often characterized as being of two kinds, declarative and procedural.

Declarative knowledge refers to facts and concepts, including facts and concepts about one's own functioning. For example, knowing that an apple is red or that it is a fruit would be examples of declarative knowledge. In modern theories of knowledge representation, declarative knowledge is typically represented in the form of semantic propositional networks (see, e.g., Anderson, 1980) in which the items of information are represented as nodes in the network and the interconnections among the items of information are represented as links between those nodes. The complexity of the semantic network should be a function of the amount, elaboration, and organization of a child's declarative knowledge (see Chi, 1984; Chi & Koeske, 1983).

Procedural knowledge refers to both general and domain-specific strategies and procedures for thought and action. For example, knowing how to solve a long-division problem, or knowing how to knit a scarf, are instances of procedural knowledge. Such knowledge is usually represented either as flow charts (e.g., Miller, Galanter, & Pribram, 1960; Siegler, 1978, Sternberg, 1977) or as production systems (e.g., Anderson, 1976; Klahr, 1978; Newell & Simon, 1972). A flow chart is a "box diagram" in which the steps for solution of a given problem are represented as a sequence of successive boxes. A production system is a set of condition-action rules in which each condition is tested, in order, until a particular condition is satisfied; at this point, the action is executed, and control returns to the first production; at this point, testing down the list of productions can resume.

Both Piagetian and information-processing psychologists have tended, historically, to downplay the role of knowledge content in intellectual development. The former have concentrated upon prelogical and logical schemes; the latter have concentrated upon sequences of information processes. During the last several years, however, there has been increasing recognition upon the part of psychologists of both persuasions that the role of knowledge in development has probably been underestimated. One of the most well known studies that made this point was done by Chi (1978), who found that children who were chess experts had much better memory for chess positions than did adults who were chess novices, despite the fact that the children had lower digit spans than did the adults. Their chunking of chess information, but not of digit information, was more effective than the chunking by adults. Clearly, memory for information could not be separated from the content of that information. This work extended earlier work by DeGroot (1965) and Chase and Simon (1973) with adults, which found that experts had superior memory for chess positions when compared with novices, despite the fact that the chess experts did not have better memories overall. Indeed, the superiority of the experts' memory for chess positions held only when the board positions were sensible. When chess pieces were randomly arranged, there was no difference in recall between experts and novices.

The importance of knowledge availability can easily be seen in the domain of reasoning as well as in that of memory. In investigating children's reasoning with logical connectives, both Paris (1973) and Sternberg (1979) have found that sheer knowledge of the meanings of the logical connectives accounts for much of the observed quality of "reasoning" performance. The same holds true for quantifiers. Quite simply, children cannot reason with connectives whose meanings are unknown to them. The role of knowledge extends to inductive as well as deductive reasoning. It is a well-known fact, for example, that many tests of verbal reasoning, such as verbal analogies and classifications, are at least as much tests of knowledge as they are of reasoning skills (Sternberg, 1977). The tests become measures of reasoning only when word knowledge ceases to be an issue. But for the large majority of examinees, such knowledge is a major issue, if not *the* major issue.

Finally, the importance of knowledge availability can be seen in the domain of problem solving. Siegler's (1976) research on Piaget's balance-scale problem (Inhelder & Piaget, 1958) is a nice example of the importance of procedural knowledge in the development of problem solving. In this research, Siegler identified four basic procedures, or "rules," by which children could solve the balance-scale task. He found a clear progression in the use of successively more sophisticated rules as children grew older. In the present terminology, children were able to bring to bear increasingly sophisticated procedural knowledge in the solution of a complex problem.

In sum, then, the availability of knowledge plays an important role in intellectual development. Mental processes act upon a knowledge base, and the knowledge base at the same time can facilitate or hinder (because of its impoverishment or incorrectness) the functioning of the mental processes. We therefore believe that the trend to assign a greater role to knowledge is a healthy one, so long as the tendency to understate the role of knowledge is not replaced by a tendency to overstate its role. We have seen at least some examples where we believe its role has, in fact, been overstated.

Functional Capacity of Working Memory

Many measures of intellectual level — such as analogies, transitive inference problems, prediction problems, and tests of reading comprehension — require the child or adult temporarily to retain certain information in working memory, and then to process this information in some way so as to reach a solution. In almost all of these tests, the functional capacity of working memory will play a significant role in level of observed performance. For example, Wagner (1980) has shown that children's success in solving schematic-picture analogies can be directly linked to the working memory demands of the items, and to the extent of the children's working memories. Trabasso (Bryant & Trabasso, 1971; Riley & Trabasso, 1974; Trabasso, Riley, & Wilson, 1975) has shown that success of young children in solving transitive inference problems is at least as dependent upon the children's functional working memory capacities as it is upon their inferential skills. Brainerd (1981) has used variations of Piaget's (1950) random-draws task to show that working memory capacity plays at least as large a role as knowledge in children's probability judgments. And Daneman and Carpenter (1980) have shown that level of reading comprehension can be predicted at an extraordinarily high level by a measure of functional working memory capacity.

Working memory is so important in task performance because the "work space" activated by a particular task will almost always have a limited capacity (Osherson, 1974). Storage and processing demands compete for this limited capacity (Baddeley & Hitch, 1974; Case, 1974). If space-demanding processes use a large portion of the available capacity, then the amount of additional information that can be stored will decrease. Space-demanding processes may also generate intermediate processes that further interfere with the retention of new information.

The functional capacity of working memory appears to increase with age (Case, 1974; Pascual-Leone, 1970). (We emphasize here the word *functional* because the evidence regarding sheer size or capacity of working memory as a function of age is quite mixed; see Chi, 1976.) As functional capacity increases, it becomes increasingly easy to utilize and possibly to acquire more complex executive (meta) processes. The gradual increase in functional working memory capacity (which seems to follow Piaget's four major periods of development) stems from an increase in automaticity of the basic operations a child is capable of executing. Case (1978) has suggested that a certain level of operational automaticity at one period of development is prerequisite for the transition to the next period.

In sum, functional working memory capacity appears to be an important competence factor affecting observed performance. Its effects are sometimes unobvious and even insidious. But they are nevertheless there, and need to be taken into account in assessing the full range of children's competences.

Representational Formats

Information must be represented in some internal format before it can be processed. Many different formats are possible, for example, propositions, images, characteristic features, defining features, dimensions, and the like (see Anderson, 1978; Kail & Bisanz, in press). We believe that the availability of various representational formats changes with age.

We have previously discussed some of the representational changes that occur with age, namely, the shift from holistic to analytic representation in the perceptual domain (Shepp, 1978) and the shift from syntagmatic to para-digmatic organization in the conceptual domain (Anglin, 1970). Obviously, availability of representational formats interacts with the metaprocess of representation selection: Individuals can only select from among those repre-sentations available to them. The format also interacts with the knowledge base, in that certain representations may be more suitable than others for various kinds of knowledge. An example of the interaction between represen-tation and knowledge base can be seen in the development of word knowl-edge. Keil and Batterman (1984) have found that as children grow older, they become more likely to rely on defining rather than characteristic features in making judgments about meanings of words. Apparently, younger children often grasp the idea of a concept without quite grasping the essence of that concept. (See Mandler, 1983, for an extended discussion of the development of conceptual and other kinds of representation.)

THE PERFORMANCE COMPONENT

Our model of the performance component of intellectual development is an attempt to provide an integrated account of the cognitive, affective, and en-vironmental factors that influence how competence is applied in a given task or situation. This account deals with eight factors that we believe mediate the utilization of competence: process execution, knowledge accessibility, usable capacity of working memory, accessibility of representations, motivation, goals, cognitive styles, and external resources.

Efficacy of Process Execution

Mental processes can be executed with greater or lesser efficacy. "Efficacy" of process execution is not a single entity, but rather seems to comprise five aspects: accessibility of the processes, speed of process execution, accuracy of process execution, activation of processes, and feedback from processes.

Accessibility.   By accessibility, we refer to the ease with which a given process or set of processes can be applied in a given situation. It is possible to have a given process available in the sense of its being potentially usable in task performance; but if the process is inaccessible, it may, in fact, not be called upon when needed.

Brown and Campione (1980) have distinguished between two kinds of process accessibility. Reflective accessibility is (self-) knowledge about what cognitive resources one possesses and awareness of how these resources can be brought to bear upon a particular task or situation. Multiple accessibility involves the flexible use of the information and skills one has available in a variety of tasks and situations. Brown (1978, 1979; Campione & Brown, 1974) and Butterfield and Belmont (1977) have claimed that mental retardation is largely a problem of insufficient multiple accessibility of processes: Retarded children have various processes available, but do not know when (and sometimes how) to use them. For example, Belmont and Butterfield (1971) found that retarded children can use rehearsal quite well, but do not spontaneously apply it. Moreover, it has also been found that even when retarded children are taught to use rehearsal in a given situation and thus to improve their recall, they do not seem to generalize this instruction — as do normal children — to other similar situations.

It is often empirically difficult to distinguish unavailability (a competence limitation) from inaccessibility (a performance limitation) of a given process. Successful attempts to distinguish the two involve providing the child with multiple opportunities to show that he or she can apply the given process in any of a variety of situations (Feuerstein, 1979). If no situation can be found in which the child applies the process, it is reasonable to conclude that the process is unavailable (although of course one can never prove this).

Speed.   Speed simply refers to the rate at which a given process is executed. More efficacious execution of processes is usually associated with greater speed of execution, although exceptions have been found (as noted earlier for encoding). Increased speed of processing is usually associated with higher efficacy of information processing for two reasons. First, increased speed means that more inputs can be processed per unit time, so that the total processing time of the mental system is decreased. Second, when inputs are presented at a rapid rate, greater speed of processing enables the individual to attend to a greater proportion of these inputs and thereby to ignore a smaller proportion. Consider, for example, listening to a lecture (an important form of information presentation in schooling). A person who is rapidly able to process inputs from the lecture is likely to attend to more and miss less in the lecture; a person who processes inputs slowly is likely to miss large parts of the lecture, and possibly to lose track of what is going on, because he or she is still processing old information long after it has been presented and the lecturer has moved on to new information. The same logic applies to reading as well as listening comprehension; indeed, the two are very highly correlated (Jackson & McClelland, 1979).

Speed of processing does appear to be at least weakly related to performance on a number of different aptitude measures (Carroll & Maxwell, 1979; Hunt, Frost, & Lunneborg, 1973; Hunt, Lunneborg, & Lewis, 1975; Keating & Bobbitt, 1978; Keating, Keniston, Manis, & Bobbitt, 1980). For example, investigators have typically found a correlation of about $-.3$ between time of access to lexical information in long-term memory and psychometrically measured verbal ability (Hunt et al., 1975). Even basic choice-reaction time tasks seem to provide a measure of one aspect of intellectual functioning (Jensen, 1979).

Although we believe that speed can be an important aspect of intellectual functioning, our own view is that if anything, the role of speed in intelligence has been overemphasized in information-processing (but not Piagetian) research. We have three reasons for this belief. First, correlations between various measures of speed of processing and intellectual ability, although significant, have been relatively modest, usually about .3. Thus, the speed of basic information processing only accounts for about 10% of the variance in measured intellectual ability. Second, as noted earlier, whether greater or lesser speed is desirable depends upon the process being executed, and the situation in which it is being executed. There are any number of examples of processes and situations for which lesser speed is associated with more efficacious information processing (Sternberg, 1977, 1981; Sternberg & Davidson, 1982; Sternberg & Rifkin, 1979). Finally, the kinds of criteria that are used to assess the importance of speed would, if anything, tend to overestimate its importance. For example, information-processing parameters are often correlated with IQ test scores. But since the IQ tests are themselves speeded, part of the obtained correlation may, in some studies, simply reflect the shared speed demands of the information-processing task and the psychometric test. Few tasks one encounters in the real world require the kinds of very highly speeded performance required in laboratory and testlike tasks.

Accuracy. Accuracy simply refers to the correctness with which a given process is executed. More efficacious execution of processes is virtually always associated with greater accuracy of process execution. In tasks requiring sequential execution of a number of processes, accuracy of process execution can be particularly important in the early stages of task performance. An inaccurately executed process early on can result in all subsequent process executions being essentially worthless.

Inaccurate execution of processes can be traced to any of a number of causes, such as inadequate knowledge, carelessness, and faulty representation of information. In our own experience, a major cause of inaccurate process execution is premature termination in the execution of that process: The individual ceases execution of a given process before sufficient aspects of the stimulus (or a relation between stimuli) have been considered. For example, Sternberg (1977) found that almost all errors made in an analogical reasoning task could be traced to premature termination of execution of performance processes. Test developers are aware of this source of errors, and frequently construct distractors in multiple-choice tests so that they will represent answers to partial problems. In other words, individuals who solve only a part of the presented problem will see the answer they have arrived at among the distractors: The answer is the correct one, but to just a subproblem of the full problem.

It is well known that speed and accuracy trade off against each other in problem solution (Pachella, 1974). Faster processing is often (although not always) associated with increased error rate. Speed and accuracy thus need to be considered interactive. Optimal problem solution requires finding a tradeoff between speed and accuracy that is suitable both for the problem and for the situational constraints presented with it (for example, the severity of the consequences of a Type I versus a Type II error). Note that on this view, speed and accuracy are clearly performance rather than competence variables. One does not merely have available a certain speed or accuracy of processing. Rather, one's speed and accuracy are determined by task and situational factors. This is not to say that competence does not enter into speed and accuracy, but rather that its role is mediated by performance considerations. Indeed, all performance factors are necessarily affected by competence, since competence is the ultimate basis for performance.

Process Activation and Feedback. Our theory of intellectual development posits that all process activation is initiated by metaprocesses, and that all process feedback returns to these metaprocesses. In other words, performance and acquisition processes act "in the service" of metaprocesses. For example, a metaprocess decides to execute a certain strategy, and the strategy, comprising a sequence of performance processes, is then executed. On this view, efficacy of process execution will depend in part upon the quality of communication between metaprocesses, on the one hand, and performance and acquisition processes, on the other (as well as between different metaprocesses). Consider, for example, the solution of a reasoning problem such as an analogy. If one is missing the point of the analogy, solution quality will depend upon one's realizing that one is missing the point, and upon one's ability to localize in what performance process or processes errors are being made. Localization, on the current view, depends upon feedback of performance processes to metaprocesses. The metaprocesses "find out" how success-fully each of the performance processes has been executed. If feedback from the performance processes to the metaprocesses is inadequate, it may be quite difficult to localize the source of the error (Sternberg, 1980c).

Knowledge Accessibility

If stored knowledge is not organized in a manner that is compatible with the requirements of a task, that knowledge may not be able to be retrieved from memory when it is needed. Thus, the needed information might be available but not accessible (Tulving & Thomson, 1973). In order for information to be retrieved from memory, an individual must (a) specify what knowledge must be accessed, (b) match this specification to a particular unit in memory, and (c) evaluate whether the memory unit accessed does indeed provide the infor-mation needed for the given task (Norman & Bobrow, 1979). Failure in any of these three steps can thwart retrieval of the needed information.

Much of the research that has been done on retrieval failure has been done by Tulving and his colleagues. For example, Tulving and Pearlstone (1966) asked subjects to learn a list of words belonging to several categories. When subjects failed to recall all of the words, they were shown the category names. Because subjects had encoded and then stored the words in memory accord-ing to category units, the category names enabled them to retrieve more words. Tulving and Thomson (1973) showed the effects of retrieval failure even more dramatically. It is well known that recognition of a list of words is virtually always better than recall of that same list of words. But Tulving and Thomson showed that if the retrieval environment in recognition does not match the environment in which the words were encoded, it is possible to re-verse dramatically the usual difficulty of task ordering, and to show that re-call can actually be better than recognition of the same words!

Usable Capacity of Working Memory

One is unfortunately rarely in a position to perform a task with absolutely no competing demands on one's attention. Sometimes these competing de-mands can be ignored; other times they cannot be. When the competing de-mands need to be attended to, they are likely to be for processing and work-ing memory capacity. (For example, as we write this chapter, we find ourselves subject to innumerable phone calls, knockings on our office doors, and other assorted distractions. Indeed, we sometimes felt as though intrud-ers had saved up their distractions just for when we had to write the chapter!) Thus, competing task demands will limit the working-memory capacity one can bring to bear on a given problem.

Research on resource competition has generally been conducted using a secondary-task paradigm. One performs a primary task while simultaneously performing a less important, but nevertheless attention-demanding, secondary task. The investigator studies degradation in task performance as a function of primary and secondary task characteristics, as well as studying individual differences in susceptibility to task interference. For example, Manis, Keating, and Morrison (1980) had second and sixth graders, as well as adults, perform a letter-matching (primary) task at the same time that they performed an auditory probe (secondary) task. Of particular interest to us here is the finding of a developmental increase in the attentional resources individuals could bring to bear upon the dual-task processing situation.

Accessibility of Representations

Many problems can be solved in alternative ways involving alternative representations for information. If a given individual has these alternative representations available (a competence consideration), then performance factors are likely to determine which representation or representations are used. Consider some examples.

Consider sentence-picture verification items, where subjects are presented with a sentence and a picture. The subjects' task is to indicate whether the picture correctly represents what is stated in the sentence. For example, in the item, "Star is above plus $\overset{*}{+}$," the picture does provide a correct representation; in the item, "Star is not above plus $\overset{*}{+}$," the picture does not provide a correct representation. Early research suggested that these items are solved primarily using a linguistic strategy (Carpenter & Just, 1975; Clark & Chase, 1972), but subsequent research has shown that at least some subjects use a spatial strategy rather than a linguistic one (MacLeod, Hunt, & Mathews, 1978; Mathews, Hunt, & MacLeod, 1980). Which strategy subjects use appears to depend upon several factors, including the way in which the items are presented (sentence and picture simultaneous or sentence followed by a pause and only then followed by the picture), subjects' respective competencies with linguistic and spatial representations, and even subjects' age (Hunt & Davidson, 1981), which may reflect changing patterns of competencies (Horn, 1968).

Similarly, linear syllogisms such as "John is taller than Pete. Pete is taller than Bill. Who is tallest?" can be solved using either a linguistic strategy, a spatial strategy, or a mixed linguistic-spatial strategy. The form of representation subjects use appears to depend upon variables such as task instructions (Sternberg & Weil, 1980), the adjective relating the subject to the predicate (Egan & Grimes-Farrow, 1982), and possibly competence in using the alternative forms of representation (although there is no solid evidence as yet to show such an effect). Surprisingly, available evidence suggests that age is not a factor in the form of representation used (Riley, 1976; Sternberg, 1980a). On the whole, the most efficacious strategy appears to be one combining both linguistic and spatial representations (Sternberg, 1980b).

Motivation

One of the main constraints on an individual's showing his or her full competence is the individual's motivation for a task at hand. Anyone who has taught knows that intellectual and other kinds of competence are worth little in the absence of motivation to pursue academic or other work. Motivation can be partitioned in any of a number of ways. For example, Murray's (1938) system of needs (such as for power, affiliation, and succorance) can be viewed as one way of partitioning motivation. Much of the work during the past few decades on achievement motivation (see, e.g., Atkinson, 1964; McClelland, 1961) derives from Murray's personological perspective. More relevant to present considerations is the partitioning of motivation into extrinsic and intrinsic sources (see, e.g., Flavell, 1977).

Extrinsic motivation refers to an individual's expectation of a reward for making a particular response or set of responses. The main factors affecting level of extrinsic motivation are the amounts and kinds of external rewards offered. Intrinsic motivation refers to internal drive toward a goal. Intrinsic motivation can spring from curiosity, anxiety, need to achieve, and the like. Most people are of course driven by both kinds of motivations, and the two kinds of motivations probably interact in complex ways.

It is believed that as children grow older, they become increasingly intrinsically motivated and decreasingly extrinsically motivated (Zigler, 1969). Psychologists and educators have often used token economies and other kinds of extrinsic reward systems in order to increase children's motivation, hoping gradually to wean the children from the reward system so that intrinsic motivation would come to replace the extrinsic motivation developed through the system of rewards. Evidence suggests, however, that extrinsic rewards may undermine rather than increase children's intrinsic motivation (Lepper, Greene, & Nisbett, 1973).

It has been known for a long time that reduced motivation is one important source of underachievement in children whose cognitive levels would lead one to expect better of them. But motivational patterns can also restrict the expression of competence in children with reduced cognitive levels. Zigler (1968, 1969) has suggested that in part because retarded children tend to be more socially deprived than normal children, the retarded children are more extrinsically motivated and less intrinsically motivated than are normal children. The retarded child is particularly eager to receive attention and praise, and seems less interested in providing correct answers for the intrinsic satisfaction such answers provide. Motivational interventions can increase the performance level of retarded individuals (Zigler, 1971).

Selection of Goals

It is impossible to separate the role of goals from that of motivation. Yet, the role of goals has received surprisingly little consideration in the cognitive-developmental literature. We have strong reason to believe that goals are a major source of reduced (or increased) intellectual performance. Consider, for example, the literature on IQ differences between majority and minority groups in this country, and between members of our culture and of other cultures. Many investigators have been inclined to attribute score differences in large part to genetic differences between populations (see, e.g., Jensen, 1969). There is now ample evidence to suggest that one's cultural milieu strongly affects one's goals, which in turn can affect one's motivation to perform well on intellectual tasks (Cole & Scribner, 1974; Laboratory of Comparative Human Cognition, 1982). Members of non-Anglo cultures may in some cases be more inclined to work in groups rather than individually, less inclined to pursue tasks with abstract, ecologically irrelevant materials, less inclined to try to please outside examiners, and less inclined to accept IQ-test like tasks in the spirit in which they are presented (namely, that of a test) (see Cole & Means, 1981). Under these constraints, it is little wonder that the tests can be of dubious validity for members of groups other than those for which the tests were originally prepared.

Cognitive Styles

It is well known that intellectual performance can be affected by the cognitive styles individuals bring to problem solution (see, e.g., Neimark, 1979; Warr, 1970). It has been found, for example, that some individuals tend to be more impulsive and others more reflective. Impulsive individuals tend to perform tasks rapidly, but at the expense of making errors; reflective individuals tend to perform tasks more slowly, but also more accurately (Kagan, Rosman, Day, Albert, & Phillips, 1964; see also Messer, 1976). Excessive impulsivity can thus lead to poor scores on tests that stress highly accurate performance, as is the case with most intelligence tests; and indeed, excessive impulsivity does seem to lead to reduced performance on many cognitive tasks (see Baron, 1982; see also Brodzinsky, 1980).

Another cognitive style related to intellectual performance is that of field independence (Witkin, 1950; see also Goldstein & Blackman, 1978). Field independence refers to an individual's ability to achieve cognitive separation from the structure of a prevailing visual field. One measure of the construct is the rod-and-frame test. In this test, an individual is seated in a completely dark room, where he or she views a luminous rod within a luminous frame. The rod and frame are both viewed in a tilted position, and the individual has the ability to retilt each separately. The individual's task is to adjust the rod to the vertical position independent of the position of the frame. In general, higher degrees of field independence are associated with higher cognitive performance. For example, Liben (1978) found field independence associated with higher performance on spatial tasks.

Although research on cognitive styles has tended to emphasize individual-difference determinants of cognitive styles, clearly, task and situational variables can enter in as well. As noted earlier in our discussion of speed-accuracy tradeoff, the relative seriousness of Type I and Type II errors would also seem to affect how likely an individual is to perform either impulsively or reflectively. We suspect that in problem solving, individuals are often both impulsive and reflective, but at different stages of problem solution. A determinant of success in solving problems may be that of knowing exactly when to be impulsive and when to be reflective.

External Resources

The effects of external resources on problem-solving performance have become increasingly evident in recent years: Using calculators and then computers, scientists and others have been able to solve problems that in earlier times would have defied solution within any individual's lifetime. But external resources go beyond the availability of obvious computational aids. Individuals are born into and grow up in highly variable environments that make available to them widely varying resources for learning and development. These resources can and almost certainly do have major effects on everyone's cognitive development (Scarr, 1981). Whatever may be one's genetic competence, for example, the environment in which one is raised is likely to lead to only some fraction of that competence being realized. Unfortunately, we still have very little idea of the extent to which external resource availability limits the expression of this genetic competence (Scarr & Carter-Saltzman, 1982).

CONCLUSION

In conclusion, we have presented a model of the competence factors that we believe play a key role in intellectual development, and of the performance factors that mediate the expression of competence. Because these two kinds of factors interact in complex ways, it is often hard to separate them theoretically, and even harder to separate them empirically. Nevertheless, we believe that the metatheoretical distinction is an important one, because of the different implications competence and performance factors have for both theory and research. At present, the best that can be hoped for is a suggestive model for ways in which competence and performance might be distinguished; a definitive model seems way beyond our present reach.

One question that almost inevitably arises in considering a model such as the present one is that of whether it is sufficiently parsimonious. Is there really a need not only to divide up the bases of functioning into competence and performance factors, but then to specify as many factors as we do? We believe that, if anything, our model is too parsimonious, and could not possibly deal with all of the factors that affect competence and limit performance. At the present early stage of model development, we are not convinced that any highly beneficial purpose is served by great parsimony. Rather, we believe that the immediate goal ought to be to find and evaluate as many aspects of competence and performance as seem reasonably important in intellectual development. As our understanding of these constructs becomes more sophisticated, we would hope to be able to pare from the list of aspects those that are inessential, and perhaps to add others that might have formerly been slighted or even ignored.

We view research on the competence-performance distinction in intellectual development as needing further expansion in at least three directions, one theoretical, a second one operational, and a third one educational.

In terms of theoretical development, it is clear that conceptualizations of the competence-performance distinction are still in their infancy. Indeed, we see this volume as an attempt to hasten the growth of the infant! Our own prediction is that further development of this distinction will best proceed by careful analysis of the interface between Piagetian and information-processing psychologies. Piagetian psychology has provided an elaborate theory of competence that gives too short shrift, we believe, to performance factors. Information-processing psychology has provided elaborate theories of performance that give too short shrift to competence factors. Research that combines the two approaches (e.g., Siegler, 1976) seems to represent a suitable means of taking into account the roles of both competence and performance factors. The difficult part, of course, will be that of determining just what these roles are.

In terms of operational development, we see an urgent need for measurement devices that separate competence from performance factors. Feuerstein's (1979) Learning Potential Assessment Device seems to provide an important step in this direction, as do recently developed tests that attempt accurate psychometric assessment of competencies specified by Piaget's theory of intelligence (e.g., Pinard & Sharp, 1972; Tuddenham, 1970). Our own efforts in this domain will probably be directed toward the measurement of information-processing aspects of competence and performance.

In terms of educational development, there is a pressing need for educational programs that integrate Piaget's insights with findings of information-processing research regarding the processing limits of human performance. We believe that as integrated theoretical development proceeds, it will be possible to design educational programs for improving thinking skills that capitalize upon individuals' levels of competence and performance. Aptitude-treatment interaction (ATI) research has represented an initial attempt to provide such a capitalization (see Cronbach & Snow, 1977). But we believe it has proceeded in the absence of sufficiently sophisticated theories to support the research. We are at least hopeful that the time is at hand when such theories will be available for educational research and intervention. We share with other contributors to this volume the hope that the volume will represent a turning point in the development of the theoretical basis for the kinds of educational interventions we believe are possible, if not yet quite feasible.

REFERENCES

Achenbach, T. M. (1970). The children's associative responding test: A possible alternative to group IQ tests. *Journal of Educational Psychology, 61,* 340–348.

Achenbach, T. M. (1971). The children's associative responding test: A two-year followup. *Developmental Psychology, 5,* 477–483.

Anderson, J. R. (1976). *Language, memory, and thought.* Hillsdale, NJ: Lawrence Erlbaum Associates.

Anderson, J. R. (1978). Arguments concerning representations for mental imagery. *Psychological Review, 85,* 249–277.

Anglin, J. M. (1970). *The growth of word meaning.* Cambridge: MIT Press.

Atkinson, J. W. (1964). *An introduction to motivation.* New York: American Book Co.

Baddeley, A. D., & Hitch, G. (1974). Working memory. In G. H. Bower (Ed.), *The psychology of learning and motivation* (Vol. 8). New York: Academic Press.

Baron, J. (1982). Intelligence and cognitive style. In R. J. Sternberg (Ed.), *Handbook of human intelligence.* New York: Cambridge University Press.

Bartlett, F. C. (1932). *Remembering: A study in experimental and social psychology.* Cambridge: Cambridge University Press.

Belmont, J. M., & Butterfield, E. C. (1971). Learning strategies as determinants of memory deficiencies. *Cognitive Psychology, 2,* 411–420.

Bourne, L. E., Jr. (1966). *Human conceptual behavior.* Boston: Allyn & Bacon.

Bower, G. H., Black, J. B., & Turner, T. J. (1979). Scripts in comprehension and memory. *Cognitive Psychology, 11,* 177–220.

Brainerd, C. J. (1981). Working memory and the developmental analysis of probability judgment. *Psychological Review, 6,* 463–502.

Brodzinsky, D. M. (1980). Cognitive style differences in children's spatial perspective taking. *Developmental Psychology, 16,* 151–152.

Brown, A. L. (1978). Knowing when, where, and how to remember: A problem in metacognition. In R. Glaser (Ed.), *Advances in instructional psychology* (Vol. 1). Hillsdale, NJ: Lawrence Erlbaum Associates.

Brown, A. L. (1979). Theories of memory and the problems of development: Activity, growth, and knowledge. In L. S. Cermak & F. I. M. Craik (Eds.), *Levels of processing and human memory.* Hillsdale, NJ: Lawrence Erlbaum Associates.

Brown, A. L., Bransford, J., & Ferrara, R. (1982). Intelligence and mental retardation. In R. J. Sternberg (Ed.), *Handbook of human intelligence.* New York: Cambridge University Press.

Brown, A. L., & Campione, J. C. (1980). Inducing flexible thinking: A problem of access. In M. Friedman, J. P. Das, & N. O'Connor (Eds.), *Intelligence and learning*. New York: Plenum Press.

Brown, A. L., & DeLoache, J. S. (1978). Skills, plans, and self-regulation. In R. Siegler (Ed.), *Children's thinking: What develops?* Hillsdale, NJ: Lawrence Erlbaum Associates.

Brown, A. L., & Smiley, S. S. (1977a). Rating the importance of structural units of prose passages: A problem of metacognitive development. *Child Development, 48,* 1–8.

Brown, A. L., & Smiley, S. S. (1977b). *The development of strategies for studying prose passages.* Unpublished manuscript, University of Illinois.

Bruner, J. S., Goodnow, J. J., & Austin, G. A. (1956). *A study of thinking.* New York: Wiley.

Bryant, P. E., & Trabasso, T. (1971). Transitive inferences and memory in young children. *Nature, 232,* 456–458.

Butterfield, E. C., & Belmont, J. M. (1977). Assessing and improving the executive cognitive functions of mentally retarded people. In I. Bialer & M. Sternlicht (Eds.), *Psychological issues in mental retardation.* New York: Psychological Dimensions.

Butterfield, E. C., Wambold, C., & Belmont, J. M. (1973). On the theory and practice of improving short-term memory. *American Journal of Mental Deficiency, 77,* 654–669.

Campione, J. C., & Brown, A. L. (1974). The effects of contextual changes and degree of component mastery on transfer of training. In H. W. Reese (Ed.), *Advances in child development and behavior* (Vol. 7). New York: Academic Press.

Campione, J. C., & Brown, A. L. (1977). Memory and metamemory development in educable retarded children. In R. V. Kail, Jr., & J. W. Hagen (Eds.), *Perspectives on the development of memory and cognition.* Hillsdale, NJ: Lawrence Erlbaum Associates.

Campione, J. C., & Brown, A. L. (1979). Toward a theory of intelligence: Contributions from research with retarded children. In R. J. Sternberg & D. K. Detterman (Eds.), *Human intelligence: Perspectives on its theory and measurement.* Norwood, NJ: Ablex.

Carpenter, P. A., & Just, M. A. (1975). Sentence comprehension: A psycholinguistic processing model of verification. *Psychological Review, 82,* 45–73.

Carroll, J. B., & Maxwell, S. E. (1979). Individual differences in cognitive abilities. *Annual Review of Psychology, 30,* 603–640.

Case, R. (1974). Mental strategies, mental capacity, and instruction: A neo-Piagetian investigation. *Journal of Experimental Child Psychology, 18,* 372–397.

Case, R. (1978). Intellectual development from birth to adolescence: A neo-Piagetian interpretation. In R. Siegler (Ed.), *Children's thinking: What develops?* Hillsdale, NJ: Lawrence Erlbaum Associates.

Chase, W. G., & Simon, H. A. (1973). The mind's eye in chess. In W. G. Chase (Ed.), *Visual information processing.* New York: Academic Press.

Chi, M. T. H. (1976). Short-term memory limitations in children: Capacity or processing deficits? *Memory and Cognition, 4,* 559–572.

Chi, M. T. H. (1978). Knowledge structures and memory development. In R. Siegler (Ed.), *Children's thinking: What develops?* Hillsdale, NJ: Lawrence Erlbaum Associates.

Chi, M. T. H. (1984). Representing knowledge and metaknowledge: Implications for interpreting metamemory research. In F. E. Weinert & R. Kluwe (Eds.), *Learning by thinking.* West Germany: Kuhlhammer.

Chi, M. T. H., Glaser, R., & Rees, E. (1982). Expertise in problem solving. In R. J. Sternberg (Ed.), *Advances in the psychology of human intelligence* (Vol. 1). Hillsdale, NJ: Lawrence Erlbaum Associates.

Chi, M. T. H., & Koeske, R. D. (1983). Network representation of a child's dinosaur knowledge. *Developmental Psychology, 19,* 29–39.

Clark, H. H., & Chase, W. G. (1972). On the process of comparing sentences against pictures. *Cognitive Psychology, 3,* 472–517.

Cole, M., & Means, B. (1981). *Comparative studies of how people think.* Cambridge, MA: Harvard University Press.

Cole, M., & Scribner, S. (1974). *Culture and thought.* New York: Wiley.

Collins, A., Warnock, E. H., Aiello, N., & Miller, M. S. (1975). Reasoning from incomplete knowledge. In D. G. Bobrow & A. M. Collins (Eds.), *Representation and understanding.* New York: Academic Press.

Commons, M. L., & Armon, C. (1983). *Beyond formal operations: Late adolescent and adult cognitive development.* New York: Praeger.

Commons, M. L., Richards, F. A., & Kuhn, D. (1982). Systematic and metasystematic reasoning: A case for levels of reasoning beyond Piaget's stage of formal operations. *Child Development, 53,* 1058–1069.

Cronbach, L. J., & Snow, R. E. (1977). *Aptitudes and instructional methods.* New York: Irvington.

Crowder, R. G. (1976). *Principles of learning and memory.* Hillsdale, NJ: Lawrence Erlbaum Associates.

Daneman, M., & Carpenter, P. A. (1980). Individual differences in working memory and reading. *Journal of Verbal Learning and Verbal Behavior, 19,* 450–466.

De Groot, A. D. (1965). *Thought and choice in chess.* The Hague: Mouton.

Egan, D. E., & Grimes-Farrow, D. D. (1982). Differences in mental representations spontaneously adopted for reasoning. *Memory and Cognition, 10,* 247–307.

Feuerstein, R. (1979). *The dynamic assessment of retarded performers: The learning potential assessment device, theory, instruments, and techniques.* Baltimore: University Park Press.

Feuerstein, R. (1980). *Instrumental enrichment: An intervention program for cognitive modifiability.* Baltimore: University Park Press.

Flavell, J. H. (1977). *Cognitive development.* Englewood Cliffs, NJ: Prentice-Hall.

Flavell, J. H. (1981). Cognitive monitoring. In W. P. Dickson (Ed.), *Children's oral communication skills.* New York: Academic Press.

Flavell, J. H., & Wohlwill, J. (1969). Formal and functional aspects of cognitive development. In D. Elkind & J. H. Flavell (Eds.), *Studies in cognitive development: Essays in honor of Jean Piaget.* New York: Oxford University Press.

Ford, M. E., & Keating, D. P. (1981). Developmental and individual differences in long-term memory retrieval: Process and organization. *Child Development, 52,* 234–241.

Furth, H. G. (1970). *Piaget for teachers.* Englewood Cliffs, NJ: Prentice-Hall.

Gallagher, J. M., & Wright, R. J. (1979). Piaget and the study of analogy: Structural analysis of items. In J. Magary (Ed.), *Piaget and the helping professions* (Vol. 8). Los Angeles, University of Southern California Press.

Gelman, R. (1978). Cognitive development. *Annual Review of Psychology, 29,* 297–332.

Gelman, R., & Gallistel, C. R. (1978). *The child's understanding of number.* Cambridge, MA: Harvard University Press.

Gentner, D. (1977). Children's performance on a spatial analogies task. *Child Development, 48,* 1034–1039.

Goldstein, K. M., & Blackman, S. (1978). *Cognitive style.* New York: Wiley.

Holyoak, K. J. (1984). Analogical thinking and human intelligence. In R. J. Sternberg (Ed.), *Advances in the psychology of human intelligence* (Vol. 2). Hillsdale, NJ: Lawrence Erlbaum Associates.

Horn, J. L. (1968). Organization of abilities and the development of intelligence. *Psychological Review, 75,* 242–259.

Hunt, E. (1974). Quote of the raven? Nevermore! In L. W. Gregg (Ed.), *Knowledge and cognition.* Hillsdale, NJ: Lawrence Erlbaum Associates.

Hunt, E., & Davidson, J. E. (1981, November). *Age effects on sentence verification strategies.* Paper presented at the Psychonomic Society Meetings, Philadelphia, PA.

Hunt, E. B., Frost, N., & Lunneborg, C. (1973). Individual differences in cognition: A new approach to intelligence. In G. Bower (Ed.), *The psychology of learning and motivation: Vol. 7. Advances in research and theory.* New York: Academic Press.

Hunt, E., Lunneborg, C., & Lewis, J. (1975). What does it mean to be high verbal? *Cognitive Psychology, 7,* 194–227.

Inhelder, B., & Piaget, J. (1958). *The growth of logical thinking from childhood to adolescence.* New York: Basic Books.

Inhelder, B., Sinclair, H., & Bovet, M. (1974). *Learning and the development of cognition.* Cambridge, MA: Harvard University Press.

Jackson, M. D., & McClelland, J. L. (1979). Processing determinants of reading speed. *Journal of Experimental Psychology: General, 108,* 151–181.

Jensen, A. R. (1969). How much can we boost IQ and scholastic achievement? *Harvard Educational Review, 39,* 1–123.

Jensen, A. R. (1979). *g:* Outmoded theory or unconquered frontier? *Creative Science and Technology, 2,* 16–29.

Kail, R. V. (1979). *The development of memory in children.* San Francisco: W. H. Freeman.

Kail, R. V., & Bisanz, J. (in press). Information processing and cognitive development. In H. W. Reese & L. P. Lipsett (Eds.), *Advances in child development and behavior* (Vol. 17). New York: Academic Press.

Kail, R. V., & Hagen, J. H. (1977). *Perspectives on the development of memory and cognition.* Hillsdale, NJ: Lawrence Erlbaum Associates.

Kagan, J., Rosman, B., Day, D., Albert, J., & Phillips, W. (1964). Information processing in the child: Significance of analytic and reflective attitudes. *Psychological Monographs, 78* (1, Whole No. 578).

Keating, D. P., & Bobbitt, B. L. (1978). Individual and developmental differences in cognitive-processing components of mental ability. *Child Development, 49,* 155–167.

Keating, D. P., Keniston, A. H., Manis, F. R., & Bobbitt, B. L. (1980). Development of the search-processing parameter. *Child Development, 51,* 39–44.

Keil, F. C., & Batterman, N. (1984). A characteristic-to-defining shift in the development of word meaning. *Journal of Verbal Learning and Verbal Behavior, 23,* 221–236.

Klahr, D. (1978). Goal information, planning, and learning by pre-school problem solvers or: "My socks are in the dryer." In R. Siegler (Ed.), *Children's thinking: What develops?* Hillsdale, NJ: Lawrence Erlbaum Associates.

Laboratory of Comparative Human Cognition. (1982). Culture and intelligence. In R. J. Sternberg (Ed.), *Handbook of human intelligence.* New York: Cambridge University Press.

Larkin, J., McDermott, J., Simon, D. P., & Simon, H. A. (1980). Expert and novice performance in solving physics problems. *Science, 208,* 1335–1342.

Lepper, M. R., Greene, D., & Nisbett, R. E. (1973). Undermining children's intrinsic interest with extrinsic reward: A test of the overjustification hypothesis. *Journal of Personality and Social Psychology, 28,* 129–137.

Liben, L. (1978). Performance on Piagetian spatial tasks as a function of sex, field dependence, and training. *Merrill-Palmer Quarterly, 24,* 97–110.

Lovell, K. (1961). A follow-up study of Inhelder and Piaget's "The growth of logical thinking." *British Journal of Psychology, 52,* 143–153.

Lunzer, E. A. (1965). Problems of formal reasoning in test situations. In P. H. Mussen (Ed.), *European research in cognitive development. Monographs of the Society for Research in Child Development, 30* (2, Serial No. 100).

MacLeod, C. M., Hunt, E. B., & Mathews, N. N. (1978). Individual differences in the verification of sentence-picture relationships. *Journal of Verbal Learning and Verbal Behavior, 17,* 493–507.

Mandler, J. (1983). Representation in children. In P. H. Mussen (Ed.), *Carmichael's handbook of child psychology.* New York: Wiley.

Manis, F. R., Keating, D. P., & Morrison, F. J. (1980). Developmental differences in the allocation of processing capacity. *Journal of Experimental Child Psychology, 29,* 156–169.

Markman, E. M. (1977). Realizing that you don't understand: A preliminary investigation. *Child Development, 48,* 986–992.

Markman, E. M. (1979). Realizing that you don't understand: Elementary school children's awareness of inconsistencies. *Child Development, 50,* 643–655.

Mathews, N. N., Hunt, E. B., & MacLeod, C. M. (1980). Strategy choice and strategy training in sentence-picture verification. *Journal of Verbal Learning and Verbal Behavior, 19,* 531–548.

McClelland, D. (1961). *The achieving society.* Princeton: D. van Nostrand.

Messer, S. B. (1976). Reflection-impulsivity: A review. *Psychological Bulletin, 83,* 1026–1052.

Miller, G. A., Galanter, E., & Pribram, K. H. (1960). *Plans and the structure of behavior.* New York: Holt, Rinehart & Winston.

Murray, H. A. (1938). *Explorations in personality.* New York: Oxford University Press.

Neimark, E. D. (1979). Current status of formal operations research. *Human Development, 22,* 60–67.

Nelson, K. (1977). The syntagmatic-paradigmatic shift revisited: A review of research and theory. *Psychological Bulletin, 84,* 93–116.

Newell, A., & Simon, H. A. (1972). *Human problem solving.* Englewood Cliffs, NJ: Prentice-Hall.

Norman, D. A., & Bobrow, D. G. (1979). Descriptions: An intermediate stage in memory retrieval. *Cognitive Psychology, 11,* 107–123.

Oppenheimer, J. R. (1956). Analogy in science. *American Psychologist, 11,* 127–135.

Osherson, D. N. (1974). Logical abilities in children (Vol. 2): *Logical inference: Underlying operations.* Hillsdale, NJ: Lawrence Erlbaum Associates.

Overton, W. F., & Newman, J. L. (1982). Cognitive development: A competence-activation/utilization approach. In T. Field (Ed.), *Review of developmental psychology.* New York: Wiley.

Pachella, R. G. (1974). The interpretation of reaction time in information processing research. In B. Kantowitz (Ed.), *Human information processing: Tutorials in performance and cognition.* Hillsdale, NJ: Lawrence Erlbaum Associates.

Paris, S. G. (1973). Comprehension of language connectives and propositional logical relationships. *Journal of Experimental Child Psychology, 16,* 278–291.

Paris, S. G., & Lindauer, B. K. (1977). Constructive processes in children's comprehension and memory. In R. V. Kail & J. W. Hagen (Eds.), *Perspectives in the development of memory and cognition.* Hillsdale, NJ: Lawrence Erlbaum Associates.

Paris, S. G., Lindauer, B. K., & Cox, G. L. (1977). The development of inferential comprehension. *Child Development, 48,* 1728–1733.

Pascual-Leone, J. A. (1979). Mathematical model for the transition rule in Piaget's developmental stages. *Acta Psychologica, 63,* 301–345.

Pellegrino, J. W., & Kail, R. (1982). Process analyses of spatial aptitude. In R. J. Sternberg (Ed.), *Advances in the psychology of human intelligence* (Vol. 1). Hillsdale, NJ: Lawrence Erlbaum Associates.

Piaget, J. (1950). Une expérience sur la psychologie du hasard chez l'enfant: Le tirage au mort des couples. *Acta Psychologica, 7,* 323–336.

Piaget, J. (1952). *The origins of intelligence in children.* New York: International Universities Press.

Piaget, J. (1972). Intellectual evolution from adolescence to adulthood. *Human Development, 15,* 1–12.

Piaget, J. (1976). *The psychology of intelligence.* Totowa, NJ: Littlefield, Adams.

Piaget, J., & Inhelder, B. (1970). *The early growth of logic in the child: Classification and seriation* (E. A. Lanzer & D. Papert, Trans.). London: Routledge, Kegan Paul. (Originally published 1964).

Piaget, J. (with Montangero, J., & Billeter, J.). (1977). Les Correlâts. *L'abstraction réflèchissante*. Paris: Presses Universitaires de France.

Pinard, A., & Sharp, E. (1972). IQ and point of view. *Psychology Today, 6,* 65–68, 90.

Resnick, L. R., & Ford, W. W. (1981). *The psychology of mathematics for instruction.* Hillsdale, NJ: Lawrence Erlbaum Associates.

Resnick, L. B., & Glaser, R. (1976). Problem solving and intelligence. In L. B. Resnick (Ed.), *The nature of intelligence.* Hillsdale, NJ: Lawrence Erlbaum Associates.

Riley, C. A. (1976). The representation of comparative relations and the transitive inference task. *Journal of Experimental Child Psychology, 22,* 1–22.

Riley, C. A., & Trabasso, T. (1974). Comparatives, logical structures, and encoding in a transitive inference task. *Journal of Experimental Child Psychology, 17,* 187–203.

Scarr, S. (1981). Testing *for* children: Assessment and the many determinants of intellectual competence. *American Psychologist, 36,* 1159–1166.

Scarr, S., & Carter-Saltzman, L. (1982). Intelligence and behavior genetics. In R. J. Sternberg (Ed.), *Handbook of human intelligence.* New York: Cambridge University Press.

Shepp, B. E. (1978). From perceived similarity to dimensional structure: A new hypothesis about perspective development. In E. Rosch & B. Lloyd (Eds.), *Cognition and categorization.* Hillsdale, NJ: Lawrence Erlbaum Associates.

Siegler, R. S. (1976). Three aspects of cognitive development. *Cognitive Psychology, 4,* 481–520.

Siegler, R. S. (1978). The origins of scientific reasoning. In R. Siegler (Ed.), *Children's thinking: What develops?* Hillsdale, NJ: Lawrence Erlbaum Associates.

Smith, L. B., & Kemler, D. G. (1978). Levels of experienced dimensionality in children and adults. *Cognitive Psychology, 10,* 502–537.

Spiro, R. J., Bruce, B. C., & Brewer, W. F. (Eds.) (1980). *Theoretical issues in reading comprehension.* Hillsdale, NJ: Lawrence Erlbaum Associates.

Sternberg, R. J. (1977). *Intelligence, information processing, and analogical reasoning: The componential analysis of human abilities.* Hillsdale, NJ: Lawrence Erlbaum Associates.

Sternberg, R. J. (1979). Developmental patterns in the encoding and combination of logical connectives. *Journal of Experimental Child Psychology, 28,* 469–498.

Sternberg, R. J. (1980a). The development of linear syllogistic reasoning. *Journal of Experimental Child Psychology, 29,* 340–356.

Sternberg, R. J. (1980b). Representation and process in linear syllogistic reasoning. *Journal of Experimental Psychology: General, 109,* 119–159.

Sternberg, R. J. (1980c). Sketch of a componential subtheory of human intelligence. *Behavioral and Brain Sciences, 3,* 573–584.

Sternberg, R. J. (1981). Intelligence and nonentrenchment. *Journal of Educational Psychology, 73,* 1–16.

Sternberg, R. J. (1982). A componential approach to intellectual development. In R. J. Sternberg (Ed.), *Advances in the psychology of human intelligence* (Vol. 1). Hillsdale, NJ: Lawrence Erlbaum Associates.

Sternberg, R. J., & Davidson, J. E. (1982, June). The mind of the puzzler. *Psychology Today,* 37–44.

Sternberg, R. J., & Downing, C. J. (1982). The development of higher-order reasoning in adolescence. *Child Development, 53,* 209–221.

Sternberg, R. J., & Nigro, G. (1980). Developmental patterns in the solution of verbal analogies. *Child Development, 51,* 27–38.

Sternberg, R. J., Powell, J. S., & Kaye, D. (1982). The nature of verbal comprehension. *Poetics, 11,* 155–187.

Sternberg, R. J., & Rifkin, B. (1979). The development of analogical reasoning processes. *Journal of Experimental Child Psychology, 27,* 195–232.

Sternberg, R. J., & Weil, E. M. (1980). An aptitude-strategy interaction in linear syllogistic reasoning. *Journal of Educational Psychology, 72,* 226–234.

Terman, L. M., & Merrill, M. A. (1973). *Stanford-Binet intelligence scale: Manual for the third revision.* Boston: Houghton-Mifflin.

Trabasso, T., Riley, C. A., & Wilson, E. G. (1975). The representation of linear order and spatial strategies in reasoning: A developmental study. In R. Falmagne (Ed.), *Reasoning: Representation and process.* Hillsdale, NJ: Lawrence Erlbaum Associates.

Tuddenham, R. D. (1970). A "Piagetian" test of cognitive development. In W. B. Dockrell (Ed.), *On intelligence.* Toronto: Ontario Institute for Studies in Education.

Tulving, E., & Pearlstone, I. (1966). Availability versus accessibility of information in memory for words. *Journal of Verbal Learning and Verbal Behavior, 5,* 381–389.

Tulving, E., & Thomson, D. M. (1973). Encoding specificity and retrieval processes in episodic memory. *Psychological Review, 80,* 352–373.

Vurpillot, E. (1968). The development of scanning strategies and their relation to visual differentiation. *Journal of Experimental Child Psychology, 6,* 632–650.

Vygotsky, L. S. (1978). *Mind in society.* Cambridge MA: Harvard University Press.

Wagner, W. J. (1980). *Reasoning by analogy in the young child: A study of the relationship between the development of working memory capacity and the ability of children to reason by analogy on figural analogy problems.* Toronto, Ontario: Unpublished Thesis, Department of Educational Theory, University of Toronto.

Warr, P. B. (Ed.) (1970). *Thought and personality.* Harmondsworth, Eng.: Penguin.

Werner, H., & Kaplan, E. (1952). The acquisition of word meanings: A developmental study. *Monographs of the Society for Research in Child Development,* No. 51.

Witkin, H. A. (1950). Individual differences in ease of perception of embedded figures. *Journal of Personality, 19,* 1–15.

Zigler, E. (1968). Mental retardation. In P. London & D. Rosenhan (Eds.), *Foundations of abnormal psychology.* New York: Holt.

Zigler, E. (1969). Developmental versus difference theories of mental retardation and the problem of motivation. *American Journal of Mental Deficiency, 73,* 536–556.

Zigler, E. (1971). The retarded child as a whole person. In H. E. Adams & W. K. Boardman, III (Eds.), *Advances in experimental clinical psychology* (Vol. 1). New York: Pergamon Press.

II POTENTIAL MODERATORS

4 Culture and Performance

Jacqueline J. Goodnow
Judith Cashmore
Macquarie University

The results to be concentrated on in this chapter stem from studies where psychologists have taken tasks developed in Western culture — Piagetian, psychometric, or experimental — and given them to members of another culture. The basic plan of the chapter is to outline three types of result that have occasioned rethinking, providing with each a description of some of the questions, concepts, and directions for new work that have been occasioned. The first type of result — the first challenge to one's usual ways of thinking — takes the form of the second culture giving performances that are at a lower level or that lag behind those of the first culture. The second takes the form of uneven differences: The two cultural groups are alike on some tasks or some forms of a task, but not on others. The third takes the form of members of the second culture not accepting the tasks: in effect, declining to "perform."

We have selected these three types of result because each — in its own way — has forced a reexamination of ideas within the field of cross-cultural comparisons. That might seem a problem only for a small group of psychologists. Cross-cultural comparisons, however, are only a technique for exploring questions of interest to all psychologists: namely, questions about the forms of experience that make a difference to performance or development, the processes by which effects occur, and the measures or tasks that are reasonable to use as indicators of the way people think. All that cross-cultural comparisons do is to provide a sharper set of contrasts in conditions or experiences than is usually available within a culture. In effect, the current state of interesting ferment in the cross-cultural field has implications for all developmentalists. It also has implications for the way one looks at one's own culture: at its assumptions about tasks and measures and at the way in which people are socialized to give performances of a particular kind.

Although the chapter is divided into three main sections (related to the three types of result and the challenge they provide), there is a recurring theme. In each case, the starting point for re-thinking is a discrepancy between the results obtained and the hopes and expectations with which the cross-cultural comparison started. We accordingly provide now a brief introduction to some of those hopes and expectations, expanding on these in the later material.

To start with, the underlying theoretical goal is usually one of being able to say that some particular aspect of culture affects some particular aspect of performance, by some specifiable process. The surface form of that search may vary a great deal. People have asked, for example, if the nature of the physical environment affects the development of concepts of space by way of a demand for the invention of navigational aids; if acquiring a written language changes the strategies used in remembering by way of the provision of new "tools for thought"; if the experience of being an apprentice tailor or potter affects judgments of amount or length by way of familiarity with operations involving these properties; if growing up in a non-authoritarian environment encourages the development of thought in general by way of leaving unsuppressed a natural tendency to be curious and to search for order in the events one experiences.

Regardless of the specific form of the question, the general goal is constant: locate an x, a y, and link the two. For that goal to be feasible, however, it will be helpful if the descriptions of culture, of process, and of performance follow certain lines or meet certain expectations.

If we take first the area of performance and its measures, it will clearly be helpful if performances can be grouped in some way. It will be helpful, for example, if performances turn out to be interrelated, to show some consistency or some general level rather than varying widely each time the question or the task material is changed. It will also be helpful if the task giver and the task taker start from some of the same assumptions about how both parties should behave or perform. As we shall see, both these hopes may be frustrated, raising serious questions about consistency across tasks, and about the learning or socialization that precedes task giving and task taking.

The second area where hopes are often initially high — although not always made explicit — is the description of culture and of process. It will clearly be helpful if there is a reasonable limit to the number of possible processes to be considered, and to the number of cultural factors. It is, for example, easier to think of describing culture in terms of some general "level of stimulation" than to list all the tasks that people are given. To this minimal hope, many cross-cultural scholars would add others. There is, as a start, the hope (indeed the need) to have a description of culture and of process that somehow fit together. That point has been recently made with special force by

Bronfenbrenner (1981), commenting that it is difficult to move from a description of culture in terms of "address labels" (nationality, suburb, workplace) to any description of process. Second, it would be an advantage to go beyond describing the features of a given environment and ask, what gives rise to those features? How does it come about, for example, that children in one culture are being given experience of a different kind from that given in another? Third, it will be helpful if we emerge at the end with an interpretation of performance that contains respect for the performance of others rather than an assumption of superiority. For many cross-cultural scholars, that hope means that results should fit the initial assumption that all people are equal, if not alike, in capacity. Finally, it will be a step forward if the description of process leaves some room for the individual to take an active part; if cultural experience, for instance, is described not only as something that impinges on individuals but also as something that is shaped or acted upon by them.

The next three sections start from the three broad types of results. Each contains points relevant to the reexamination of ideas in two areas: the nature of performance and its measures; the description of culture and of the processes by which its features have an effect. Each section also contains points relevant to the issue of relationships between performance and capacity, with one major link occurring by way of taking as a description of process Overton and Newman's (1982) proposal that one way in which cultural factors may give rise to diversity in performance is through their differential activation or utilization of an underlying capacity or competence. That proposal is intuitively appealing, and it will be used as a starting point for asking what would need to be added to such a picture in order to come to grips with cross-cultural data.

CHALLENGE 1: A LOWER PERFORMANCE ON ALL TASKS GIVEN

A psychologist may select a large battery of tests, designed to be measures of several aspects of *intelligence*. Alternately, he or she may opt for a small set, selected because on theoretical grounds these measures are indicative of underlying levels of development. The former procedure is usually in the tradition called psychometric, the latter more in the tradition called Piagetian. In either case, the result has frequently been one where the members of the new culture give a "lower" or a "younger" performance than, say, people of the same age in the culture where the tests were developed. The profiles of performance on several tasks look alike, but the one lies below or "lags behind" the other. Psychometric examples may be found in Vernon (1969).

Greenfield's (1966) study of the Wolof is one example based more on Piagetian tasks; Dasen's (1975) comparison of concrete operational development in three cultures is another.

How is such a result related to the original hopes and expectations? If one had hoped to find that cultural factors had relatively little effect, the result is clearly a disappointment. The description of development in terms of internal, biological, or inherent factors cannot be regarded as sufficient. The task of locating cultural factors will have to be faced. If one had hoped to show that under a surface layer of variety, all people are relatively equal in ability, the results are again a disappointment. The choice may have to be faced of modifying a belief in equality or a belief in one's tasks as adequate measures of ability. For a look at the way these basic challenges have been perceived and responded to, we start with proposals about the description of culture and process, and then proceed to proposals about the nature of performance and its measures.

Cultural Factors and Processes

In the early days of cross-cultural comparisons, one could offer accounts of lower performances in terms of the given nature of the other individuals — their genetic inferiority or their more primitive mentalities, offset though these might be by some unusually skilled performances on tasks of *perception* or *rote memory*. Such explanations are no longer easy to live with, both on ideological grounds (they are arrogant and ethnocentric) and on the grounds that they involve a set of distinctions among tasks (e.g., perception and cognition, higher and lower mental processes) that psychologists no longer accept as given.

With this type of explanation ruled out, the source of next interest is the nature of the culture. What could its critical features be?

We noted earlier that one of the hopes, in locating environmental factors, is that one can locate general features: features that cut across a variety of tasks or experiences. There have been several proposals of this type, each encountering some difficulties or leading to still more questions.

Within comparisons of subcultures, for example (white and blacks in one country; working class and middle class), one favored proposal used to be that differences existed in the "level of stimulation." That proposal has not worked out well. It is, for one thing, based on an underlying metaphor that may be challenged: the metaphor of young humans as sluggish, tending to be mentally inert unless prodded. That metaphor may be no more valid than its opposite: the notion that infants are by nature in an over-alert state, in need of calm and relative isolation if they are to avoid becoming "jangled." In addition, the notion of "level of stimulation" has tended to have added to it the further notion that "more must be better." There is, however, grave doubt about this notion. It has, in fact, produced comments on a phenomenon that is our major reason for mentioning levels of stimulation. In an environment where a great deal is happening, it has been pointed out, individuals react by "tuning out." Babies learn to turn their heads away from "stimulating" mobiles; children learn not to listen. We note this form of response as important because it marks, for the first time in this chapter, two of the complications we would wish to introduce into the notion of culture as activating capacity: (a) the individual takes an active part in selecting what aspects of the environment to respond to and may, in fact, decide not to respond at all; and (b) the environment may have a negative effect, beyond an effect of simply failing to activate or to utilize.

What alternatives are there to the notion of cultures differing in the level of stimulation? An early Genevan concept is worth considering. This is the proposal that the main effort of education should be toward avoiding negative effects: in particular, the negative effect of dampening a child's natural tendency to wonder about the events experienced (cf. Inhelder, in Tanner & Inhelder, 1956, p. 85). Some related but more extended proposals have recently been offered by Dasen (1980).

Dasen (1980) describes a distinction by Lautrey among three environments: one in which events occur randomly, one in which the relationships between events are simple and rigid, and one ("flexible" rather than "random" or "rigid") that contains enough order to allow people to predict the consequences of their actions but enough irregularity to demand attention. Lautrey, in Dasen's (1980) description, has used these distinctions to analyze the daily life of French children, examining, for instance, the presence of rules about events ranging from table manners to TV watching. His results indicate a relationship to social class and, irrespective of class, a relationship to several Piagetian measures of cognitive development (Dasen, 1980).

For his own current research among the Kikuyu, Dasen (1980) offers a proposal similar to Lautrey's, but related to a different aspect of daily life. He is primarily concerned with the balance of work and play, and with the extent to which assigned tasks are explained or placed in a structured sequence. The equivalent of Lautrey's flexible environment, Dasen suggests, may be one in which there is a mixture of work and play, and the opportunity to structure activities. Least favorable among the Kikuyu may be the environments for young boys (no set tasks, no attempts by adults to help in the structuring of free time) and for the oldest girls in a family ("given work almost continuously, often without an explicit goal or an obvious sequencing of chores": Dasen, 1980, p. 84).

Such proposals provide examples of a specific form that activation might take (namely, encouragement and opportunity to establish a structure). Some questions, however, are left unanswered.

The first of these is the way in which a link is established between a relatively specific feature of an environment (e.g., the allocation of chores) and a general level of thinking (e.g., about material of several kinds or at least about material unrelated to chores). One possibility is that ways of thinking about one aspect of experience generalize to other aspects. A second is that the particular experiences chosen for analysis—whether these are family rules or the nature of a work load—are indicative of the quality of a wider range of experiences. Kikuyu girls, for example, may in many contexts not have events explained to them, not be given the opportunity to sequence or vary their activities. They may even be discouraged from asking "why."

If cultures have such pervasive features, however, how can they be described? And how do they come about? Why is it, for instance, that Kikuyu girls are not given an explanation of the goal or sequence of work?

The last question can take one into analyses of the social status and roles of girls and children (a direction illustrated by the anthropologist Blount, 1972), or into analyses of how cultures preserve a power structure by establishing norms for the ownership of knowledge or of chores (a direction illustrated in Sheridan's (1980) account of the sociologist Foucault). Such directions, as Glick (this volume) makes clear in his discussion, are very much needed in psychology. They help counter the notion that difficulties in acquiring knowledge rest mainly in the capacity of the learner. They also offer possibilities for the description of pervasive features to the situations children encounter. The pervasive feature may, for instance, be a conviction on the part of adults that children "don't need to know why," that certain forms of knowledge are "not for children" or "not for girls" (either because of appropriateness or difficulty), or that children learn best by trying things out for themselves.

Descriptions of a culture in terms of the prevailing ideas about how children learn and what they should learn are attractive to psychologists for several reasons. One is that they provide a link with historical studies, studies that relate the provision or denial of various kinds of experience for children to the prevailing ideas about the nature of childhood and the obligations of parenting (e.g., Ariès, 1962; Kessen, 1979). A second is that there are some relevant data available. This comes from an E.T.S. study of families within the United States. Parents were presented with a set of vignettes designed to elicit parents' ideas about how children learn (e.g., how they learn social rules or the reasons some objects float while others do not) and about how parents may teach. The kinds of explanations parents give, it has been proposed, can be reduced to degrees of belief in the notion that children learn by a "constructivist" process: actively observing events and abstracting principles, able to understand explanations but benefiting from doing at least part of the explanatory work themselves. This pervasive belief in the way learning proceeds can then be correlated with background features of the parents, with parents' actions on teaching tasks, and with children's cognitive development, using basically Piagetian measures (McGillicuddy-de Lisi, 1982; Sigel, 1982).

The several sets of data from this large E.T.S. study give rise to a number of modifications to any simple model of consistent ideas translated completely into parental actions and levels of development, modifications predominantly in the direction of specificity to effects. Ideas about constructivism, for instance, do vary with the material to be learned; parents' teaching actions are highly task-specific; fathers display more correspondence between ideas and actions than mothers do; the correlations with measures of cognitive development are higher for some measures than for others. Nonetheless, what does emerge is some consistency in the way parents describe themselves as teaching and children as learning, and a link is established between these reports and the way parents help children on tasks.

A Different Type of Proposal. In most of the work mentioned so far, the stress has been on the individual actively engaged in experience: abstracting, generalizing, constructing an ordered reality. Cultural environments have appeared as varying in the extent to which they encourage the individual to act in this way, and in the extent to which the amount of order present makes the task feasible.

This view of events, however, has been regarded as limited. The limits, in turn, have led to new directions of work.

The primary statement of limits is that the image of individuals constructing reality contains too little allowance for the presence of other people. The individual is too solitary. If one grants this, however, there is the obligation to take the next step, to ask the next questions: What are these other people doing? And what guides their actions?

One possibility is that other people are arranging the conditions that make discovery possible. They "scaffold" tasks or "pace" the individual, deftly supplying a framework or a set of tools needed for discovery or learning to take place and then, with equal deftness, rearranging these early props so that the individual may manage without them or may make them his or her own. This language of "tools," of "scaffolding," and of "supportive others," is primarily associated with the name of Vygotsky (cf. Vygotsky, 1978). It has suggested a new direction of research for sources of performance, with particular stress on the way mothers provide and remove "scaffolding" as they help their children learn to cope with a physical or social environment (cf. Gardner & Rogoff, 1982; Wertsch, 1979; Wood, Bruner, & Ross, 1976).

A second possibility stems from some neo-Piagetian positions. People are again arranging the conditions for learning. They do so, however, by providing the degree of practice needed to bring some parts of a performance to a level of smooth automatization that frees energy and attention for the steps needed to change or upgrade the performance. It is difficult, for instance, to work out a complex arithmetic problem if the basic steps of addition and subtraction require a great deal of attention. In this case, the culture makes possible a redistribution of effort and a change in the way capacity is used. The reader interested in Piaget will recognize this type of argument as an extension of curriculum arguments by Case (1978) and by Pascual-Leone (cf. Chapman, 1981).

The third and last possibility is related to the argument that the classical Piagetian view of development is too "a-historical." It is as if worlds are reinvented each generation, with no allowance for the way knowledge is accumulated by being passed on from generation to generation. The argument again prompts a change of research direction. Smillee (1982), for instance, in a recent reexamination of Piagetian work on infant cognitive development, argues that since the basic process is one of the transmission rather than the construction of ideas, the primary research problem should be the nature of communication between adults and infants. An interest in transmission as a process appears also in some work at Macquarie (Cashmore, 1982) on the degree of agreement between ideas held by parents and ideas held by children, work to be described in a later section of this chapter.

In effect, there is no shortage of ways in which we could consider people as being involved in the child's abstracting of invariants or principles from daily experience. In addition, each of these ways is translatable into research and prompts still further questions.

The questions that have attracted our own particular attention — and that of Ninio (1979) in Israel — are as follows: What guides the provision of practice, tools, or scaffolding at particular ages or at particular moments on a task? What are the observations that adults are making? What are the ideas that underlie what they make available and when they decide to see if a child can manage without the help provided or is ready for a new task?

This type of question is the same as that asked earlier in relation to Dasen's (1980) description of the Kikuyu allocation of chores: namely, what prompts or guides the provision of different types of experience? At that time, we proposed that one background factor consists of the views held by adults about the way in which children learn and the areas of knowledge or skill they should acquire. We shall now add some further suggestions. One factor is certainly *age norms:* the expectations adults have about what children are capable of at different ages, expectations that are known to vary from one cultural group to another (cf. Goodnow, Cashmore, Cotton, & Knight, in press; Hess, Kashigawi, Azuma, Price, & Dickson, 1980). Another is the *perceived responsibility* to provide help: a factor found important in Rosemary Knight's current studies at Macquarie of perceived influence among parents, and in Ghuman's (1975) comparison of Punjabi with English parents in the United Kingdom. A third is the possibility that adults provide not simply what they see as assimilable but also what they see as *useful.* Brown's (1958) comments on money terms are an example, suggesting that parents shift from nonspecific terms such as *money* to more specific terms (20 cents, 5 cents, etc.) when they consider the knowledge relevant to the child's activities (saving or spending). Finally, it is possible — in fact almost certain — that adults are guided by the *social value* of performance, regardless of its practical value or of the child's capacity to understand. "Proper" table manners and "proper" speech are examples.

The Nature of Performance and its Measures

We have been dealing so far with the way people have responded to the need to locate cultural factors and processes that could account for a difference between performances that takes the form of one culture appearing to be at a lower level or to lag behind another. This is not the only area, however, where reexamination has occurred. New thinking is occurring also in ideas held about the nature of performance.

We shall separate out two aspects: ideas about how performances are interrelated, and ideas about the value of various kinds of measures.

Ideas about the interrelationships of performance may not be much disturbed by a "lag" or "level" type of result. (They are primarily challenged by the second type of result, namely an uneven pattern of similarities and differences as the comparison moves from one task to another.) If the profile of results is much the same in the two cultures, one may, for instance, continue to hold the hypothesis of a general factor to intelligence (especially if the intercorrelations among tasks are similarly high in both cultures), or the hypothesis of a universal order of difficulty to several tasks (conservation of weight always more difficult, for example, than conservation of amount).

What will be disturbed, however, is one's acceptance of the usual tasks as measures of capacity. The disturbance will be particularly marked if a scholar starts from the belief that all cultures are equal in capacity, or if one notes that in everyday life, the people giving "poor" scores display mastery of some complex material (kinship systems are a prominent example).

What options have been proposed? One is abandoning the notion that the psychologists' usual measures are indicative of capacity, accepting them instead as useful predictors to performances in equally "Western" or "modern" settings such as formal schooling or industrial employment. That is not an unpalatable proposal.

A second option consists of discarding the usual measures and turning attention completely to the study of everyday life, noting within it the problems that arise and the way these are solved. This is, for instance, the direction of Sylvia Scribner's current work. A softer version of such an option is to ask about the way people in everyday life make comparisons among children (e.g., choose one child rather than another to deliver a complex message) and then to correlate these rankings with the scores on various standard tasks, giving possible preference to those tasks that do correlate positively with local ratings. This is, for instance, a direction within work both in Africa (cf. Serpell, 1976) and in Guatemala (Nerlove, Roberts, Klein, Yarbrough, & Habicht, 1975). The last option to be considered is that of improving one's measures, adapting them by changing the instructions or the material to a point where they give "reasonable" results. Although it seems the simplest, this option had been left to the last because we wish to underline a question it raises that will recur: To what point do people adapt measures? We suggest that they do so until the tasks fit some underlying criteria ("normal" distribution, "sensible" factor structure, "reasonable comparability with everyday life," "reasonable fit" with some other measure in which one has more confidence). These underlying criteria, however, are often far from explicit, even though they guide both the work of test adaptation and the surprise felt when the members of another culture do not display the behavior expected. Their more explicit statement is a much needed task.

A Summary of Responses to Challenge 1

At this point, what do we have in terms of the hopes held at the beginning for unraveling relationships between culture and performance?

We have, at the least, a range of new ideas about changes that might be made in the selection of measures and in the inferences drawn from performance.

We have as well a set of proposals of how one might describe culture and the processes by which its features have an effect upon performance. For example, culture might profitably be described in terms of its rigid/flexible qualities, in terms of the way access of knowledge is controlled, or in terms of the ideas about childhood and learning that guide adults' provision of experience. For the description of process, we can add considerably to the first notion of activation/utilization. On the one hand, the area provides some specifics of how the facilitation of performance may take place: by way, for instance, of providing tools or scaffolding, or by providing the automatizing practice that frees the mind for other work. It provides also some amplification to the idea that a culture may not simply operate by activating capacity in an "on" or "off" fashion. The process may be one of active suppression. It may also — as in Lautrey's "random" environments (Dasen, 1980) — be one of frustration, encouraging the individual to believe that there is little or no point to the effort to understand. Finally, we have made a beginning toward suggesting how the individual may take an active role in the course of interactions with culture, even though that role as agent is so far limited to turning aside from an environment with more happening or more disorder than one can cope with. More scope for this possibility emerges in the next section, dealing with a different type of result: namely, an uneven pattern of similarities and differences in performance across cultures.

CHALLENGE 2: DIFFERENCES ON SOME TASKS BUT NOT OTHERS

Comparisons across cultures often yield, not a difference in overall level or in age of achievement, but an uneven pattern. Moreover, a difference may occur on some forms of a task but not others. A classification task with one set of material, for instance, elicits a different performance from that shown on the "same" task with other material; a numbers task with the problem given in one language elicits a different performance from the "same" problems given in another. Examples of many such variations may be found in work by Serpell (1979), in Rogoff's (1982) review of "contextual" approaches to performance, and within the publications of the Laboratory for Comparative Human Cognition (e.g., Cole, Hood, & McDermott, 1978; LCHC, 1979, 1980). For cross-cultural comparisons, the overall result is one of a shifting image: equality with some task forms but not with others.

As with the first type of result, we consider what such results do to views about performance and its measures and to descriptions of the nature of culture and the processes by which effects occur. Since this second type of result has a particular effect on views of performance, we start with that area, reversing the order of points followed in the previous section.

The Nature of Performance and its Measures

When one culture exhibits performances that are highly context-specific and another gives performances that are intercorrelated, it is inevitable that people will begin to wonder which is the "natural" state. When evidence begins to appear of performance being context-specific even in the culture thought to display unity, it is likely that the balance will seem to shift toward context-specificity as the "natural" or the "first" state. This is, for instance, the impact of work discussed by Donaldson (1978) showing that among children in Scotland the level of performance may be considerably altered by using, say, a cops-and-robbers format for the traditional three-mountains task as a way of determining whether children can take the visual perspective of another individual.

If one starts, however, from a view of performance as context-specific (in either a natural or a first state), problems soon arise on both theoretical and empirical grounds. Theoretically, one runs the risk of becoming "submerged in a mass of unmanageable material" (Jahoda, 1980, p. 126). Empirically, one has the problem of accounting for those occasions where performances are interrelated.

The latter problem, as Rogoff (1982) points out, means a return to looking more closely at the notion of generalization, a return that has thrown up several proposals that affect the way culture and performance are perceived to interact. The proposals deal primarily with what may be happening within cognitive development.

One proposal is that the individual develops, not a single level of skill, but a repertoire of skills and strategies from which a selection is made to suit a particular occasion (cf. Goodnow, 1972). The sharpest example of such selection is probably the use of various forms of speech to fit relationships between two speakers. To the notion of repertoire, one could add the suggestion of alternative ways of action that do not necessarily co-exist peacefully until called for, but may be competitive with one another. The metaphor comes from Susan Isaacs' (1970) argument that earlier ways of thinking are not absorbed into later ways, as most Piagetian theory proposes. Instead, the earlier ways continue to exist, breaking through at times when the task-situation allows them to or when the individual is tired or upset and does not expend the usual energy required to inhibit them.

A second proposal is that an important part of cognitive development consists of developing some sense of how contexts or situations are related to one another. This type of proposal appears, for instance, in Bronfenbrenner's (1979) study. Any society, he argues, may be described as a collection of settings. What develops, depending on the links provided between settings and the individual's capacity to perceive them, is a more or less differentiated view of how one setting (with its characteristic tasks and roles) is related to another. That proposal can be fitted with an argument such as Donaldson's (1978) to the effect that cognitive development is marked by "decontextualization," by the recognition that the same principle applies to several contexts. It is also compatible with a proposal from Harris and Heelas (cited by Dasen, 1980), to the effect that consistency in performance occurs primarily in "valleys of construction": "progress in any one of the valleys has a constructive stage-like character but there is little communication between valleys" (Dasen, 1980, p. 81). There is, however, a difference between Dasen (1980) and Donaldson (1978) in what is seen as giving rise to some interrelationships among performances. In Dasen's (1980) description, the implication is that the unification of performance within a valley owes a great deal to an internal push, from within the individual, for bringing order into the universe and into one's ideas. In contrast, a proposal such as Donaldson's (1978) looks more to an external pull. In Donaldson's view, institutions such as schools insist upon and reward decontextualization: children are taught that "locating the general principle" is a good thing.

These are, of course, not the only possible proposals that could be made about how performances might come to depart from a state of being extremely specific to a task situation. One could add points made in a related debate about consistency in social behavior, a debate that includes, for instance, attention to differences in the degree of importance given to consistency in various domains, in the definition of consistency, and in the dimensions that give rise to some situations being seen as calling for similar behaviors whereas others do not (cf. Forgas, 1979). We are not working toward an exhaustive set of proposals. The point we wish to make is that the finding of specificity in behavior must bring with it a rise of interest in how performances come to be interrelated. The area of cross-cultural comparisons, once discussion moves away from differences in a general level or stage of performance, is no exception. The area must also — and this pressure may be more unique — come to terms with the task of specifying the features of culture that may affect generality/specificity in performance and the way in which these features have an effect.

The Choice of Measures. We have been dealing so far with the reexamination of ideas about how performances are interrelated. That is the issue where the most wide-ranging proposals have appeared for the intertwining of culture and performance. Also up for review, however, have come the choice of measures and the inferences made as to what tasks measure. For anyone interested in "standard" measures that may be used across many cultures, the notion of performance as highly contextual may in fact produce a state close to despair. Even choosing tasks that are in some way familiar to a culture may not solve the problem. In fact, the notion of familiarity itself has come under review, with people asking whether it applies to the task material or to the operation and whether it may elicit an unthinking "poor" performance rather than giving the advantage one expects (cf. Greenfield, 1974). All told, the notion of performance as intrinsically context-specific makes it very difficult to speak at all of some measures as more indicative of capacity than are others. For a strong contextualist, the notion of some measures as indicating "underlying capacity" and others "utilized capacity" would hardly arise at all.

A reexamination of measures, however, does lead in some positive directions. The move to adapt tasks, altering their features to a point where they elicit the performances that people are expected to be able to give, has led to a second look at how children in our own culture come to know about the usual features of tasks; come to know, for example, that some features are likely to be irrelevant, that the solution is more likely to be found in some parts of the problem rather than others, that certain strategies are worth trying on almost any task, that the later problems in a series are likely to be harder than the first. Such learning about the features of tasks and expected performances seems to take place so smoothly that only the unexpectedly poor performance of a new group makes one realize how much learning has taken place. For children within our own Western culture, Gelman (1978) supplies a number of examples of such research and of its application to ways of accounting for age differences in performance.

Cultural Factors and Processes

Suppose culture were described as a collection of contexts or settings, each with characteristic tasks, props, casts of people, and roles. Such a description occurs in Bronfenbrenner's (1979) description of the "ecology of childhood." It clearly fits well with "contextual" views of performance.

How then would contexts have an effect? What processes might be involved? We distinguish two broad types of proposal. The first points to the way that some contexts involve demands for specific skills. The second moves in a quite different direction, asking instead, How do people come to be in some contexts or settings rather than others?

The first type of proposal is most sharply illustrated by studies of physical environments. Some physical environments, for instance, require movement away from home-base and across particular types of ground (ice, water, or desert: all containing few obvious landmarks or shifting landmarks). Such environments are seen as demanding that people develop more elaborate and more abstract concepts of space than are needed in a world where movement is restricted to home-base or to well-trodden paths (cf. Berry, 1976; Gladwin, 1970; Lynch, 1960; Munroe & Munroe, 1971). Such arguments could also be given a more "social" turn. A "village" type of environment, for instance, may make few demands for seeing space from another's point of view, of the type required, say, in giving directions to a stranger or a voyager.

The second type of proposal moves research in a different direction. The basic question is, How do people come to be in different contexts or settings?

One may begin by describing where people are. An example is Rogoff's (1981) description of where children varying in age and gender are to be found in a Guatemalan village.

In a more theoretical vein is a hypothesis about process: a process termed context selection (LCHC, 1980). The term *context selection* may actually be used to cover two processes. In one, the stress is on the individual as selecting contexts. The individual takes an active part in "ecological niche-picking" (Cole, Hood, & McDermott, 1978). It is this concept that gives rise, for instance, to a case study of how children select tasks within a cooking club and how, in particular, a boy with a reading disability selects and alters activities so that his difficulties are not obvious (Cole & Traupmann, 1979). This seems the clearest example to date of self-selection of contexts, although one might wish to add to it examples of children in a family choosing activities that are *not* those of their siblings (cf. Scarr & Grajek, 1982).

The other sense of the term context selection may be thought of as *context assignment*. Adults and peers assign a given child to a given task, setting, or role. Such assignment becomes of particular interest if we accept the Vygotskian notion that one of the important functions of adults is their selection and arrangement of situations that provide varying degrees of support in the learning of a skill (cf. Vygotsky, 1978). To this direction of interest, investigators have tagged the further question, What gives rise to the assignment of children to some contexts rather than others? That question underlies research asking, Who goes to school in an elective situation? (cf. Sharp, Cole, & Lave, 1979). It leads also to our own research into the ages at which children are expected to master certain skills or to be assigned various household chores (Goodnow et al., in press). The starting assumption in such research is that assignment is influenced by several factors. One is a factor noted earlier, namely the ideas held about children and about what is "appropriate," "natural," "good" or "useful" for certain children. To these we would now add some others particularly prompted by discussions of context selection or assignment. One is that assignment by parents or adults is often in the service of *their* needs in addition to — or in preference to — those of the child, a point made especially by Whiting (1974) in commenting on factors that influence a child's being given access to various parts of a house. Another is the type of factor noted by Glick in his discussion: namely, that assignment may take a negative form, i.e., take the form of exclusion and of closing doors as well as opening them. The marking of mathematics as inappropriate or as difficult for girls (cf. Parsons, Adler, & Kaczala, 1982) provides an example within Western culture.

A Summary of Responses to Challenge 2

What do we now have added to our understanding of relationships between culture and performance? We have, at base, a strong challenge to the notion that performances tend to be interrelated, at least to any degree that would allow one to talk about general stages or levels. We have, as well, a strong challenge to the hope of designing standard measures and a clear indication that we should look to see how children in any culture come to know the expected forms of any task. In an equally positive vein, we have a description of culture as a collection of contexts or settings, a description that allows us to ask about the tasks, props, roles, and demands of a setting and about the ways in which one context is seen as linked to others. We also have a description of process either in terms of a demand for skills or in terms of context selection: selection by oneself or assignment by others. The first of these gives the largest room so far for an active part played by the individuals: they emerge to some extent choosing the cultural conditions they experience. The second (context assignment) again raises questions about factors that influence assignment, factors ranging from adults' needs to ideas about the nature of childhood.

CHALLENGE 3: TASKS DECLINED

The tasks offered by psychologists may be declined as absurd or evaded with courtesy, leaving the giver in either case with the sense of somehow having lost status as a sensible, intelligent adult. The phenomenon has been noted among the Kpelle when asked to work on reasoning tasks (Cole, Gay, Glick, & Sharp, 1971) and among Puerto Rican mothers asked to complete an interview schedule (Hertzig, Birch, Thomas, & Mendez, 1963). The case most often cited is the response of Russian peasants, living in the Urals in the 1930s, to Luria's reasoning tasks (Luria, 1976). These adults saw no point, for example, in working out how many hours it took to go by rail from their village to, say, Tomsk, if in real life they did not themselves travel to Tomsk by any means.

This particular type of result adds little to what has already been said about the way performances are interrelated or about the fate of various measures of ability. If all tasks are declined, for example, one learns nothing about the interrelations of performances. If some are accepted but others declined, one is back to the problem of context, puzzling over how to specify the difference between one task situation and another. The new facet added to the culture-performance question lies in the questions raised about describing the nature of culture and its effects, and it is on these that we concentrate.

Cultural Factors and Processes

To say that the difference between "accepting" and "non-accepting" cultures is one of "motivation" seems to add no new information. Something new is added by proposals that particular components of culture are responsible for changes in the acceptance of tasks as worth working on. Luria (1976), for instance, saw industrialization as accounting for the task acceptance he observed when he returned to the same area at a later time. (Scholars such as Buck-Morss, 1975, would add the comment that the "alienation" of modern work from "real" concerns sets the stage for accepting disembodied psychometric tasks.) As a further component in such task acceptance, formal schooling has been proposed. Formal schooling, it has been argued, sets problems that are out of context and unrelated to practical needs. It also rewards children for success on such tasks, leading to a general acceptance of tasks that seem like those set in school (Bruner, 1966).

Beneath these specific suggestions lies a pervasive process that is so far little explored by psychologists but has been noted by other social scientists. This is the way cultures designate some problems as more worth working on than others, more "serious" or more "prestigious" than others. Kuhn (1968), for instance, has argued that the designation of some research problems as "worthwhile" (while others are "trivial") is one index of a prevailing scientific paradigm. Arnheim (1971) has remarked on the way Western culture divides activities into arbitrary groups, coupled with a "better-poorer dimension": "the hard sciences" and "the soft arts," for instance. Berger, Berger, and Kellner (1974) have noted the way "modern" culture insists on a separation between "work" and "play," between "learning" and "doing nothing." Jackson and Marsden (1958) have commented that something general is said about a culture when it is found to teach music only to the lower streams of a class.

Comparisons across cultures give one the same sense that the acceptance of tasks—the categorization of some as more or less worth working on, more or less appropriate to one's age and status—indicates some general underlying views: views about the nature of "skill," about the nature of "good," "sensible" performance, and about the nature of obligations between people when task requests are made. There is a great deal yet to be learned about such underlying views, both the views that others hold and the views that lead members of one culture to present to others, particular tasks as worthy of effort. There is as well a great deal to be learned about the way in which such views are acquired or are transmitted from one generation to another.

To end with the proposal that "there is a great deal to be learned," however, is hardly satisfactory. We should be able to provide something more specific, namely, advice on a specific type of research problem. One highly feasible research area deals with the transmission of ideas, a process noted as important in the earlier discussion of whether ideas are abstracted or constructed by the enquiring individual, rather than handed down in more historical and less individualist fashion. There are, in fact, studies of agreement between generations on what is regarded as important, primarily by sociologists and under the label of congruence in values (primarily political and religious values). Within these studies, one may find analyses of the effects of such conditions as the importance, to the older generation, of the message to be transmitted, the likelihood of its being verbalized, or the "vested interest" of the younger generation in turning a deaf ear. Recent reviews have been provided by Bengston and Troll (1978) and Troll and Bengston (1979). For our current purposes, the points to note are that the parental messages can provide one way of describing culture, the child's expression of the same messages or values can be treated as a form of social cognition (one view of the social world), and transmission can be regarded as the linking process. Such a position has the advantage of describing culture and cognition in the same terms, avoiding the difficulty noted earlier of attempting to map on to one another descriptions that use different dimensions or qualities. Such a view of cognition, however, leaves out—as Glick notes—a great deal of what is usually covered in Piagetian accounts of cognitive development.

Cross-generation studies—especially in their stress on transmission as a process—seem at first remote from the idea of the enquiring individual searching among the experiences that a culture may or may not provide. It is, however, possible to locate a bridge. Within cross-generation studies, there are a few scholars (e.g., Scheck & Emerick, 1976; Tedin, 1974) who argue that one critical factor must be the child's perception of the adult message about what is important. In some recent work by Cashmore (1982), that does indeed turn out to be the case. The best predictor of what children themselves regard as important is, in almost all cases, their perception of the views that parents hold rather than the views parents report themselves as holding. The exceptions appear to fall into the "vested interest" category. Children for instance, do not see "being neat" or "being obedient" as having the same importance that parents give to these qualities. Such studies do not specify what tasks our own culture specifies as appropriate or as worth working on. They do, however, give us an indication of factors involved in the acquisition of ideas about areas that are more rather than less worthy of the effort of performance. They also begin to spell out what may need to be explored if we accept the notion of transmission as a process by which some features of a culture (namely its values or its prevailing ideas) may affect the way a new generation thinks and performs in task situations.

GENERAL COMMENTS

At this point, we wish to draw together a number of the points already made and to bring them to bear more sharply on the notion of culture as an influential factor in activating or utilizing capacity, and on the distinction between capacity or competence and performance.

We have used as a starting point Overton and Newman's (1982) notion of culture as activating or utilizing capacity, and have asked what would need to be added to such a notion in order to have a broader picture of how cultural or environmental factors may influence performance. We have added, for instance, the notion of a negative effect: an effect not simply of failure to activate but also of suppression, a point expressed even more strongly in Glick's discussion. We have added the presence of the individual as an agent, taking an active part in the selection or avoidance of experience. We have added the metaphor of transmission of ideas to the pervasive metaphor of an "on-or-off" switch, incorporating a stress on the knowledge of others and moving away somewhat from the picture of individuals constructing reality largely from their own active experience with physical and social events. In line with that shift, we have asked what it is that the "significant others" provide to the individual (ranging from tools to scaffolding and ideas about what is worth working on and what represents good performance). Finally, we have pointed to a recurring question that arises as soon as we begin to see culture as consisting of people who provide (or deny) various forms of experience:

namely, what guides the provision of experiences? Are there, for instance, underlying ideas about the nature of childhood and learning that we should investigate further?

All of these proposals have to do with the way in which we might describe a culture and the processes by which effects occur. What has also emerged — in the rethinking that currently marks a great deal of cross-cultural work — is a set of proposals about "performance." The phenomena of interest may not be simply the behaviors observed on standard tasks but also the ideas people hold about task performance. Of equal interest may also be the task performance of everyday life. Pervasive throughout is a sense of caution about inferring levels of performance from any particular set of measures.

That sense of caution brings us to the final point: the distinction between *competence* and *performance*. One of us (JG) has a strong preference for not using the distinction at all, partly because of the difficulty in establishing criteria that will designate some performances as more indicative of capacity than others. To say that one does not feel comfortable about a distinction, however, is hardly positive. What are the alternatives?

One alternative is to recognize that the distinction is intended to convey a conviction that the thinking people display is the result of both internal and external factors. In Overton and Newman's (1982) description of factors in development, there is always — in addition to environmental demands — some "internal push" for change in thought, some "necessary and inherent" activity. The assumption of such an "internal push" (like the assumption of biological factors and of qualitative differences between the thinking of 2-year-olds and 10-year-olds regardless of all the help given) seems to be a matter of belief that we would share with Overton. It need not, however, lead to a distinction between *competence* and *performance*.

A second alternative is to follow Lefebvre-Pinard and Pinard's suggestion (this volume): namely, collapse the two terms, adopting Descartes' proposal that the use of a capacity is a part of capacity itself and avoiding the Aristotelian distinction between capacity and its use.

A third alternative is to shift the distinction to another pair of terms, a pair that may lead to more manageable research and be more closely related to the concerns that push one toward a competence/performance distinction. At least in the cross-cultural area, the phenomenon that brings many psychologists to a concern with *capacity* is a sense of surprise at the performances observed. The nub of the experience is a sense of discrepancy between "behavior observed" and "behavior expected." Given that, perhaps the critical questions to work on are the pair: What are the expectations we brought to the situation? And on what are they based? Such questions turn inquiry back to one's own culture and theory, a step that seems essential if relationships between culture and performance are to be untangled in a satisfying way.

REFERENCES

Ariès, P. (1962). *Centuries of childhood*. London: Jonathon Cope.

Arnheim, R. (1971). *Visual thinking*. Berkeley: University of California Press.

Bengston, V. L., & Troll, L. (1978). Youth and their parents: Feedback and intergenerational influence in socialization. In R. M. Lerner & G. B. Spanier (Eds.), *Child influences on marital and family interaction: A life-span perspective*. New York: Academic Press.

Berger, P., Berger, B., & Kellner, H. (1974). *The homeless mind*. Harmondsworth: Penguin.

Berry, J. W. (1976). *Human ecology and cognitive style*. New York: Sage-Halsted.

Blount, B. G. (1972). Parental speech and language acquisition: Some Luo and Samoan examples. *Anthropological Linguistics, 14,* 119–130.

Bronfenbrenner, U. (1979). *The ecology of human development*. Cambridge, MA: Harvard University Press.

Bronfenbrenner, U. (1981). *The evolution of research models in field studies of human development*. Unpublished manuscript, Cornell University.

Brown, R. (1958). How shall a thing be called? *Psychological Review, 65,* 14–21.

Bruner, J. S. (1966). On cognitive growth. In J. S. Bruner, R. R. Olver, & P. M. Greenfield, *Studies in cognitive growth*. New York: Wiley.

Buck-Morss, S. (1975). Socio-economic bias in Piaget's theory and its implications for cross-cultural studies. *Human Development, 18,* 35–49.

Case, R. (1978). Intellectual development from birth to adulthood: A Neo-Piagetian interpretation. In R. S. Siegler (Ed.), *Children's thinking: What develops?* Hillsdale, NJ: Lawrence Erlbaum Associates.

Cashmore, J. (1982). *Factors in agreement between parents and children on values and sources of skill*. Unpublished doctoral thesis, Macquarie University.

Chapman, M. (1981). Pascual-Leone's theory of constructive operators. *Human Development, 24,* 145–155.

Cole, M., Gay, J., Glick, J. A., & Sharp, D. W. (1971). *The cultural context of learning and thinking*. New York: Basic Books.

Cole, M., Hood, L., & McDermott, R. P. (1978). *Ecological niche picking: Ecological invalidity as an axiom of experimental cognitive psychology*. Unpublished manuscript, University of California, San Diego (LCHC).

Cole, M., & Traupmann, K. (1979). Comparative cognition research: Learning from a learning disabled child. *Minnesota Symposium on Child Development* (Vol. 12). Minneapolis: University of Minnesota Press.

Dasen, P. R. (1975). Concrete operational development in three cultures. *Journal of Cross-Cultural Psychology, 6,* 156–172.

Dasen, P. R. (1980). Psychological differentiation and operational development: A cross-cultural link. *The Quarterly Newsletter of Laboratory of Comparative Human Development, 2,* 81–86.

Donaldson, M. (1978). *Children's minds*. Glasgow: Fontana.

Forgas, J. P. (1979). *Social episodes: The study of interaction routines*. London: Academic Press.

Gardner, W. P., & Rogoff, B. (1982). The role of instruction in memory development. *The Quarterly Newsletter of Laboratory of Comparative Human Development, 4,* 6–12.

Gelman, R. (1978). Cognitive development. *Annual Review of Psychology, 29,* 297–332.

Ghuman, P. (1975). *The cultural context of thinking*. Windsor-Berks.: National Foundation for Educational Research.

Gladwin, T. (1970). *East is a big bird*. Cambridge, MA: Belknap.

Goodnow, J. J. (1972). Rules and repertoires, rituals and tricks of the trade: Social and represen-tational aspects of cognitive and representational development. In S. Farnham-Diggory (Ed.), *Information processing in children*. New York: Academic Press.

Goodnow, J. J., Cashmore, J., Cotton, S., & Knight, R. (in press). Mothers' timetables in two cultural groups. *International Journal of Psychology.*

Greenfield, P. M. (1966). On culture and conservation. In J. S. Bruner, R. R. Olver, & P. M. Greenfield (Eds.), *Studies in cognitive growth.* New York: Wiley.

Greenfield, P. M. (1974). Comparing dimensional categorization in natural and artificial contexts: A developmental study among the Zinacantecos of Mexico. *Journal of Social Psychology, 93,* 157–191.

Hertzig, M. E., Birch, H. G., Thomas, A., & Mendez, O. A. (1963). Class and ethnic differences in the responsiveness of preschool children to cognitive demands. *Monographs of Society for Research in Child Development, 33,* (Whole No. 117).

Hess, R. D., Kashigawi, K., Azuma, H., Price, G. G., & Dickson, W. P. (1980). Maternal expectations for mastery of developmental tasks in Japan and the United States. *International Journal of Psychology, 15,* 240–258.

Issacs, S. (1970). *Intellectual growth in young children.* London: Routledge & Kegan Paul.

Jackson, B., & Marsden, D. (1958). *Education and the working class.* Harmondsworth: Penguin.

Jahoda, G. (1980). Theoretical and systematic approaches in cross-cultural psychology. In H. C. Triandis & W. W. Lambert (Eds.), *Handbook of cross-cultural psychology* (Vol. 1). Boston: Allyn & Bacon.

Kessen, W. (1979). The American child and other inventions. *American Psychologist, 34,* 815–820.

Kuhn, T. S. (1968). *The structure of scientific revolutions.* Chicago: University of Chicago Press.

Laboratory of Comparative Human Cognition. (1979). Cross-cultural psychology's challenges to our ideas of children and development. *American Psychologist, 34,* 827–833.

Laboratory of Comparative Human Cognition. (1980). *Culture and cognitive development.* Unpublished manuscript, University of California, San Diego.

Luria, R. A. (1976). *Cognitive development: Its cultural and social foundations.* Cambridge, MA: Harvard University Press.

Lynch, K. (1960). *The image of the city.* Cambridge, MA: MIT Press.

McGillicuddy-de Lisi, A. V. (1982). Parental beliefs about developmental process. *Human Development, 25,* 192–200.

Munroe, R. L., & Munroe, R. H. (1971). Effect of environmental experience on spatial ability in East African society. *Journal of Social Psychology, 83,* 15–22.

Nerlove, S. B., Roberts, J. M., Klein, R. E., Yarbrough, C., & Habicht, J. P. (1974). Natural indicators of cognitive development: An observational study of rural Guatemalan children. *Ethos, 2,* 265–295.

Ninio, A. (1979). The naive theory of the infant and other maternal attitudes in two subgroups in Israel. *Child Development, 50,* 976–980.

Overton, W. F., & Newman, J. (1982). Cognitive development: A competence-activation/utilization approach. In T. Field, A. Houston, H. Quay, L. Troll, & G. Finley (Eds.), *Review of human development.* New York: Wiley.

Parsons, J. E., Adler, T. F., & Kaczala, C. M. (1982). Socialization of achievement attitudes and beliefs: Parental influences. *Child Development, 53,* 310–321.

Rogoff, B. (1981). Adults and peers as agents of socialization: A Highland Guatemalan profile. *Ethos, 9,* 18–36.

Rogoff, B. (1982). Approaches to integrating context and cognitive development. In M. E. Lamb & A. L. Brown (Eds.), *Advances in developmental psychology* (Vol. 2). Hillsdale, NJ: Lawrence Erlbaum Associates.

Scarr, S., & Grajek, S. (1982). Similarities and differences among siblings. In M. E. Lamb & B. Sutton-Smith (Eds.), *Sibling relationships.* Hillsdale, NJ: Lawrence Erlbaum Associates.

Scheck, D. C., & Emerick, R. (1976). The young male adolescent's perception of early child-rearing behavior: The differential effects of socioeconomic status and family size. *Sociometry, 39,* 39–52.

Serpell, R. (1976). *Culture's influence on behavior.* London: Methuen.

Serpell, R. (1979). How specific are perceptual skills: A cross-cultural study of pattern reproduction. *British Journal of Psychology, 70,* 365–380.

Sharp, D., Cole, M., & Lave, C. (1979). Education and cognitive development: The evidence from experimental research. *Monographs of the Society for Research in Child Development, 44* (Whole No. 178).

Sheridan, A. (1980). *Michel Foucault: The will to truth.* London: Tavistock.

Sigel, I. E. (1982). The relationship between parental distancing strategies and the child's cognitive behavior. In L. M. Laosa & I. E. Sigel (Eds.), *Families as learning environments for children.* New York: Plenum.

Smillee, D. (1982). Rethinking Piaget's theory of infancy. *Human Development, 25,* 282–294.

Tanner, J. M., & Inhelder, B. (Eds.). (1956). *Discussions on child development* (Vol. 1). London: Tavistock.

Tedin, K. L. (1974). The influence of parents on the political attitudes of adolescents. *American Political Science Review, 68,* 1579–1592.

Troll, L., & Bengston, V. (1979). Generations in the family. In W. R. Burr, R. Hill, F. I. Nye, & I. L. Reiss (Eds.), *Contemporary theories about the family* (Vol. 1). New York: Free Press.

Vernon, P. E. (1969). *Intelligence and cultural environment.* London: Methuen.

Vygotsky, L. S. (1978). *Mind in society; The development of higher psychological processes.* Cambridge, MA: Harvard University Press.

Wertsch, J. V. (1979). From social interaction to higher psychological processes: A clarification and application of Vygotsky's theory. *Human Development, 22,* 1–22.

Whiting, B. B. (1974). Folk wisdom and child rearing. *Merrill-Palmer Quarterly, 20,* 9–19.

Wood, D., Bruner, J. S., & Ross, G. (1976). The role of tutoring in problem solving. *Journal of Child Psychology and Psychiatry, 17,* 89–100.

5 Culture and Cognition Revisited

Joseph Glick
Cuny Graduate School

An understanding of the relationship between culture and cognition requires the understanding of three basic elements. We require a clear understanding of *cognition,* of *culture,* and of the various means by which they may interact.

None of these primitives to the equation is fully understood. So it is not surprising that we are far from having satisfactory notions of how to proceed in order to advance knowledge in this fundamentally important area of inquiry. It is not that we are ignorant. We do know a great deal about culture and cognition. The problem is the "way" that we know.

The standard form of scientific knowing requires certain intellectual tactics that strongly determine the ultimate form of "what is known." Generally, and succinctly put, we gain knowledge in an area by being able to delimit sharply the boundaries of what we wish to know about. The operations of delimitation affect both the topic of study and the means by which the topic is studied.

By delimiting the topic, we work in areas where we can have a strong theory of the phenomena in question. In much the same way that Chomsky's advances in understanding language require a field of data that has definite boundaries so that one can distinguish between "real competence" and "performance errors," inquiries in other fields require a strong enough boundary so that essential phenomena can be differentiated from the accidental. In this way we save ourselves from investigations that amount to no more than unordered catalogues of miscellaneous "facts."

Similarly, we delimit the topic by choosing within a restricted range of methods that are deemed adequate to studies of the chosen topic. Certain ways of studying a topic gain ascendancy, others are considered to be "too loose" or "off topic." Since judgments of this sort strongly determine what can and will be published in our professional journals, the cumulative wisdom about a given topic is constrained.

This chapter is not intended as an attack either on current theory or on contemporary methods of study. However it does attempt to look beyond current conceptualizations and practices in order to prepare the way for an understanding of culture-cognition relationships in ways that are not currently provided for by our available conceptual arsenal.

In particular this chapter examines the potentialities for understanding culture/cognition relationships afforded by Piagetian theory as it has been developed to date. After this examination it proceeds to seek for expansions of and alternatives to this powerful theory of cognition in order to open the way more appropriately for a treatment of cognition and culture that has some greater promise of success.

Piagetian theory has had an exceedingly strong influence on current conceptualizations of the development of cognition. For many it has provided precisely the sort of "strong theory" that allows for sharp delimitation of core facts from accidental phenomena that theoretical progress requires. Even detractors of the theory often couch their arguments within the conceptual framework provided by the theory.

However, Piagetian theory, for reasons to be developed in the following sections, is not a good candidate for being the sort of theory that will allow progress in understanding the relationships between culture and cognition. Although it may be a perfectly fine sort of theory for understanding cognition (of a certain sort) it does not provide the kind of conception of cognition that allows for the incorporation of cultural factors. This limitation is not an accidental property of the theory, occurring only because Piagetians, in the main, have not concentrated on issues of culture. The reasons are deeper, more fundamentally connected to the kinds of things that the theory attempts to be a theory about.

PIAGETIAN THEORY: AN OVERVIEW

Any theory of mind and its development is, of necessity, a theory that is posed within the basic parameters of understanding of some particular cultural group. Although theories seldom reference their own cultural origins, those origins are nonetheless operative at all points in the inquiry. Piagetian theory exists firmly within the tradition of thinking about thinking that began with the Greek philosophers, reached clear formulation in the work of Plato and Aristotle, and modern expression in the critiques of Kant. In many respects Piaget's work can be seen as the empirical extension of these deliberations with the added feature of attempting to posit mechanisms that could allow us to understand how mind can be "acquired."

The basic insight developed in this tradition of inquiry is that mind operates by principles that are often "abstract." Much of what is known has, as principal components, many features that go "beyond the information given." Indeed this tradition of inquiry goes to great pains to demonstrate the fundamentally abstract characteristic of knowledge by demonstrating that what is known cannot possibly be likened to what is perceived. Most of the phenomena investigated by Piaget — the object concept, conservation, logical operations and the like — share the common feature that they are phenomena of mind that do not seem to depend at all on the "surface features" of our perceptual experience.

Given this formulation of the problem it would seem that these abstract and nonperceptual features of our knowledge system would therefore have to be considered, in some manner, "innate." Piaget rejected this formuation of the issue and attempted to prepare the ground for a developmental theory of the origins of mind by demonstrating, on the one hand, that these presumably innate features show an orderly developmental regularity, and once having demonstrated development, he sought, on the other hand, to posit mechanisms of acquisition that could account for the mystery of how nonperceptually based knowledge could work.

Initially great excitement attended Piaget's demonstration that these fundamental features did indeed undergo a developmental progression from a point where they were "nowhere in sight" to a period where rudimentary forms can be shown to exist, to a period where these features were fully in competence. What remained to be shown was the sort of developmental mechanisms that could account for the development of abstract knowledge.

The requirements for the description of such mechanisms are quite complex and difficult. The development of fundamental forms that are considered to be both *abstract* and *universal* requires positing acquisition mechanisms that can fully explain this development in a manner that does not simply appeal to biological pre-wiring.

Piaget ingeniously solved the theoretical problem of finding a non-innate, universal basis for knowledge by positing a constructive system that operated upon "reflections upon actions." We elaborate this achievement of the theory and where it seems to fail in a later section of this chapter. For now, however, it is instructive to take a look at what psychologists have attempted to do in following up Piaget's theoretical attempts.

The Piagetian position is, in its essential form, one that takes structures of thought as an outcome of two component variables: biological structures (which generate actions in the nervous system) on the one hand and environmental occasions for action on the other (Piaget, 1974). The theory can be tested, it seems, in two ways. The first and by far most difficult way would be to find some way to "vary" biological factors, holding everything else constant and seeing if different "logical structures" appear. There are understandably few attempts to do this though there have been some efforts along these lines (e.g., DeLemos, 1969; Jensen, 1969).

The second way, and the one most frequently opted for, is to seek for environmental variation coupled with variation in cognitive outcome. Two related courses of action have been taken in this regard. One can produce variation in environments either by introducing various "training" formats for experience (Beilin, 1978) or by seeking natural variation in environments such as occur in different cultures (Dasen, 1972). The former approach takes off from the notion that some variation in cognitive outcome exists and that this can be traced, in some measure, to the environment considered as a "socializing agent." We have recently seen an extension of this approach by looking at the influence of socialization as it can exist between peers (e.g., Doise, Mugny, & Perret-Clermont, 1975).

The second approach is to test for the presence or absence of various cognitive structures in cultural groups that differ considerably in both material environment and socializing environment. As the results of these studies came in, it seemed that considerable variation in cognitive outcome could be found (Dasen, 1977; Newman, Riel, & Martin, in press).

These efforts occurred in parallel with other efforts (beyond training studies) that were pursued within culture. The effect of environmental variation was pursued "within task," seeking variation in measured cognitive ability coupled with variation in the topic of a task (e.g., conservation of weight vs. conservation of volume) or with variations in task arrangements so that mini-environmental differences and their impact upon cognitive functioning could be assessed.

From these sorts of efforts new topics for developmental psychologists were engendered. For those committed to the Piagetian view of things the fundamental problems became described as problems of *decalage* (why do tasks that seem to have an underlying structural unity not show a concurrent acquisition in competence?). For those not committed to the Piagetian view, problems of decalage and the demonstration that measured cognitive ability depended on the nuances of task arrangements were used to supplant the Piagetian notions of structure with competing notions of "particular skills" (Cole, 1981; Donaldson, 1978; Gelman, 1969; Klahr & Wallace, 1972; Siegler, 1981).

Goodnow's paper (this volume), and the Overton and Newman paper she discusses, very well reflect the current state of affairs. One of the major viable responses to the twin issues of decalage and the identification of "component skills" is to attempt to find some way of reconciling the structural insights of Piagetian theory with the sort of empirical variation that tests of that theory have encountered.

One reasonable way to do this is to come up with a "structure" plus "activation" model that conserves notions of structure and accounts for their somewhat problematic empirical status by looking at the influence of local arrangements of task topic and task conditions as factors that influence the activation of those structures in the task at hand. This author has tried several variations of that approach (Cole, 1981; Glick, Gay, Glick, & Sharp, 1971). Fischer (1980) too has tried this as well, coupling structures with skills in a mixed model.

This approach has its problems as well. The fundamental problem is to make sure that the notion of activation is not used simply as a bail-out to account, in a nonprincipled way, for encountered variations. What the approach needs, if it is to be at all convincing and successful, is a *theory of occasions* so that one could predict precisely which arrangements, and so forth, could serve as "activators" for which structures.

One major candidate for this sort of theory development is to take cultural description as a way of helping to detail the sorts of mappings between occasion and structure that exist within cultural practice. It could be that cultural analysis could be precisely the sort of "theory of occasions" that is needed.

Goodnow's chapter (as well as a closely associated paper by Goodnow, 1983) represents some first steps toward building such a theory. She takes the unusual step of assuming that culture is not something that is known in an automatic and self-evident fashion by either analyst or culture member. Her focus is rather on the transmission process by means of which cultural "messages" are given and on the degree of understanding of these messages by children. Rather than starting with cognition and taking culture as background she takes culture as foreground.

Whatever the advantages of this approach, there are difficulties with it. First, it is by no means clear what level of cultural description is relevant to culture-cognition issues. As I see it, the level of description that Goodnow is striving for is at the level of cultural "ideology." In this approach, what is taken as important is the announced values and expectations of adult culture members about issues of thinking. There are culture theorists, however, who see culture as being determined not so much by ideologies as by the material conditions that form the material basis of the culture, with ideology being seen as a superstructure on that base.

Although the sort of problem discussed above is characteristic of all cultural issues in the social sciences, there is a yet more fundamental problem to be dealt with as well.

Even if we could gain a truly elegant understanding of culture and an equally elegant understanding of cognition, we would still need to develop a range of theoretical constructs that would allow us to understand the manner in which culture and cognition interact. When we can achieve data statements of the form "the x believe y and therefore they perform in such and such a way on cognitive tasks," we are left with an essentially mysterious connection between cultural statement and cognitive outcome. How does belief translate into performance? It should be noted here that the somewhat expanded form of this statement, e.g., "the x believe y and therefore train their children in the skills demanded in tasks that fulfill y" is empty unless we can find a way of bridging the relationship between *belief* on the one hand and *training* on the other, and between belief-driven training and the details of cognitive performance.

The following sections of this chapter focus on the sorts of problems just described. The theoretical development is predicated on the conviction that "mixed metaphors" combining theoretical constructs of different types may not be the most promising way to make theoretical advances at this time, particularly for those who have been struck by the fundamental and basic insights of the Piagetian position.

The approach taken here might be best described as one that looks for the grounds by which culture and cognition interact by taking a stringent look at what Piagetian cognitive theory is all about and seeking cultural influences within the core phenomena posed by the Piagetian position. At the very least this approach can firmly identify what it is that Piagetian theory is a theory of and can "fix it up" in part by defining the proper boundaries of that theory.

BACK TO BASICS

BASIC 1: There is an essential feature of the Piagetian theory that has gotten lost in modern discussion of the theory, and is lost only at peril for theory builders, savers, and modifiers.

Piagetian theory has only a tangential relationship to Piagetian tasks. The theory has, as its conceptual center, the problem of accounting for the necessity of human cognitive (logical) judgments. This central problem did not derive as an empirical generalization from a number of task performances. Rather it derived from a *critique* where essential features of human cognition were identified by *hermeneutic means* (in the sense that Gadamer, 1982, uses the term). The issues within the critique did not arise with Piaget, nor will they go away with Piaget's passing. They may even survive the efforts of Piagetians and their opponents.

The terms of the Piagetian critique are quite similar to those developed by Plato and Kant. There are undeniably features of human cognition wherein the perceptual structure of appearances is penetrated by a higher order knowledge system. Systems of knowing are developed wherein unseen and unseeable things are found to exist, discovered by systems of inference that lead inevitably and inescapably to conclusions that have a necessity. These systems can be characterized structurally and do not appear to derive from any direct training.

BASIC 2: Although all of the above may be true, the degree to which critique-identified systems of knowing actually characterize the thinking processes of ordinary people is a matter of conjecture.

A critique serves the necessary function of identifying the essential characteristics of an identified system of thought. In doing so it severely constrains the type of developmental theory that would be adequate to account for the occurrence of such a system. In Piaget's theory the topic, or conceptual object, of the theory is the description of and coming to grips with the development of abstract necessary judgments.

What the theory does not, cannot, nor even attempt to do is to tell us the degree to which the "critique-defined" topic is typical of the thinking of any given human being, or group of human beings. The question of typicality is an essentially normative question, one that bears little relationship to the precise identification of a cognitive area of functioning.

Much of the empirical confusion surrounding Piaget's theory stems directly from treating the theory as if it were a normative theory and not a theory that has a precisely defined topic. Inevitably, when normative questions are raised psychologists become obsessed with details and conditions of measurement and quickly lose sight of the basic non-normative aspects of the problem that the theory initially set out to deal with.

It seems that what is needed at this juncture is an "expanded" critique that sets the forms of knowledge that Piaget was interested in within the context of other forms of knowledge that his theory may not have addressed. In this manner, we might more clearly understand the Piagetian contribution (once it is freed of its normative interpretation) and at the same time make some progress in understanding the relationships that may exist between culture and cognition.

To shift focus to an expanded critique it is useful to start initially with the limits that may be properly drawn around the ground covered by Piagetian theory in its classic form. In order to do so, the next section delves into the acquisition mechanism stressed by Piaget: the theory of reflective abstraction.

REFLECTIVE ABSTRACTION AND BEYOND

A fundamental tenet of the Piagetian position is that one cannot gain necessary knowledge from contingent (perceptual/empirical) experience. From this basic standpoint Piaget found it necessary to posit an acquisition mechanism that bridges the relationship between experience of things (contingent experience) and knowledge of logical form. In order to maintain a constructivist position and not to lapse into innatism, some role for experience must be found, but that role has to be compatible with a logical system that is governed by rule of necessity.

This conceptual demand is fulfilled by the notion of reflective abstraction. This basic notion asserts that logical forms can be built in experience by the mind operating on (reflecting on) actions done in the real world. The notion of reflective abstraction then fulfills a basic theoretical requirement by coupling action (which is connected to experiences in the "real world") with a reflection upon the forms of action (which could be of a different order of organization than actions themselves).

Actions are constrained by the nature of the empirical world (actions occur in actual settings, encountering actual results, and being constrained by actual empirical conditions) and by the nature of the nervous system (only some kinds of actions and their combinations are afforded by our nervous system). Yet, at the same time there is some degree of distance between the action system and the empirical conditions within which it operates.

Actions may engage the same empirical conditions in different ways. The choice of action is somewhat organism-determined, and a given empirical condition may afford any number of actions that are successful within it. Since this is the case, action is *constrained* by the empirical world but is not fully *determined* by it. Hence, reflection on such actions, and their systematic interrelationships, may yield knowledge that is "experience-constrained" but not "experience-determined." The systematic patterning of actions is determined as much by the organismic factors (choice of action, neural programming limitations on what actions and action combinations are possible) as by the empirical conditions within which actions occur.

The reflective abstraction model, although stressing the interaction between the organism and the world, is most firmly fixed on the organism side of the equation. The environment is treated as a somewhat neutral ground upon which the organism can act, and within which the organism can discover the underlying principles of the system of its own actions. As long as this focus is maintained within the context of the environment considered as a physical environment only, there are no serious problems raised by the model. The laws of physics operate everywhere.

But the situation presupposed by the reflective abstraction model is a fundamentally acultural one. Cultural constraints do not operate in the same way that physical constraints do. Cultural constraints, being social-historical *creations,* are more arbitrary than physical constraints. Moreover, they are not "universal" and vary from cultural group to cultural group, and apply differentially to different status of membership within cultural groups. Because cultural constraints are socio-historically created, they may also be incoherent in important ways. Cultures are never created at once, as a whole fabric. Rather, they are constructed over time, by different agents, with different conditions applying at the time of creation.

In coming to grips with the differences between cultural constraint and physical constraint we can see sharply the limitations of the reflective abstraction model. Although the model might serve quite well for some aspects of the cognitive system, it cannot serve for all of the cognitive system. Some portion, probably huge, of our cognitive system is "cultural" in a non-trivial way. The possibilities for knowledge gained by reflective abstraction within a physical system are quite different from the possibilities within a cultural system.

This point may be developed by working through a metaphor contrasting physical and cultural constraints. Imagine a pendulum and a child. The pendulum, as a physical object, acts in way that is isomorphic to the actions performed upon it. By swiping at the pendulum, the child might learn that the direction of action determines the direction of pendulum motion. Similarly, the child might discover that the force of action is directly related to the extent that the pendulum swings. By opposing directions of action, the child might "reflectively abstract" primitive notions of negation, and by ordering degrees of force, the child might similarly abstract ideas of ordering, and so forth. The key to all of these discoveries is that the pendulum reacts isomorphically to actions upon it; and that therefore the systematism of action and its implications for cognitive organization might thereby be discovered.

However, not all pendulums are simply physical objects. We can construct in imagination some pendulums-with-a-difference. Let us imagine that the pendulum is one that exists within a culture. The pendulum may not simply be there for the using, it may be owned. At the very least, in this cultural situation, there exists the possibility that freely chosen action may be constrained by the cultural situation. The owner may want to be paid for the use of the pendulum. Hence, we can project the need for actions that obey cultural constraint, but have little to do with physical constraint. The child, in order to discover negation, ordering, and the like, may first have to discover how to pay for the use of the pendulum. Whether it be by begging, smiling in a winning way, or finding an odd job, some action *non*intrinsic to action on the pendulum will have to be performed. It is conceivable that this action, which is not intrinsic to discovery but nonetheless necessary to its occurrence, will come to be integrated into knowledge of the pendulum and actions upon it. The consequence of this integration is some degree of confusion between the necessary and culturally arbitrary aspects of experience.

This confusion can be engendered in a number of ways. Most reflectively abstracting, freely acting children have mothers. Mothers have ideas of their own about what children can and cannot do, and have ideas of their own about how children should go about doing what they are allowed to do.

Thus, the intervention of another person may channel the activities that the child may be allowed to perform on the pendulum. Some actions will take priority, whereas others may be the kind of things that you have to do when someone is not looking. At the least we can see some confusion creeping in about what is properly discoverable through the pendulum and the cultural and social constraints that surround that discovery.

Finally, as long as we have infused our discussion of pendulums and children with "culture" in a number of forms, we can take the next logical step and ask how representative of the world are objects like pendulums (when they are not owned or mother directed). The free and easy swinging pendulum is, it might be argued, a rarity. The cultural world is populated with artifacts that have been constructed with some degree of complexity. As a metaphor for that sort of object, let us consider that the pendulum has gears. A pendulum with gears is considerably different from a pendulum without gears. A gear is a hidden part of the pendulum apparatus. Though hidden, it will, in a major way, influence the sort of mappings that can exist between action and physical reaction. If the gear is sometimes in forward and sometimes in reverse, an action in the same direction will negate itself for *completely hidden* reasons. If the pendulum is sometimes in first gear and sometimes in overdrive, the ordering relationship is similarly confused. The only corrective available in such a situation is one that is, in principle, not available to the reflective abstraction model. The actor would need an "informant" to explain the notion of gears. Such cultural transmission of knowledge would have to be integrated into the self-discovered knowledge system.

From the development of the pendulum examples above, it seems clear that, at the least, there is a diversity of conditions under which knowledge is acquired. If this diversity is accepted, then some guidance to an expanded critique of knowledge has been gained. It is likely that the human knowledge system is *diverse,* composed of mixed kinds with different sorts of acquisition conditions and constraints underlying it.

Although it is possible that Piaget has provided an elegant, and perhaps the only possible solution to the acquisition of the formal logic system, it is now feasible that the solution to that problem will not apply mutatis mutandis to other sorts of knowledge. Formal knowledge is one sort of knowledge among many that the child or adult who lives within a culture will have. We do not have any a priori or even clear way of knowing "how much" of knowledge is of the formal sort, nor is it by any means clear how and when any knowledge-eliciting occasion (like an experiment) taps formal knowledge to the exclusion of other sorts of knowledge. Again, it must be reiterated that Piagetian theory is *not* a normative theory. It is not a theory about knowledge on occasions. It *is* a theory about the origins of a sort of knowledge whenever that knowledge happens to be displayed. This should not be regarded as an attempt to minimize the importance of Piagetian theory. Formal knowledge does, most certainly, exist and because it does, no theory of knowledge can be complete without dealing with it. Just as certainly as reflective abstraction will not solve the problem of cultural knowledge, so too will cultural transmission theories not solve the problem of necessary knowledge.

This way of putting the issues argues for the possibility of **multiple theories of the growth of mind.** Cultural research that deals with socially organized action may be a necessary supplement to the acultural transcendental approach of Piaget. In the remainder of this chapter we develop the outlines of such an approach. However, at the outset it should be clear that the attempt is not so much to account for the *influence* of culture on cognition as it is to develop a theory of "cultural cognition."

CULTURAL COGNITION

In a cultural world action is meaningful. Actions are not simply selected and performed under the dictates of the individual's need to discover, or need to act. There is another level of selectivity operating. Actions have significance for others and are "tokens" in a social discourse. Individuals can be held accountable for their actions. Thus, actions have meanings in the social world.

Similarly, the conditions within which actions, whether they be socially meaningful or not, occur are complexly organized. The principles of operation of the cultural environment for action are not fully accessible to the actor. Some knowledge is simply passed on from generation to generation (from cultural actor to cultural actor) because it is not accessible to individual discovery. This chapter, for example, did not wait for the reader to discover or construct it. Rather, it was written so as to take the reader into a framework of ideas generated from outside of the reader's discoveries, to provide a socially organized framework within which the reader can make further discoveries, now constrained in some way by the massive building of a framework for discourse that the chapter has tried to achieve.

The objects in a social and technological world are not directly accessible to discovery. Their understanding requires embedding of individual knowledge in cultural frameworks, and knowledge about states of affairs communicated by others. Although the causal linkages between a lightbulb lighting up and an electrical switch being thrown are physically exact, they are undiscoverable without some imported knowledge about electricity and electrical connections.

From these observations it seems that we require a special sort of theory in order to deal with the phenomena of cultural cognition. The class of problems described above requires some theory that will take account of the facts of "cultural mediation." At the same time we need a theory that can articulate the relationships that exist between culturally mediated knowing and the "transcendental" features of knowing, which is the proper topic of Piagetian research.

Perhaps the greatest pathway toward progress is the relatively conservative path of attempting to develop theoretical constructs to deal with cultural matters in a way that is closely linked to those constructs already developed to deal other aspects of cognition. As a matter of intellectual strategy, it is worth at least an initial attempt to treat cultural and transcendental theories in close relationship to one another.

Transcendental and Mediated Knowledge Systems.   One of the hallmarks of transcendental knowledge systems is their ability to deal with form in a manner that is differentiated from the contents that "fill" the forms. One of the hallmarks of mediated systems of knowing is that they rest upon organized (formed) contents.

All cultural communication occurs in some embodied form. We communicate by words, pictures, diagrams, and so on. At the same time, individually constructed knowledge (à la Piaget) may be represented in a manner that is fundamentally different from the manner in which cultural communications are organized.

As an example, we may take some recent work by Beilin (1982) and his students. These studies have investigated the relationship between operational thinking and culturally mediated thinking about the "same" topic. In one of these studies children are presented with a conservation of continuous quantity task, each stage documented by a polaroid photograph. When children in the appropriate age range are left to their own devices, they conserve. However, when these same children are shown the photo-documentation of the task, with a false picture (implying non-conservation) inserted, they show a strong tendency to give up their individually constructed answers and to believe that they must have been wrong because photographs don't lie.

It seems as if a powerful system of reasoning (the logical system) can be confuted by a powerful system of cultural representation. The thing that gives photographs their power is the cultural knowledge that photographs render reality by means of a mechanical process, and that, accordingly, they are more accurate than perceptions. It seems here as if the photograph has power over the presumably nonperceptual logical system as well.

The issue behind these studies is not, as some might think, whether conservation can be extinguished. Rather, what is called into question is the relationship between knowledge as it is "constructed" and knowledge as it is culturally mediated. The studies point out that we are quite sensitive to the power of cultural mediators to define our view of the way that things are, and have to be.

Findings similar to those presented above have been obtained in other areas as well. A recent dissertation (Fulani, 1984) investigated the relationship between children's operational knowledge of numbers and the sign systems by which numbers are usually displayed in culture.

The study did an inventory of the manner in which numbers are encountered in everyday life. As one might, with a bit of reflection, expect, numbers encountered in life are different from numbers encountered in school number-learning situations. The numbers met with in everyday experience are quite diverse, ranging from the names for buses, trains, and TV channels, to telephone numbers, to street addresses, to numbers fulfilling school criteria for operations (interval scale numbers). From the outside, on the surface, all of these numbers look alike. Yet, from the point of view of mathematical operations, it makes quite a difference if the number in question is merely the coded "name" for something (nominal scale) or actually represents a quantity. The study showed that some of the difficulties that children encounter surround a confusion between the cultural use of numbers and their operational use.

Children were sometimes confused by the varying messages of the number orthography system. In some cases children would assert that if you were to add a #1 bus and a #2 bus you would have three buses or you would have only two buses (but they would be faster than other buses); and sometimes children would deal with the issue in expected ways by asserting that you would have only two buses since the number on the bus was only a name for it.

There is some suggestion in this data that younger children encounter difficulties in arithmetic operations by importing everyday knowledge into the school sphere. Older children are not exempt from these problems. However, they import school knowledge into the everyday sphere (e.g., they are more likely to add buses and the like).

Adults experience difficulties in the same domain, but in more sophisticated ways. Reber and his associates (see Reber & Glick, 1979, for a review of some of these studies) have studied college students' abilities to "extract" information about structures (rules) underlying complexly organized displays of nonsense strings. Subjects were exposed to long sequences of letters (e.g., *XXYZZUM*), which were generated by an abstract, complex, underlying grammar. In a number of those studies, it has been shown that when subjects were instructed to simply let the information "sink in," they showed great ability to know the system and were able to make highly accurate judgments of the grammaticality of new strings. This knowledge, however, was implicit in that subjects were unable to give the reasons or rules that lay behind their "rule-governed" judgments. In contrasting conditions where subjects were instructed to "find out the rules" of the system, there was much less evidence of structure extraction. Judgments of grammaticality were explicitly defended, but were most often wrong. It seemed as if the attempt to generate explicit hypotheses interfered with subjects' ability to grasp the underlying structure. The rule-finding instruction directed subjects to deal with the surface structure of the information, when the rules were to be found in deep structure relationships.

In follow-up studies using strings of numbers instead of strings of nonsense letters, performance across the board was quite poor, with subjects in the "sink in" (implicit learning) conditions doing as poorly as those in the explicit learning condition. In this case, the probable reason for this finding is that the orthography (mediational form) of the experiment demanded explicit processing in both conditions. Although it is possible to think of strings of letters as being "just there" to be passively apprehended, it is virtually impossible for a college student to think of numbers in that way. Numbers are things to be operated upon, to form hypotheses about, and to be explicit about.

These examples demonstrate some of the complexities of cognition when mediated systems intervene in cognitive processing. The relationship between these systems is one of the major misunderstood topics in cognitive enquiry, and one that may lie at the heart of the empirical uncertainties surrounding Piaget's theory (see Donaldson, 1978, for even more examples).

Transcendental and Mediated Systems: The Sign.   The close connections and possible direct competitions between operational and culturally mediated knowledge presented in the examples above suggest that a theory that can encompass both, and give them a proper place in the cognitive economy, is much to be desired.

There are significant leads to such a theory embodied in the work of two theorists who are not usually referenced in contemporary discussions of cognitive theory: Claude Levi-Strauss and Heinz Werner.

In his seminal work, *The Savage Mind,* 1966, Levi-Strauss developed his views on the nature of cognition and the manner in which cognition interfaces with culture. In keeping with his structural orientation, Levi-Strauss stressed that human mentality, wherever expressed, will obey the same underlying structural rules (a logic of binary oppositions). To quote a characteristic formulation (Levi-Strauss, 1963):

> Prevalent attempts to explain the alleged differences between the so-called primitive mind and scientific thought have resorted to qualitative differences between the working processes of the mind in both cases, while assuming that the entities which they were studying remained very much the same....our view...(is), that the kind of logic in mythical thought is as rigorous as that of modern science, and that the difference lies, not in the quality of the intellectual process but rather in the nature of the things to which it is applied....In the same way we may be able to show that the same logical processes operate in myth as in science, and that man has always been thinking equally well; the improvement lies, not in the alleged progress of man's mind, but in the discovery of new areas to which it may apply its unchanged and unchanging powers. (p. 230)

The posited manner in which the "things" to which cognition is applied produces the ostensive differences between scientific and "primitive" thinking is of immediate relevance to our concerns here. This difference is akin to the difference between transcendental and mediated systems of knowing that we have developed above. In the opening chapter of *The Savage Mind,* 1966, Levi-Strauss argues that the symbolic medium (sign system) is of decisive importance for determining how the same underlying logical rules can have markedly different surface appearances.

The surface difference between scientific and "concrete" thinking is seen to reside in the changing relationships that exist between three entities: the percept, the sign, and the concept. Thinking uses either signs or concepts to transcend the perceptual given. A concept, characteristic of the scientific tradition, stands in somewhat "distant" relationship to the object or idea that it refers to; it is capable, therefore, of being dealt with abstractly, hypothetically, and arbitrarily. Since there is no substantial tie between the concrete form of the concept and its referent, these tactics of intellectual flexibility are not impeded. The sign, on the other hand, bears a substantial relationship to its referent. It perceptually resembles the referent and as such, is limited in its flexibility. It cannot do arbitrary things so long as it is somewhat bound to actual states of affairs. The differences between scientific and mythic thinking are seen to reside in the dependence of the former on the concept, and of the latter on the sign.

This view of the matter is not unlike some developmental formulations (e.g., Bruner, 1966), which see the course of ontogenetic development being determined, in part, by shifts in the representational processes that children function with at different ages. Indeed it is tempting, as Bruner has done, to try to account for children's progress through Piagetian stage development as being a direct function of differences in mediational systems. This task would be worked out in two related ways. Changes in mediation could be seen as being determined by level of development, on the one hand, and by cultural programming on the other. The developmental aspect would chart the child's propensity for functioning with mediators of a given sort (for reasons yet to be determined), and the cultural aspect would chart the means by which such mediators are provided by cultural agents (technologies, curricula, interactional strategies derived from child-lore, and the like).

However, this view of the matter is, perhaps, too deterministic. It does not clearly provide for the sorts of variations that both developmental and cultural phenomena display (see for example, Cole et al., 1971). More dynamic and dialectical views of mediated functioning have been developed by Vygotsky (1962), Werner (1948), and Werner and Kaplan (1963).

Werner's theory (1948, Werner & Kaplan, 1963) shared the stress on mediation that we have developed in the preceding sections of this chapter. Psychological organization is seen as being composed of overlapping systems that mutually influence one another. The overlapping systems would represent co-existing developmentally different levels of functioning. Psychological functioning on any given task or occasion is seen from this view as a microgenetic process wherein systems representing different developmental levels are applied successively to the task at hand. The finally achieved level of development will depend on such things as time constraints (how many levels does the time allow) and the kinds of mediational systems that are available in the task surround, as well as the levels of structural development that the child has achieved.

Werner's intention was to look at development from a dynamic, process viewpoint. The inputs of developmental level, concurrent determiners like time and mediation, are seen as inputs to a fluid system that assembles itself to solve a task at hand. The resultant behavioral manifestation (task solution or failure, etc.) is seen to depend upon the ways that these forces work themselves out. In this way, a determiner, such as mediation, could have a variable role depending upon the degree it has been acted upon by other components of the system. A given mediator could be treated as a "sign" (in Levi-Strauss' sense) or a concept depending upon the extent of the microgenetic processes operating. This point of view sees the relationship of mediator to psychological process as one of "dual schematization" (Werner & Kaplan, 1963) wherein the medium both structures and is structured by the psychological system. Influences flow in two directions: from the mind to the medium, and the medium to the mind. Thus, the relationships between culture and cognition would be seen as a dynamic interplay of influences. It is the analysts' task to sort this complexity out. The sorting out would, of necessity, operate upon concrete moments of functioning, and would not talk only of disembodied structures.

The child in our culture is embedded in a world where objects, symbolic media, and actions have both an epistemological and a cultural meaning. The systems of cultural significance may serve both to enhance and to delimit the possibilities of thought. This demands that developmental psychologists, and even genetic epistemologists, shift attention to precisely detailing the ways in which emerging structures play into actual situations, laden with cultural meaning.

REFERENCES

Beilin, H. (1978). Inducing conservation through training. In G. Steiner (Ed.), *Psychology of the 20th century: Vol. 7. Piaget and beyond.* Zurich: Kindler. (in German)

Beilin, H. (1982, March). *Toward a developmental theory of pictorial comprehension.* Paper presented at AERA meeting. New York.

Bruner, J. (1966). *Toward a theory of instruction.* New York: Norton.

Cole, M. (1981). *Society, mind and development*. Center for human information processing. University of California, San Diego, CHIP report 106.

Cole, M., Gay, J., Glick, J., & Sharp, D. (1971). *The cultural context of learning and thinking*. New York: Basic Books.

Dasen, P. (1972). Cross-cultural Piagetian research: a summary. *J. Cross-Cultural Psychology, 3*(1), 23-29.

Dasen, P. (Ed.) (1977). *Piagetian psychology: Cross-cultural contributions*. New York: Basic Books.

De Lemos, M. M. (1969). The development of conservation in aboriginal children. *International Journal of Psychology, 7*, 255-269.

Doise, W., Mugny, G., & Perret-Clermont, A. (1975). Social interaction and the development of cognitive operations. *European Journal of Social Psychology, 5*, 367-383.

Donaldson, M. (1978). *Children's minds*. New York: Norton.

Fischer, K. W. (1980). A theory of cognitive development: The control and construction of heirarchies of skills. *Psychological Review, 87*(6), 477-531.

Fulani, L. (1984). *Everyday and school number*. Doctoral dissertation, CUNY Graduate School.

Gadamer, H. G. (1982). *Truth and method* (2nd ed.). New York: Crossroad.

Gelman, R. (1969). Conservation acquisition: A problem of learning to attend to relevant attributes. *Journal of Experimental Child Psychology, 7*, 167-187.

Glick, J. (1981). Functional and structural aspects of rationality. In I. Sigel, D. Brodzinsky, & R. Golinkoff (Eds.), *New directions in Piagetian theory and practice*. Hillsdale, NJ: Lawrence Erlbaum Associates.

Glick, J., Piaget, J., Vygotsky, L. S., Werner, H. (1983). In S. Wapner & B. Kaplan (Eds.), *Toward an holistic developmental psychology*. Hillsdale, NJ: Lawrence Erlbaum Associates.

Jensen, A. R. (1969). How much can we boost IQ and scholastic achievement? *Harvard Educational Review, 39*(Winter), 1-123.

Klahr, D., & Wallace, J. G. (1972). Class inclusion processes. In S. Farnham-Diggory (Ed.), *Information processing in children*. New York: Academic Press.

Levi-Strauss, C. (1963). *Structural anthropology*. New York: Basic Books.

Levi-Strauss, C. (1966). *The savage mind*. Chicago: University of Chicago Press.

Newman, D., Riel, M., & Martin, L. (in press). Cultural practices and Piaget's theory: The impact of a cross-cultural research program. In D. Kuhn & J. Meacham (Eds.), *On the development of developmental psychology*. Basel: Karger.

Piaget, J. (1974). *Biology and knowledge*. Chicago: University of Chicago Press.

Reber, A., & Glick, J. (1979, June). *Implicit learning and stage theory*. Paper read at the ISSBD conference, Lund, Sweden.

Siegler, R. S. (1981). Developmental sequences within and between concepts. *Monographs of the Society for Research in Child Development,* (Serial No. *189*).

Vygotsky, L. S. (1962). *Thought and language*. Cambridge, MA: MIT Press.

Vygotsky, L. S. (1978). *Mind in society*. Edited by M. Cole, V. John-Steiner, S. Scribner, & E. Souberman. Cambridge, MA: Harvard University Press.

Werner, H. (1948). *The comparative psychology of mental development*. Chicago: Follett.

Werner, H., & Kaplan, B. (1963). *Symbol formation*. New York: Wiley.

6 Extreme Décalage: The Task by Intelligence Interaction

Herman H. Spitz
Edward R. Johnstone Training and Research Center,
Bordentown, NJ

> *There is no such thing as a brain (natural or artificial) that is*
> *good in any absolute sense — it all depends on the circumstances*
> *and on what is wanted. Every faculty that a brain can show is*
> *"good" only conditionally, for there exists at least one environ-*
> *ment against which the brain is handicapped by the possession*
> *of this faculty* *(Ashby, 1962, p. 264).*

For Piaget, intelligence is what matures. Consequently, and logically, he could title a book on development *The Psychology of Intelligence.* This is quite the opposite of the conceptions of intelligence produced by the psychometric tradition, which conceives of intelligence as a relatively stable capacity, expressed differently at different ages, but measurable by the individual's position on the Gaussian curve; that is, by the performance of an individual compared with other individuals of the same chronological age. Imagine for a moment identical normal curves for each year from ages 7 to 15, so that they produce a superstructure of normal curves, one above the other, with an individual's position on each curve relatively unchanged. In this image, Piagetian tasks that reflect changes with age produce the rising, *vertical* dimension (across curves), and individual differences on these (or other) tasks produce the spreading *horizontal* dimension (within curves).

A number of attempts to bridge this difference in approach have been made (see, for example, Elkind, 1969, 1981), but the difference is so profound that it is not easy for psychologists schooled in one tradition to enter the world of the other. To complicate matters, there is a third conception of intelligence, represented by information processing theory, which although it

117

draws from both these traditions is more interested in thoroughly describing the processes involved in intelligent behavior, even if the behavior is emitted by robots.

Piaget developed the stage approach partly because he was dissatisfied with the psychometric approach. He and Inhelder pointed out that the IQ test was "an excellent and quick way of observing mental level" (p. 401), but it was too limited (Piaget & Inhelder, 1947). Consequently, the concept of mental age (MA) was also insufficient. Based on a heterogeneous collection of subtests that changed from year to year, the MA concept could not describe the process of mental development as did, for example, their conservation tests, in which the advance to higher levels is dependent upon the integration of lower level concepts. To describe the intellectual level of a child they preferred the stage concept, in which the attainment of a particular stage guaranteed the attainment of earlier stages, and where the sequence of stages was universal.

There is however one place where the two conceptions meet, and that is in the area of extreme differences, as reflected in the performances of mentally retarded individuals or intellectually gifted children. Although to my knowledge Piaget did not perform studies directed toward the understanding of individual differences (there is just so much that one person can do in a single lifetime), his colleagues certainly did, and it is difficult to distinguish between their solution and Binet's, for they arrived at the familiar idea that individual differences are reflected in the rate at which individuals advance through the stages. For example, mentally retarded children advance through the stages at a slower rate, severely retarded children do not advance beyond the early stages, and mildly retarded individuals can reach the stage of concrete operations but never formal operations, as Inhelder demonstrated in her doctoral dissertation, later published in book form (Inhelder, 1943/1968).

The same principle was applied to the upper end of the intellectual spectrum. In a paper that to my knowledge has not been published in English, Piaget (1931) recognized that bright children can perform beyond the level of their chronological age (CA). He was responding to a book written by S. Isaacs in which she chronicled the performances of exceptionally bright young children who attended her school. According to her, their accelerated performance illustrated the inaccuracy of Piaget's stages. In his paper, Piaget emphasized that children are in part influenced by their physical and social environment. Furthermore, he warned that there are no general stages arrived at simultaneously in all domains, and noted that it becomes very difficult to agree, without precise terminology, upon a mean age at which a notion, operation, or any other intellectual event is most likely to occur (pp. 153–157).

Nevertheless, in his reply Piaget (1931) made it quite clear that the attainment of stages is based on MA, not CA, for despite his dissatisfaction with the psychometrically determined MA he respected it as a measure of mental level.[1]

> Dan at 5 years 9 months can correctly explain the mechanism of a bicycle, a feat which Mrs. Isaacs judges to be in contradiction to the age we assigned for comprehension of mechanical causality. . . . But since she tells us . . . that Dan . . . had an I.Q. of 142, he would have a mental age of 8 years. Now, its exactly at age 8, based on statistics formed on a large sample of children, that a correct explanation of the bicycle is expected. (p. 144)

There have been innumerable Piagetian-oriented studies with the retarded and gifted, and many studies specifically designed to measure the effects of MA and CA on performance. Yet, coming as I do from another tradition, I am surprised by the number of studies that studiously avoid giving the IQs and MAs of their subjects when such information would appear to be vital. I realize that the intelligence tests are under attack and out of favor with many workers, but it is difficult to understand how any complete account of development can ignore the concept of mental age. Consider that the stage of intuitive thought is said to range from about 4 to 7 years of age. Of course there is no magic about specific ages, but to paraphrase Piaget, a 6.5-year-old girl with an IQ of 130 has an MA of 8.5; consequently her CA places her in the preoperative intuitive stage while her MA places her in the period of concrete operations.

This is not simply an arbitrary example; when subjects are from high socioeconomic areas or are children of university faculty and students, an average IQ of 120 or more would not be unusual. Based on Brown's (1973) results, the MA criterion for stage attainment of bright children would not be valid at 4 years CA, but data from DeVries' (1971) study indicate that when very bright children reach CA 5 or 6 years they perform reliably better than average or retarded equal-CA children on a variety of Piagetian tasks, including the conservation of number and continuous quantity. A study by Little (1972) also confirms that MA increases in importance as bright children mature to about 6 years of age. Rader (1975) reported that the conservation performance of 20 first graders, ranging in IQ from 102 to 160, on the Concept Assessment Kit (Goldschmid & Bentler, 1968) correlated reliably with IQ (.64) when CA was controlled, despite ceiling effects. In Jordan and Jordan's (1975) review of 36 studies that included 44 independent groups of normal children and adolescents ranging from 3 years to 18 years of age, MA yielded higher and more consistent correlations with Piagetian test performance than did CA, accounting for about twice as much of the variance in performance. Retarded groups usually perform at or below the level of their MA

---

[1]I am grateful to Nancy J. Turner of the Educational Testing Service for translating this and other sections of Piaget's paper.

on Piagetian tasks (Weisz & Yeates, 1981; Wilton & Boersma, 1974). In sum, except for very bright 4-year-olds, who apparently lack the neural structures and/or the experience required for certain conservation tests (cf. Halford, 1980), knowing both the IQ and the CA is *at least* twice as valuable for making predictions of performance on Piagetian tasks than is knowing only the CA, even with unexceptional children.

As for performance on Piagetian formal operations tasks, Webb (1974) reported that 6- to 11-year-old children with IQs over 160 performed better than average 12-year-olds, although only four attained a formal level of functioning. Keating (1975) reported a correlation of .65 between scores on the Standard Progressive Matrices test and the formal operations scores of average and bright fifth and seventh graders. With subjects ranging in age from 10 to 30 years, Kuhn, Langer, Kohlberg, and Haan (1977) found that on formal operations tasks the amount of variance accounted for by MA, or IQ, was more than six times the amount accounted for by CA alone.

With CA controlled, then, performance differences on Piagetian tasks reflect differences in general intelligence as measured by individually administered intelligence tests. Although some workers have reported that Piagetian and IQ tests largely measure different capacities (e.g., DeVries, 1974; Stephens, McLaughlin, Miller, & Glass, 1972), in many instances factor analytic methods were used that did not extract a general factor. In studies where the general factor was extracted it was substantial (Humphreys & Parsons, 1979; Vernon, 1965a, 1965b) or moderate (DeVries & Kohlberg, 1977), particularly when large numbers of subjects were drawn from unrestricted samples (cf. Elkind, 1981; Glass & Stephens, 1980; Humphreys, 1980; Kohlberg & DeVries, 1980).

There is also some question about the MAs of the children tested by Piaget and his colleagues, and consequently about the CAs at which various stages are reached by children of average intelligence. In 1931, Piaget stated that their subjects had a mean IQ of about 100 (Piaget, 1931, p. 144). Forty years later he wrote that their research on formal operations "was, perhaps, based on a somewhat privileged population" (Piaget, 1972, p. 6). Dulit (1972, p. 297) reports a personal communication from Inhelder explaining that because their purpose was to illustrate the characteristics of the formal operations stage they did not report the performance of adolescents who failed to function at that stage. Furthermore, Piaget specifically stated that formal operations as measured by their tasks might not be reached until 15 to 20 years of age, or is sometimes not reached at all, and he proposed that the most probable explanation was that all normal individuals eventually attain formal operations "in different areas according to their aptitudes and their professional specializations" (Piaget, 1972, p. 10). Carpenters, then, would exhibit formal operational thinking in carpentry but not necessarily on the

Inhelder tasks (cf. Neimark, 1981). But surely carpenters differ from each other intellectually, about which Piagetian theory is silent.

There have been studies that included "mentally retarded" subjects who had MAs of 13 or 14 years (Stephens, Mahaney, & McLaughlin, 1972), but based on presently accepted standards (Grossman, 1977), the highest MA a retarded person can have is about 12.5 years (IQ 69 × CA 18/100), when a lenient upper CA of 18 years is used. If one uses, as we do, an upper CA of 16 years (for anyone 16 and older), the highest MA in the mental retardation range is about 11.0 years. In general, on Piagetian tasks the performance of mildly retarded adolescents and young adults who have MAs of 9 or 10 years places them at the level of concrete operations. This is another way of saying that retarded groups will usually perform at the level of nonretarded groups who are of equal MA.

However, I would like to demonstrate that there are circumstances in which groups of retarded individuals with MAs of about 9 or 10 years will perform much worse than nonretarded children with approximately equal MAs, as well as circumstances in which they will perform much better than college students. Essential to this proposal is the corollary that no accurate prediction about performance can be made without taking into account at least three variables: CA, IQ, and the requirements of the task. The first two variables correspond to the competence component, and the third variable corresponds to the performance component. (Other variables, such as gender and cognitive style, may also contribute to the variance, but are outside the scope of this paper.) In order to predict performance accurately we must understand at least the kinds of heuristics (or schemes, in Piaget's terms) and the working memory capacity of persons described by the first two variables.

Our increasing knowledge of mental retardation permits us to make certain broad statements about this syndrome, and about the mental resources retarded persons will draw upon when faced with tasks requiring some degree of thoughtful response. The critical maneuver for us is to match the requirements of the tasks to the responses likely to be generated by subjects who have developed particular heuristics or rules, and to the subjects' working memory capacity. This approach is a variant of the rule-assessment approach advocated by a number of workers (see especially Siegler, 1981), and the M-space concept of Pascual-Leone (1970). If the heuristics possessed by most members of a target population generate responses that are appropriate for the particular task, and if they have the necessary working memory capacity, then most of them will solve the problem. If the heuristics generate a response that does not match the solution, and/or if the solution requires a working memory that is beyond their capacity, they will fail, at least on initial trials. Nor does it matter whether an individual is very bright or very dull; the important thing is to match the task solution with the responses likely to be generated by a person of a given age and intelligence. If these conditions are filled, tasks can be given that produce outcomes that, to the naive observer, are totally unexpected, such as instances in which young children outperform older children or adults (e.g., Odom, Cunningham, & Astor, 1975; Siegler, 1981).

In terms of the competence/performance dichotomy, this chapter illustrates why account must be taken of the performer's CA and IQ, as well as the requirements of the task, if inferences about competence are to be drawn on the basis of performance. Once these variables are taken into account, inversions as well as exaggerations of customary results when comparing groups from the extremes of the intellectual continuum can reveal a great deal about underlying competence.

RETARDED ADOLESCENTS AND YOUNG ADULTS PERFORM BELOW THE LEVEL OF EQUAL-MA CHILDREN

Of the two proposals—(a) that there are particular tasks on which retarded groups perform less successfully than nonretarded groups of equal MA, and (b) that there are other tasks on which retarded groups perform more successfully than college groups—the first is far easier to demonstrate. Originally, we had not chosen these tasks to demonstrate an MA lag in retarded performance; they were chosen, rather, for an entirely different reason. Evidence from numerous studies in learning and memory indicated that retarded groups learned poorly largely because they failed to organize the to-be-learned material efficiently; they did not spontaneously use mnemonics or other aids, and they made less efficient use of redundancies and other information-reducing aspects of the material than did nonretarded groups of equivalent MA (Brown, 1974; Spitz, 1966, 1973). This reduced the amount of material that reached short-term memory. However, for the material that did enter short-term memory (as measured, for example, after zero delay) the slope of forgetting was no different than that of nonretarded comparison groups (Belmont & Butterfield, 1969; Ellis, 1978). In other words, differences in intelligence produced an intercept but not a slope difference.

As we now know, a substantial amount of thinking and reasoning, not simply rote memory, is responsible for efficiently memorizing even simple material, and apparently it is this thinking component that is largely (though not entirely) responsible for the poor performance of retarded groups in laboratory learning experiments. When supplied with strategies, the performance of the retarded improves rather dramatically (for reviews of these issues, see the contributions in Ellis, 1979). In general, then, retarded persons have the competence to memorize material, but lack the competence to spontaneously use strategies to organize the material for the most efficient input. In view of this we decided to study directly the strategic thinking of retarded groups. The Piagetian tasks did not seem particularly suitable for this purpose, to some extent because at the level we were interested in they seem so dependent on the kind of verbal and semantic facility that many retarded persons are not comfortable with. Consequently, we adapted a number of games, puzzles, and other problem-solving tasks that required a nonverbal response and that measured what we thought of as prototypical strategic and logical thinking. We gave these problems to mildly and moderately retarded adolescents and young adults and to comparison groups of nonretarded children.

The Logic Problem

On the logic task that we had adapted from Neimark's logic test (Neimark & Lewis, 1967), we prepared very basic practice items in order to familiarize the subjects with the procedure so that they would perform optimally on the somewhat more difficult test items. What we found was that many of our retarded subjects were having great difficulty with the practice problems (Nadler, 1980; Spitz & Borys, 1977; Spitz & Nadler, 1974), an example of which is shown in the unstriped right-hand section of Fig. 6.1 (ignore for the

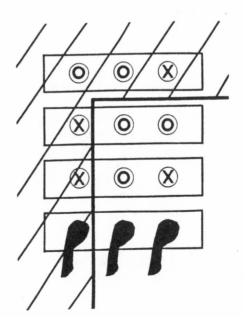

FIG. 6.1   Schematic of the Logic Task. Slanted lines denote opaque board which can be removed to turn two-pattern problems into three-pattern problems. From Spitz and Borys (1977), used with permission of the *Journal of Experimental Child Psychology*.

moment the striped area). The subject's task is to discover, by opening only one lever, which pattern (*O-O* or *O-X* in this example) is hidden beneath the levers. Either an *X* or an *O* is beneath each lever and by moving the lever the symbol is exposed. In this example, the right-hand lever is the correct one to open, because if an *X* is revealed, the *O-X* pattern must be hidden, and if an *O* is revealed, the *O-O* pattern must be hidden. Opening the left-hand lever provides no useful information.

Pretesting criteria were (a) a matching-to-sample test in which both levers were always open, different patterns were displayed over a number of trials, and subjects simply had to point to the pattern (e.g., either the *O-O* or the *O-X* pattern in the example given in Fig. 6.1) that matched the pattern revealed by the open levers; and (b) a test in which a number of trials were presented with the levers closed, but the experimenter opened the correct lever (e.g., the right-hand lever in the example given in Fig. 6.1), and, on the basis of the figure revealed by the open lever, the subject had to determine which of the upper two patterns matched the pattern under the levers. Only subjects who passed both pretests advanced to the main experiment, in which both levers were closed. Eighteen sets of patterns were presented, on each of which the subject was required to open only one lever to discover which pattern was hidden.

For subjects who passed the two-pattern task, the board (indicated by the striped lines in Fig. 6.1) was taken off the apparatus so that the three-pattern task could be presented. Following similar pretest criteria, subjects were required to open *two* of the three levers in order to discover which one of the three patterns was hidden beneath the levers. Eighteen sets of three-pattern configurations were presented.

Results of these experiments were consistent: mildly retarded individuals with MAs of about 10 years performed at the level of nonretarded, unexceptional 6- and 7-year-olds, even on the two-pattern "practice" task. On the three-pattern problem they performed at a chance level, and individuals with borderline intelligence and MAs of about 12 years performed only at the level of 6- and 7-year-olds. Figure 6.2 shows these results (Spitz & Borys, 1977).

Why is this problem such a dilemma for the retarded? What heuristic, if any, do most of them use? Even when they opened the lever that provided no information they insisted that they could tell which pattern was hidden, and they proceeded to point to one of the two patterns. Based on this fact, and on their reaction (e.g., "There, I knew it would be that one," when they were right, and surprise and disappointment when they were wrong), they, and kindergarten children, frequently regarded the task as a guessing game, despite the extensive pretesting. By guessing, of course, they were correct on about half the two-pattern problems, for when by chance they did open the correct lever they invariably pointed to the correct pattern, indicating that they could use the information that was provided but could not lawfully gen-

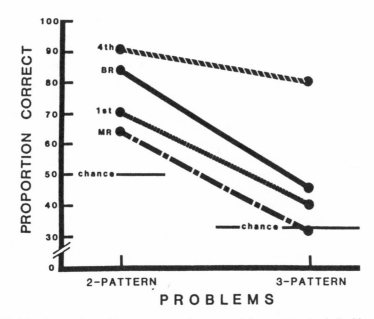

FIG. 6.2   Comparison of four groups on the two- and three-pattern Logic Problem. 4th = fourth graders, $\overline{CA}$ of 8.37; 1st = first graders, $\overline{CA}$ of 6.81, BR = borderline retarded, $\overline{CA}$ of 18.97, $\overline{MA}$ of 12.03; MR = mildly retarded, $\overline{CA}$ = 18.55, $\overline{MA}$ of 10.24. Data from Spitz & Borys (1977).

erate it. In subsequent exploratory studies we gave tokens for correct responses and took away tokens for incorrect responses, without improving performance. The use of peer interaction was also unhelpful (Borys & Spitz, 1979). When poorly performing individuals worked with a peer who had succeeded on the task, paired performance was extremely good, but when they were again left to solve the problems alone, performance plummeted to pre-pair levels. Using pictures of real objects rather than symbols or letters did not improve performance (Nadler, 1980).

For many of our retarded, then, there was no problem to be solved. In information-processing terms they never developed a problem space,[2] and the heuristic they used was the simplest heuristic of all: "guess." For the borderline retarded and first-grade nonretarded groups who could solve the two-

---

[2]A problem space is defined by Newell and Simon (1972) as the subject's internal representation of the task environment (p. 56), and they give a lengthy description of its properties (pp. 808–814). Of course these retarded subjects developed some sort of internal representation, but because they did not understand that the task was a problem that could be solved by deducing some rational means of moving from the present to the desired state, then by definition they could not develop a *problem* space. We might simply refer to their internal representations as a response space that includes guessing as one of the possible responses.

but not the three-pattern problems, determining the underlying sources of failure is more difficult. Many apparently solved the simple task without developing a general rule or principle (e.g., never open the lever under a column of symbols that are all the same, since this provides no information); or if they did develop such a rule they were apparently unable to generalize it to the three-pattern problem. Furthermore, we must recognize that making a *vertical* assessment of a series of *horizontal* patterns is, for the maturationally young, a more difficult requirement than we imagine.

The failure of our retarded subjects on this problem may also result in part from inadequate working memory, although the small amount required appears to be well within their capacity. However, limited working memory is surely implicated in their failure on many logical and strategic problems. Working memory should be distinguished from the less demanding *rote memory,* defined here as the memory skill tapped when no decisions or complex mental manipulations are required, as in repeating exactly a series of items. *Working memory,* on the other hand, is defined here as a more active process that is used, for example, in problem-solving situations to store and consider alternative paths of search (e.g., Baddeley & Hitch, 1974). Chess requires searching through a branching decision tree, keeping in mind the imagined moves and the placements of all the pieces and the possible replies of one's opponent, while at the same time deciding on the best strategy.

This type of thought process, although at a reduced level of complexity, is required by a number of problems we have presented to retarded groups. Rather than give brief descriptions of each of these problems (see Spitz & Borys, 1984), an example is drawn from our studies with the Tower of Hanoi (TOH) problem, the one problem we have examined most intensively.

The Tower of Hanoi Problem

The TOH performance of young children and retarded young adults has been subjected to a good deal of scrutiny lately (e.g., Borys, Spitz, & Dorans, 1982; Byrnes & Spitz, 1977, 1979; Klahr, 1978; Klahr & Robinson, 1981; Piaget 1974/1976; Spitz, Webster, & Borys, 1982). The TOH material consists of three pegs and any number of graduated disks (see Fig. 6.3). The player is required to transfer the disks from a start state (the configuration of the disks as presented to the subject) to a goal state (usually illustrated by the disk configuration on a second board) by moving the disks one at a time to any other peg but never placing a larger disk on a smaller one. Any number of disks can be used and start and goal state configurations can be varied, providing a large number of possible problems that vary in difficulty. In our studies subjects were not given three-disk problems unless they first passed a simple two-disk problem. As in the logic problem, many of our retarded subjects fail the basic two-disk problem (as many as 40% in our most recent

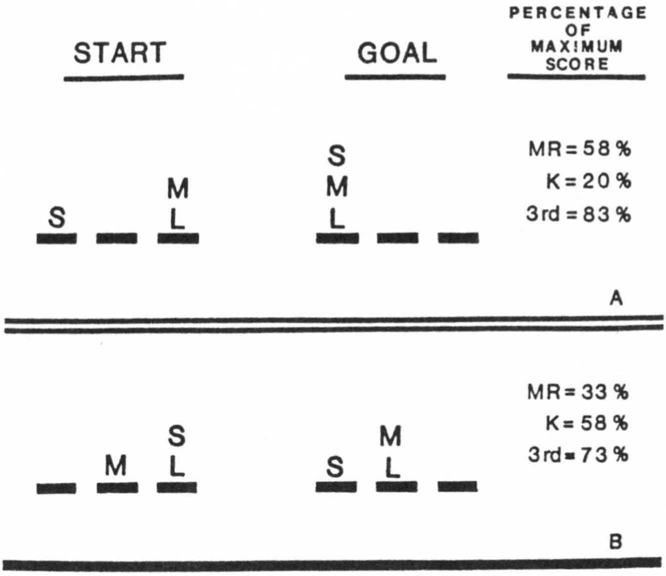

FIG. 6.3   Examples of two 6-step Tower of Hanoi problems requiring two-move depths of search to reach the first subgoals. S = small disk, M = medium disk, L = large disk. Performances of mildly retarded (MR), kindergarten (K), and third grade (3rd) groups are given at the right. Adapted from Spitz, Webster, & Borys, 1982.

study), and this again suggests that many do not develop a problem space. However, we now have a good sampling of the performance of retarded groups on three-disk problems, and it is apparent that these problems also produce an appreciable MA lag.

After much analysis we are convinced that the primary source of the retarded deficiency is a search capacity that is strained when required to search only two steps, and severely overtaxed when required to search three. Performances of all our groups, both retarded and nonretarded, correlated significantly with number of steps required to solve the problem. However, it is much more meaningful to analyze the depth of search required to accomplish the subgoal of transferring the first disk to its goal peg. In our definition, *depth of search* is always one move less than the number of actual steps, because once the goal peg is open (holds no disk) and the target disk is free to move, the transfer of the disk is automatic. In the example given at the top of Fig. 6.3 (problem A) a two-move depth of search is required to move the large disk to its goal peg (peg 1): move M to peg 2, then S to peg 2, leaving L free to move to its open goal peg. In the example given at the bottom of Fig. 6.3 (problem B) no search is required to move S to its goal peg, but this move is incorrect, as it blocks further progress. To move L to its goal peg requires a two-move depth of search: move M to peg 1, then S to peg 1. Depth of search to the first subgoal accounts for almost 70% of the variance in the performance of a retarded group on 16 different TOH problems, so we are quite certain it is a crucial variable (Spitz, Webster, & Borys, 1982).

Figure 6.4 describes performance on a number of problems requiring increasing depths of search to the first subgoal. When the first subgoal requires a one-move search, the mean percentage of maximum scores for retarded and kindergarten groups is 68%. However, when the first subgoal requires a two-move search their performance drops to 40%. Performances of these two groups are comparable despite the fact that the retarded have a mean MA of 10.23, which is more than 4 years above the mean CA of the kindergarten group. In general, the third graders search about one move farther than the other two groups.

Equality of performance between groups occasionally hides some interesting differences. For example, although both problems shown in Fig. 6.3 require two-move searches for the initial subgoal, results suggest that the strat-

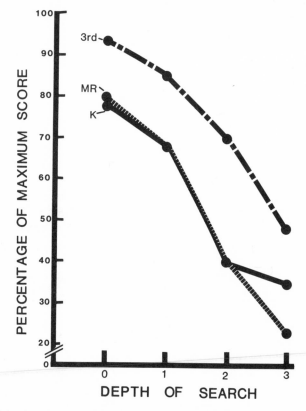

FIG. 6.4   Comparison of three groups on 16 different Tower of Hanoi problems requiring increasing depths of search to the initial correct subgoal. 3rd = third graders (and two fourth graders), $\overline{CA}$ of 9.40; K = kindergartners, $\overline{CA}$ of 5.99; MR = mildly retarded, $\overline{CA}$ of 20.19, $\overline{MA}$ of 10.33. Data from Spitz, Webster, & Borys (1982).

egy used by most of the retarded group was to *free L,* whereas the kindergartners' strategy was to *clear L's goal peg.* In problem A, the *free L* rule will produce a correct first move (M to peg 2), and *clear L's goal peg* will produce an incorrect first move (S to peg 2), which were the moves that accounted for the relatively good scores of the retarded group and the poor performance of the kindergarten group (proportion correct shown on the right of Fig. 6.3).

On problem B, the *free L* response (S to peg 1) now produces poor performance by the retarded (although, of course, they may also be simply transferring S to its goal peg prematurely), whereas the *clear L's goal peg* strategy (M to peg 1) produces relatively good performance by the kindergarten group.

In either case an inappropriate strategy could be overruled by a search of just one more move. The third graders are capable of making that extra search, and they perform well on both problems.

There are other tasks that illuminate the kinds of heuristics retarded persons draw upon. For example, on a series completion test most members of the retarded group inadequately scanned the series of items, focusing primarily on the end items to cue their response (Spitz & Semchuk, 1979). Knowledge that retarded groups tend to resort to such a limited approach can be used as a basis for structuring tasks on which they will perform at an exceptionally high level.

RETARDED ADOLESCENTS AND YOUNG ADULTS OUTPERFORM COLLEGE STUDENTS AND POSTGRADUATES

Demonstrations that there are tasks on which retarded persons perform better than college students are important primarily because they prove how deeply we understand and how accurately we can predict their behavior. To produce such results we must know the demands of the task and the kinds of responses that it will generate in persons who are at opposite ends of the intellectual spectrum.

Discrimination Learning

When the solution to a discrimination learning problem is beyond them, mildly retarded adolescents and nonretarded kindergarten children tend to regress to response alternation (Gerjuoy & Winters, 1967; Rieber, 1969); that is, they will, in a stereotyped manner, alternate their responses from one side to the other at above chance levels. Individuals who are lower in the developmental scale tend to perseverate to one side.

Two theoretical positions (at the least) are relevant here. Levine's (1969,

1975) hypotheses theory states that at the outset of a problem, subjects select a hypothesis from a universe of hypotheses, test to see if their hypothesis is correct, then retain or replace it until the correct concept is learned. There are two general classes of hypotheses: (a) prediction hypotheses, which are based on some aspect of the stimulus and which are sensitive to disconfirmation, and (b) response-set hypotheses, which are based on stimulus preferences or position sequence preferences and are insensitive to disconfirmation. Response-set hypotheses are frequently exhibited by young children and retarded individuals, whereas prediction hypotheses predominate by the time nonretarded children reach about 8 years of age (Gholson, 1980). Although response-set hypotheses are very difficult to induce in college students (Ress & Levine, 1966) they are, to the contrary, very difficult to dislodge in 5-year-olds (Gholson, Levine, & Phillips, 1972).

According to attention theory, which provides an alternative theoretical framework, the probability that subjects of low developmental level will attend to a position dimension is very high, and subjects who are developmentally more advanced are more likely to attend to object characteristics such as size, shape, and color (Zeaman & House, 1967).

Both theoretical positions produce fundamentally similar proposals: that there is a hierarchy of biases (types and kinds of hypotheses, or probability of attending to particular dimensions) that differs — both in size and order — in groups of different ages and intelligence. Based on numerous studies, response alternation is high in the hypothesis and/or attentional hierarchy of mildly retarded individuals, but low in the hierarchy of mature nonretarded individuals. It follows, then, that matching the correct solution with a bias that is high in the hierarchy of a target group should result in rapid solution, but very delayed solution — or none at all — will result if the solution is very low in a target group's hierarchy (Milgram & Furth, 1964; Schusterman, 1964).

In our experiment (Spitz, Carroll, & Johnson, 1975) we used 40 different stylized Japanese characters, divided randomly into 20 pairs in the usual discrimination learning format. Our subjects were 20 college students and 20 retarded young adults of approximately the same CA but with an average IQ of 58. The correct response on each trial (after the first) was to select the side opposite to the previously chosen stimulus.

There were 19 opportunities to alternate. As can be seen in Fig. 6.5, the college group responded at a chance level, whereas the retarded group alternated reliably above chance and reliably above the college group. When the retarded subjects who were high alternaters were asked how they knew the right answer, they pointed alternately to the left and right, or said something to the effect that "first you go here, then you go there."

Only 2 of the 20 college subjects alternated on 11 or more trials. Only one college subject discovered the correct response, and he alternated invariantly

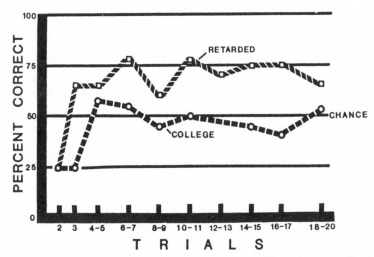

FIG. 6.5   Comparison of the performance of retarded and college subjects on a discrimination learning task in which the correct strategy was single alternation.

from the tenth trial on. Many appeared frustrated and could not understand why they were doing so poorly. Consequently, during posttest discussions we told each of them the correct response to allay their anxieties. We also asked them what strategies they had used. Some bases of choice were whether or not it was a real Japanese symbol, the number of angles, the patterns or subunits — such as two boxes or two lines, the repetition of symbols given earlier, the presence of t-shapes or two crossed lines on a t, the presence of boxes that enclosed something, the degree to which the symbol resembled an abstraction of a real life object, and whether or not a symbol had a sexual connotation.

The number of hypotheses were large and original, and no doubt college students could dredge up new ones during the course of a longer experiment. No one can doubt that college students have the competence to solve a simple position alternation problem once they attend to that dimension, but they are unlikely to try position solutions when the stimuli are rich in possibilities for inventive hypotheses. For many retarded subjects, on the other hand, single alternation is a preferred solution. Those who could not solve the problem by invariant or near-invariant alternation, nevertheless tended to alternate at above-chance rates.

Pseudoconservation of Area and Perimeter

A loop of string can be made into a square by holding it apart with the forefinger and thumb of each hand so that each finger forms one of the four corners. If the square is then transformed into a rectangle by bringing each forefinger closer to its opposing thumb while increasing the distance between the hands, most adults will insist that the area within the string remains the same. Only when the interior area almost disappears will they realize their misjudgment.

Lunzer (1968) reported that this type of misjudgment (pseudo-conservation)[3] starts to appear at about 9 years of age, and that 5-year-olds judge differences in area and perimeter in terms of the height of the figure. However, Russell (1976) reported that most of his 6-year-old subjects judged the transformed figure — the rectangle — as bigger "because you stretched it," and it made no difference whether the transformation was vertical or horizontal, so that attention to a single dimension of height or width could not alone have been responsible for the misjudgments (cf. Anderson & Cuneo, 1978).

When individuals develop to the point where transformations are routinely conserved, conservation becomes a powerful concept that can be divorced from an actual percept. In our example, mature observers know that the length of the string remains unchanged when it serves as the boundary of an area, and that no matter how drastically the area changes shape, the length of the perimeter of the transformed area must remain the same. Without really thinking about it, most observers will automatically assume that the amount of space within the string must also remain the same. Lunzer (1968) has pointed out that the reverse effect also occurs, in which it is usually assumed that when the size of an area is conserved, the length of its perimeter also must be conserved (as is demonstrated below). In sum, most mature individuals assume a principle of covariance that states, incorrectly, that if one aspect of two-dimensional figures — either the perimeter or the area — is conserved, then the other aspect must also be conserved.

We know that most retarded individuals do not readily conserve and that conservation of length — in this case the length of the string that serves as the perimeter of a shape — is a relatively difficult conservation (Goldschmid, 1967), so it is reasonable to assume that they will not conserve the perimeter of the transformed shape. The responses of individuals who do not conserve cannot be influenced by the area-perimeter covariance principle, and consequently this task becomes a good candidate for another demonstration of performance inversion. All the retarded need do is judge the differences in

---

[3]This operational pseudoconservation refers to the misapplication of conservation. Piaget and Inhelder (1966/1971) distinguish it from primary pseudoconservation (p. 262) which occurs in the preoperational stage, and which they apparently also refer to as figurative (imaginal) pseudoconservation. Examples of the latter occur when young children are so compelled to conserve a bounded figure that they find it difficult to imagine an overlapping figure intruding into its boundaries (pp. 60–63) or when they imagine that the level of a liquid will remain the same (be conserved) after transformation to a narrower jar, until they observe that it changes in height (p. 10).

size, and there is no reason to believe that mildly retarded young adults cannot make simple size discriminations.

Space Test — Nonconservation of Area.   The transformation of the loop of string, described above, was made objective with the use of a board and nails. (Full descriptions of the material, dimensions, and procedure are in Spitz, Borys, & Webster, 1982.) Four nails were placed to form a square on the top section of the board, and two separate loops of string, both of the same size, were just large enough to fit snugly around the nails. Below the square, four more nails formed a rectangle whose perimeter was the same as the square's perimeter but whose area was 1.64 times smaller than the area of the square. Below this, on the bottom section of the board, four nails formed a long, thin rectangle whose perimeter was also the same as the square's, but whose area was 4.27 times smaller than the area of the square.

With the subject observing, one of the two loops of string was taken off the square and placed around the center set of nails to form a horizontal rectangle, and subjects were asked if "the area or space inside this string (top square, experimenter points to area) and this string (middle rectangle) is the same, or does one have more area inside the string?" (the wording was counterbalanced over subjects). Subjects who replied that one had more area or space were asked which one, and all subjects were asked to justify their responses. The string was then transferred from the middle to the bottom rectangle and the questions repeated.

Area and Perimeter Tests — Conservation of Area and Nonconservation of Perimeter.   Whereas the Space Test is a measure of the effect of conserved perimeter on size judgments of the nonconserved enclosed space, the Area Test is a typical measure of the conservation of two-dimensional area. The Perimeter Test measures the effect of the conserved internal area on length judgments of the nonconserved perimeter.

A square of grey hardboard served as a standard, and a second square of the same size was cut into eight equal-sized rectangles. This dissected square was reassembled and in place on top of, and exactly covering, the standard square. With the subject observing, the eight pieces were lifted one at a time and — slightly below the square — were rearranged into a two-piece by four-piece horizontal rectangle. Subjects were asked whether the grey area or space inside "this figure" (the square) and "this figure" (the rectangle) was the same or if one figure had more grey area inside it (wording counterbalanced), and also to justify their responses. Following this, the pieces were rearranged end to end on the bottom section of the board, and the same questions were repeated. Although the areas of all figures were of course exactly the same, the perimeter of the middle rectangle was 1.25 times larger than the perimeter of the square, and of the bottom rectangle was 2.13 times larger than the perimeter of the square.

Following the Space and Area Tests, which were given in counterbalanced order across subjects, we gave the Perimeter Test. We used the same procedure and materials as in the Area Test except that when the pieces were transformed from the square to the rectangles, subjects were reminded of the responses they had given in the Area Test and were asked, "If a fly walked around the outside of this figure (square) and the outside of this one (rectangle, experimenter traces with finger around each figure), would it walk the same distance, or farther around one (wording counterbalanced)?"

The retarded subjects were students at the Johnstone Center (N = 16, mean CA = 19.57 years, mean IQ = 65). The college-educated group consisted primarily of staff members at Johnstone (N = 11, mean CA = 38.91). Two had B.A., six had M.A., and three had Ph.D. degrees.

Control for Response Bias — Retarded Group.   The 16 retarded subjects included in the experiment had passed a control test given, at the end of the experiment, only to retarded subjects. In this test, subjects observed the dissected square being taken off the standard square and reassembled into a square just below it. Only subjects who responded that the areas were the same have been included in the study.

Control for Discrimination — College Group.   A new group of college graduates (N = 12, mean CA = 33.96), drawn from the same source, were tested on the Space and Perimeter Tests, but they did not observe either the string or the cardboard pieces being taken from the square and transformed into the rectangles. Prior to testing, strings were placed around each of the three sets of nails in the Space Test, and for the Perimeter Test a solid (uncut) grey square and solid grey middle and lower rectangles were glued into place in the same locations of the figures in the previous conditions. In both tests, given in counterbalanced order across subjects, the lower rectangle was covered when the subject entered the room. As before, subjects were requested to make comparisons and provide reasons for their responses. After recording the square/middle rectangle comparison, the experimenter transferred the cover to the middle rectangle and requested square/lower rectangle comparisons. This condition served as a control for the ability to discriminate the figures when the transformation was not observed; that is, when the area-perimeter covariance principle would not be invoked because the observers had no way of knowing that the perimeters of all three string figures were the same length, or that the areas of all three cardboard figures were the same size.

Results on Simple Discrimination Task.   When the transformations were not observed, the discriminations by the college subjects of the square/lower rectangle comparisons were nearly perfect (100% correct discriminations of the areas within the strings, 92% correct discriminations of the lengths of the perimeters around the cardboard). However, discriminations of the square/middle rectangle figures were not as good (83% correct for the discrimination of areas within the strings, only 33% correct for the discrimination of the perimeters around the cardboard figures, which were in fact not greatly different from each other). Consequently, for the transformation tasks, only the results of the extreme comparisons (square/lower rectangle) are considered.

Results on the Nonconservation Tasks. The results are shown in Fig. 6.6. On both nonconservation tasks many more retarded subjects gave correct responses than did the college graduates (all the group differences shown in Fig. 6.6 are statistically reliable). On the Space (string) Test, 82% of the college students incorrectly judged that there was the same amount of space in the square as in the rectangle, whereas 75% of the retarded subjects correctly judged that there was more space in the square.

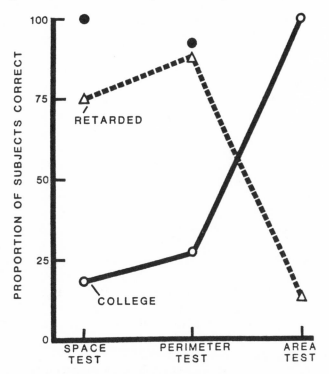

FIG. 6.6   Comparison of retarded and college graduate groups on two nonconservation tasks (Space and Perimeter Tests) and on one conservation task (Area Test). Isolated solid circles indicate performance levels of college graduates when they did not observe the transformations.

The college subjects who incorrectly conserved space justified their responses by noting that the string fitted around both figures, or that the lengths of the strings were the same. For example: "the string hasn't changed, it must outline the same area," "the string went around the top and bottom," "same string, stretched taut," "you just manipulated the length times the width, the area is the same," "the string fits the top area," "haven't changed the size of the string," "perimeter is still the same."

Most of the retarded found it difficult to verbalize reasons for their responses. Those who correctly judged that the space within the square was larger noted, for example, that "the top looks bigger and the bottom looks smaller," "the top has more, it's wider," "the bottom is skinnier," "(top) has a lot more room in there," "bottom is a rectangle, top is a square."

On the Perimeter Test, 73% of the college graduates incorrectly judged that the lengths of the perimeters around the square and lower rectangle were the same, whereas 88% of the retarded subjects correctly judged that the perimeter of the rectangle was longer. College subjects' justifications referred to the fact that the areas were the same and therefore the distances were also the same, or they noted that the same pieces that made up the square also formed the rectangle. For example: "same area, the perimeter's the same," "the squares are the same size and it still has to go around eight of them" (referring to the eight pieces), "'same area, perimeter changes shape but not total distance."

For their perimeter judgments, most of the retarded subjects simply noted that the rectangle was longer, e.g., "farther around the bottom, it's a lot bigger."

Results on the Conservation Task.   On the conservation task, the results were completely reversed. All the college subjects correctly conserved two-dimensional area, justifying their responses by noting that although shape was changed, area remained the same, or remarking that the same pieces that comprised the square also comprised the rectangle. Most of the retarded did not conserve, with 31% judging the area within the square as larger and 56% judging it as smaller than the rectangle. These results suggest that their correct nonconservation responses on the Space Test, where 75% had judged that the square was larger, were not due primarily to a bias to attend only to the height dimension. Justifications included: "the square is big, rectangle is small," "longer than the top one," "it's eight blocks" "it's straight and top is square," "bigger, by looking at it."

Discussion.   That almost all college subjects made accurate comparative judgments of the areas and perimeters in the control condition is solid evidence that the misjudgments in the primary experiment were caused by the dominating influence of the observed transformations. The misjudgments on the Space Test, where the ample square (10.16 × 10.16 cm) was judged the same size as the long, thin rectangle (1.27 × 19.05 cm), are particularly startling. During posttest discussions with each of the college students, when we pointed out the obvious discrepancy there was usually a short silence, an embarrassed laugh, and then — for most subjects — immediate recognition of what they had done. There were rationalizations as well as good-natured recriminations for our having "tricked" them, and many expressed interest in the purpose of the experiment.

Obviously, then, although the covariance principle is a powerful one in most mature individuals, it can readily be overcome. Furthermore, it is not universal; it did not affect the judgments of all our subjects, and we suspect that persons who frequently deal with the sizes of areas, or who are mathematically or scientifically inclined, will not usually demonstrate the effect. It has been reported that extreme transformations, and also training, affect the results (Lunzer, 1965; Shultz, Dover, & Amsel, 1979).

The retarded subjects based their judgments on the immediate percept. In the Space Test, for example, they apparently did not recognize that during shape transformation the length of the string was conserved. In order to verify this supposition, a new group of retarded subjects — drawn from the same source — was tested on the Space (string) Test, but this time we asked for comparison judgments of the perimeters of the square and rectangles. Also, we included a new control task, in which a second board contained the four nails of a square, plus just below it another four-nail square of exactly the same size. As in the Space Test, subjects observed one of the two loops of string taken from the top square and placed on the square just below it.

Subjects were given the Space Test (square and rectangles) followed by its control (two squares), in each of which they observed the transformations and were asked to compare the spaces inside the strings. This was followed by the Perimeter Test in which they were reminded of their responses in the Space Test and were asked to compare the distances a fly would walk around the strings, first for the Space Test, then for its control. Only subjects who responded "same" on both control tests were included in this study ($N = 14$, mean IQ = 59, mean CA = 18.64 years).

Results were clear. For the square/bottom rectangle comparison all 14 responded correctly that there was more space in the square than in the rectangle. On the Perimeter Test, only 1 of the 14 responded that the perimeters of the two figures were the same. Of the remaining subjects, 5 responded that the fly would walk farther around the square, and 8 responded that it would walk farther around the rectangle. The judgments of the retarded subjects were purely perceptual, with no recognition that the length of the string was conserved when its shape was transformed. Consequently, there was no chance that the covariance principle would influence their judgments. Even their errors were frequently unrelated; of the 14 subjects who judged the area of the square to be larger, 8 nonetheless judged that the fly would walk farther around the rectangle.

Parenthetically, it should be noted that Pinard and Chassé (1977) demonstrated pseudoconservation with three-dimensional objects, but I do not believe it has been demonstrated in classical liquid conservation tasks. Figure 6.7 illustrates the material for such an experiment. If observers were informed that the amount of paint required to paint the wide squat jar is exactly the same amount required to paint the tall narrow jar, it is likely that most of them would assume that both jars would hold exactly the same amount of water. But in fact if the water that filled the square jar were poured into the empty narrow jar there would be an embarrassing amount of spillage, perhaps giving college students some idea of what it feels like to behave at a preoperational level on the liquid transformation task. The isolated section floating above the narrow jar in Fig. 6.7 indicates how tall the narrow jar would have to be in order to contain all the water from the squat jar. Although the surface areas of both jars are exactly the same, surface area is not invariantly related to interior volume.

The existence of pseudoconservation in bright college graduates raises a number of interesting questions. Piaget and Inhelder (1966/1971, p. 333) believed that pseudoconservation at the level of concrete operations involves the "inheritance of a preoperational belief in a simple area-perimeter correspondence," and "generalization of emergent operational notions of conservation," but they gave no indication that they were aware that this phenomenon persists into the formal operations stage. In any event, what evidence is there that an area-perimeter correspondence exists preoperationally, and why should preoperational beliefs persist for this relationship and not for others? Why should these particular operational notions generalize?

The pseudoconservation demonstrated here cannot emerge until either area or perimeter is conserved, and fits therefore with Lunzer's (1968) report that it starts at about 9 years of age in nonretarded children. One can explain the results—or rather, describe them in a different way—by noting the type of stimulus that is salient at different maturational levels. This general approach stresses the influence of stimulus variables on the observer's responses (e.g., Gelman, 1969; Miller, 1978; Odom, 1978).

There is, however, a slightly different way of looking at it. The area-perimeter (as well as the volume-surface area) covariance principle is in the same family as the quantity-level covariance principle that causes young children to believe that the quantity of material is related to the level it reaches in a jar, and which consequently is responsible for their nonconservation responses (Piaget & Inhelder, 1966/1971, p. 262). In other words, for young children the nonconserved aspect dominates. If the child's assumed covariance of these two aspects is responsible for failure to conserve, then there is no reason why young children should not conserve when the level of

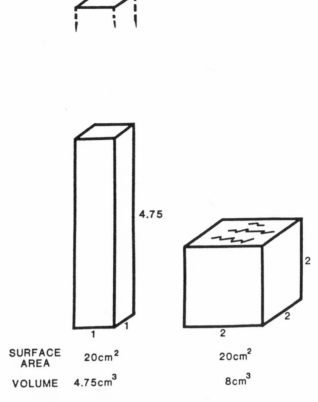

FIG. 6.7   Example of two open jars containing the same surface areas but very different interior volumes. Height required for the narrow jar to hold all the liquid from the squat jar is indicated by detached segment.

the liquid (the nonconserved aspect) is screened from view (Miller & Heldmeyer, 1975). Eventually, children who are not retarded develop to the point where the quantity-level covariance relationship shifts so that it is the conserved aspect that dominates, and shortly thereafter the domination of the area-perimeter covariance relationship also shifts from the nonconserved to the conserved aspect. Such a view gives a certain coherence and continuity to the changes that occur during development, and is consonant with Piaget's (1968) view that the natural tendency of children is to conserve unless they are confronted with a perceptually disparate display. With maturation, this natural tendency becomes so strong that it not only allows observers to ignore perceptual disparities, it also intrudes on their veridical perceptual judgments.

As noted, pseudoconservation is not always obtained and can be ephemeral, but it is competing with a very strong contrary percept. The point is that once conservation fully develops it is so powerful and pervasive that it is capable of overriding the accurate perceptual discriminations of very bright individuals.

Still, there is no obvious reason why in later development the conserved aspect should dominate the nonconserved aspect rather than the other way around, unless at a certain maturational level there is something innately compelling about it. The idea of an innately determined schedule should not be dismissed out of hand. It is not impossible that, all things being equal, certain concepts will be dominant at certain levels of development without there being any direct causal connection with previous development. This is a radical genetic viewpoint that compares the emergence of certain heuristics to the emergence of certain physical characteristics. For example, a beard will grow in all normally developing boys and searching for a cause in a boy's physical history will prove unrewarding.

Piaget (1947/1951) has pointed out that object constancy, as well as size and shape constancy, are early forms of conservation. He did not discuss their origins, but it seems to me the evidence is overwhelming that these constancies are innately given. Furthermore, the conservation concepts appear to be universal, although it has been reported that the rate and uniformity of the various conservations and other concrete operations differ in different cultures (Dasen, 1977) — findings that may be largely an artifact of methodological problems (e.g., Nyiti, 1982). The idea of innate necessity for specific types of conservation is more Chomskyian than Piagetian (see Piattelli-Palmarini, 1980). Piaget's view, as I understand it, is that although the roots of operations are derived from innate neurological functioning, the operations are finally constructed by the individual by means of a series of self-regulations, self-organizations, and equilibrations (Piaget, 1968), so long as the environment provides the minimum required material and stimulation, and so long as there is normal organic development. But whichever one's view, instances where children show delayed or no development of conservation and other operational concepts, such as occurs in mental retardation, illustrate the crucial role played by a normally developed central nervous system.

SUMMARY

Although Piaget's maturational approach to intelligence differs from the individual difference approach derived from the psychometric tradition, the two approaches meet in their descriptions of bright and dull children. Piagetians describe exceptional children by their rate of progress through the stages, which is essentially the basis (minus the discrete stages) of Binet's test of intelligence. The reality of mental age, although accepted by both traditions, is not always acknowledged by Piagetian researchers. Nevertheless, the competence of groups of individuals is related to their IQ and CA, and how this competence is expressed is determined by the requirements of the experimental task. Knowledge of the heuristics hierarchy and working memory capacity of groups with specified IQ and CA characteristics allows the experimenter to produce instances in which mildly retarded young adults perform, on the one hand, more poorly than nonretarded children of the same MA, or, on the other hand, much better than college-educated groups.

Examples of the MA lag of retarded groups were generated by the Logic Test and the Tower of Hanoi, where retarded groups were at a disadvantage because of their limited capacity for logical and strategic thinking, as well as by their limited foresight and working memory.

Superior performance by retarded than by college-educated groups was generated by discrimination learning and nonconservation tasks. In the discrimination learning experiment the competence of the intelligent adults was obscured, and the superior performance of the retarded group was obtained, by requiring a response that was at once low in the hypothesis hierarchy of the college group and high in the hypothesis hierarchy of the retarded group. In the nonconservation experiment the competence of most of the college subjects led them astray when a high level (but incorrect) conservation concept predominated over a more primitive (but correct) nonconservation percept. Most of the retarded subjects, unencumbered by the seductive conservation concept and its accompanying area-perimeter covariance principle, made a simple, correct perceptual discrimination. It is suggested that conservation and nonconservation successes and failures are related to the observed dominance of certain aspects of presented materials, the expression of which follows a very general developmental timetable so long as organic structures and environmental stimulation are intact and unimpeded.

A theoretical hierarchy of problem-solving approaches can be generated, anchored at one end by a very basic perceptual approach—favored by persons of limited intelligence—and at the other end by a less stimulus-bound conceptual approach—favored by persons of high intelligence. Within this framework the manner in which competence is expressed in performance is largely dependent on the requirements of the task. Successful performance is usually, but not always, an adequate measure of competence. Any formula that attempts to infer competence on the basis of performance must take into account the manner in which response propensities of persons at various intellectual levels will interact with the requirements of the task.

REFERENCES

Anderson, N. H., & Cuneo, D. O. (1978). The height + width rule seems solid: Reply to Bogartz. *Journal of Experimental Psychology: General, 107,* 388–392.

Ashby, W. R. (1962). Principles of the self-organizing system. In H. Von Foerster, & G. W. Zopf, Jr. (Eds.), *Principles of self-organization.* New York: Pergamon Press.

Baddeley, A. D., & Hitch, G. (1974). Working memory. In G. H. Bower (Ed.), *The psychology of learning and motivation* (Vol. 8). New York: Academic Press.

Belmont, J. M., & Butterfield, E. C. (1969). The relations of short-term memory to development and intelligence. In L. P. Lipsitt & H. W. Reese (Eds.), *Advances in child development and behavior* (Vol. 4). New York: Academic Press.

Borys, S. V., & Spitz, H. H. (1979). Effect of peer interaction on the problem solving behavior of mentally retarded youths. *American Journal of Mental Deficiency, 84*, 273–279.

Borys, S. V., Spitz, H. H., & Dorans, B. A. (1982). Tower of Hanoi performance of retarded young adults and nonretarded children as a function of solution length and goal state. *Journal of Experimental Child Psychology, 33*, 87–110.

Brown, A. L. (1973). Conservation of number and continuous quantity in normal, bright, and retarded children. *Child Development, 44*, 376–379.

Brown, A. L. (1974). The role of strategic behavior in retardate memory. In N. R. Ellis (Ed.), *International review of research in mental retardation* (Vol. 7). New York: Academic Press.

Byrnes, M. M., & Spitz, H. H. (1977). Performance of retarded adolescents and nonretarded children on the Tower of Hanoi problem. *American Journal of Mental Deficiency, 81*, 561–569.

Byrnes, M. M., & Spitz, H. H. (1979). Developmental progression of performance on the Tower of Hanoi problem. *Bulletin of the Psychonomic Society, 14*, 379–381.

Dasen, P. R. (Ed.). (1977). *Piagetian psychology: Cross-cultural contributions.* New York: Gardner Press.

DeVries, R. (1971). *Evaluation of cognitive development with Piaget-type tests: Study of young bright, average, and retarded children.* Urbana, IL: University of Illinois. (ERIC Document Reproduction Service No. ED 075 065)

DeVries, R. (1974). Relationships among Piagetian, IQ, and achievement assessments. *Child Development, 45*, 746–756.

DeVries, R., & Kohlberg, L. (1977). Relations between Piagetian and psychometric assessments of intelligence. In L. Katz (Ed.), *Current topics in early childhood education* (Vol. 1). Norwood, NJ: Ablex.

Dulit, E. (1972). Adolescent thinking à la Piaget: The formal stage. *Journal of Youth and Adolescence, 1*, 281–301.

Elkind, D. (1969). Piagetian and psychometric conceptions of intelligence. *Harvard Educational Review, 39*, 319–337.

Elkind, D. (1981). Forms and traits in the conception and measurement of general intelligence. *Intelligence, 5*, 101–120.

Ellis, N. R. (1978). Do the mentally retarded have poor memory? *Intelligence, 2*, 41–54.

Ellis, N. R. (Ed.). (1979). *Handbook of mental deficiency, psychological theory and research* (2nd ed.). Hillsdale, NJ: Lawrence Erlbaum Associates.

Gelman, R. (1969). Conservation acquisition: A problem of learning to attend to relevant attributes. *Journal of Experimental Child Psychology, 7*, 167–187.

Gerjuoy, I. R., & Winters, J. J., Jr. (1967). Response preference and choice-sequence preferences: I. Regression to alternation. *Psychonomic Science, 7*, 413–414.

Gholson, B. (1980). *The cognitive-developmental basis of human learning: Studies in hypothesis testing.* New York: Academic Press.

Gholson, B., Levine, M., & Phillips, S. (1972). Hypotheses, strategies, and stereotypes in discrimination learning. *Journal of Experimental Child Psychology, 13*, 423–446.

Glass, G. V., & Stephens, B. (1980). Reply to Humphreys' and Parsons' "Piagetian tasks measure intelligence and intelligence tests assess cognitive development." *Intelligence, 4*, 171–174.

Goldschmid, M. L. (1967). Different types of conservation and nonconservation and their relation to age, sex, IQ, MA, and vocabulary. *Child Development, 38*, 1229–1246.

Goldschmid, M. L., & Bentler, P. M. (1968). *Concept assessment kit—conservation.* San Diego: Educational and Industrial Testing Service.

Grossman, H. J. (1977). *Manual on terminology and classification in mental retardation* (rev. ed.). Washington, DC: American Association on Mental Deficiency.

Halford, G. S. (1980). A learning set approach to multiple classification: Evidence for a theory of cognitive levels. *International Journal of Behavioral Development, 3,* 409–422.

Humphreys, L. G. (1980). Methinks they do protest too much. *Intelligence, 4,* 179–183.

Humphreys, L. G., & Parsons, C. K. (1979). Piagetian tasks measure intelligence and intelligence tests assess cognitive development: A reanalysis. *Intelligence, 3,* 369–382.

Inhelder, B. (1968). *The diagnosis of reasoning in the mentally retarded* (2nd ed.) (W. B. Stephens, Trans.). New York: John Day. (Originally published, 1943)

Jordan, V. B., & Jordan, L. A. (1975, April). *Relative strengths of IQ, mental age and chronological age for predicting performance on Piagetian tests.* Paper presented at the meeting of the Society for Research in Child Development, Denver. (ERIC Document Reproduction Service No. ED 111 510)

Keating, D. P. (1975). Precocious cognitive development at the level of formal operations. *Child Development, 46,* 276–280.

Klahr, D. (1978). Goal formation, planning, and learning in pre-school problem solvers. In R. S. Siegler (Ed.), *Children's thinking: What develops?* Hillsdale, NJ: Lawrence Erlbaum Associates.

Klahr, D., & Robinson, M. (1981). Formal assessment of problem-solving and planning processes in preschool children. *Cognitive Psychology, 13,* 113–148.

Kohlberg, L., & DeVries, R. (1980). Don't throw out the Piagetian baby with the psychometric bath: Reply to Humphreys and Parsons. *Intelligence, 4,* 175–177.

Kuhn, D., Langer, J., Kohlberg, L., & Haan, N. S. (1977). The development of formal operations in logical and moral judgment. *Genetic Psychology Monographs, 95,* 97–188.

Levine, M. (1969). Neo-noncontinuity theory. In G. Bower & J. T. Spence (Eds.), *The psychology of learning and motivation* (Vol. 3). New York: Academic Press.

Levine, M. (1975). *A cognitive theory of learning: Research on hypothesis testing.* Hillsdale, NJ: Lawrence Erlbaum Associates.

Little, A. (1972). A longitudinal study of cognitive development in young children. *Child Development, 43,* 1024–1034.

Lunzer, E. (1965). Les Co-ordinations et less conservations dans le domaine de la géométrie. In V. Bang & E. Lunzer (Eds.), *Etudes d'épisstémologie génétique: Vol. 19. Conservations spatiales.* Paris: Presses Universitaires de France.

Lunzer, E. A. (1968). Formal reasoning. In E. A. Lunzer & J. F. Morris (Eds.), *Development in learning: II. Development in human learning.* New York: American Elsevier.

Milgram, N. A., & Furth, H. G. (1964). Position reversal vs. dimension reversal in normal and retarded children. *Child Development, 35,* 701–708.

Miller, P. H. (1978). Stimulus variables in conservation: An alternative approach to assessment. *Merrill-Palmer Quarterly, 24,* 141–160.

Miller, P. H., & Heldmeyer, K. H. (1975). Perceptual information in conservation: Effects of screening. *Child Development, 46,* 588–592.

Nadler, B. (1980). Effects of stimulus characteristics on the logical problem solving behavior of retarded adolescents and nonretarded children. *Child Study Journal, 10,* 27–40.

Neimark, E. D. (1981). Explanation for the apparent nonuniversal incidence of formal operations. In I. E. Siegel, D. M. Brodzinsky, & R. M. Golinkoff (Eds.), *New directions in Piagetian theory and practice.* Hillsdale, NJ: Lawrence Erlbaum Associates.

Neimark, E. D., & Lewis, N. (1967). The development of logical problem-solving strategies. *Child Development, 38,* 107–117.

Newell, A., & Simon, H. A. (1972). *Human problem solving.* Englewood Cliffs, NJ: Prentice-Hall.

Nyiti, R. M. (1982). The validity of "cultural differences explanations" for cross-cultural variation in the rate of Piagetian cognitive development. In D. A. Wagner & H. W. Stevenson

(Eds.), *Cultural perspectives on child development.* San Francisco: W. H. Freeman.

Odom, R. D. (1978). A perceptual-salience account of décalage relations and developmental change. In L. S. Siegal & C. J. Brainerd (Eds.), *Alternatives to Piaget: Critical essays on the theory.* New York: Academic Press.

Odom, R. D., Cunningham, J. G., & Astor, E. C. (1975). Adults think the way we think children think, but children don't always think that way: A study of perceptual salience and problem solving. *Bulletin of the Psychonomic Society, 6,* 545–548.

Pascual-Leone, J. (1970). A mathematical model for the transition rule in Piaget's developmental stages. *Acta Psychologica, 32,* 301–345.

Piaget, J. (1931). I.-Le développement intellectuel chez les jeunes enfants. *Mind, 40,* 137–160.

Piaget, J. (1951). *The psychology of intelligence* (M. Piercy & D. Berlyne, Trans.). London: Routledge & Kegan Paul. (Originally published, 1947)

Piaget, J. (1968). Quantification, conservation, and nativism. *Science, 162,* 976–979.

Piaget, J. (1972). Intellectual evolution from adolescence to adulthood. *Human Development, 15,* 1–12.

Piaget, J. (1976). *The grasp of consciousness: Action and concept in the young child.* (S. Wedgwood, Trans.). Cambridge, MA: Harvard University Press. (Originally published, 1974)

Piaget, J., & Inhelder, B. (1947). Diagnosis of mental operations and theory of intelligence. *American Journal of Mental Deficiency, 51,* 401–406.

Piaget, J., & Inhelder, B. (1971). *Mental imagery in the child.* (P. A. Chilton, Trans.). New York: Basic Books. (Originally published, 1966)

Piattelli-Palmarini, M. (Ed.) (1980). *Language and learning: The debate between Jean Piaget and Noam Chomsky.* Cambridge, MA: Harvard University Press.

Pinard, A., & Chassé, G. (1977). Pseudoconservation of the volume and area of a solid object. *Child Development, 48,* 1559–1566.

Rader, J. R. (1975). Piagetian assessment of the conservation skills in the gifted first grader. *Gifted Child Quarterly, 19,* 226–229.

Ress, F. C., & Levine, M. (1966). Einstellung during simple discrimination learning. *Psychonomic Science, 3,* 77–78.

Rieber, M. (1969). Hypothesis testing in children as a function of age. *Developmental Psychology, 1,* 389–395.

Russell, J. (1976). Nonconservation of area: Do children succeed where adults fail? *Developmental Psychology, 12,* 367–368.

Schusterman, R. J. (1964). Strategies of normal and mentally retarded children under conditions of uncertain outcome. *American Journal of Mental Deficiency, 69,* 66–75.

Shultz, T. R., Dover, A., & Amsel, E. (1979). The logical and empirical basis of conservation judgments. *Cognition, 7,* 99–123.

Siegler, R. S. (1981). Developmental sequences within and between concepts. *Monographs of the Society for Research in Child Development, 46* (2, Serial No. 189).

Spitz, H. H. (1966). The role of input organization in the learning and memory of mental retardates. In N. R. Ellis (Ed.), *International review of research in mental retardation* (Vol. 12). New York: Academic Press.

Spitz, H. H. (1973). Consolidating facts into the schematized learning and memory system of educable retardates. In N. R. Ellis (Ed.), *International review of research in mental retardation* (Vol. 6). New York: Academic Press.

Spitz, H. H., & Borys, S. V. (1977). Performance of retarded adolescents and nonretarded children on one- and two-bit logical problems. *Journal of Experimental Child Psychology, 23,* 415–429.

Spitz, H. H., & Borys, S. V. (1984). Depth of search: How far can the retarded search through an internally represented problem space? In P. H. Brooks, R. Sperber, & C. McCauley (Eds.), *Learning and cognition in the mentally retarded.* Hillsdale, NJ: Lawrence Erlbaum Associates.

Spitz, H. H., Borys, S. V., & Webster, N. A. (1982). Mentally retarded individuals outperform college graduates in judging the nonconservation of space and perimeter. *Intelligence, 6,* 435–444.

Spitz, H. H., Carroll, J. G., & Johnson, S. J. (1975). Hypothesis testing from a limited set: An example of mentally retarded subjects outperforming college subjects. *American Journal of Mental Deficiency, 79,* 736–741.

Spitz, H. H., & Nadler, B. T. (1974). Logical problem solving by educable retarded adolescents and normal children. *Developmental Psychology, 10,* 404–412.

Spitz, H. H., & Semchuk, M. T. (1979). Measuring the use of a principle by retarded adolescents and nonretarded children on a redundancy series test. *American Journal of Mental Deficiency, 83,* 556–560.

Spitz, H. H., Webster, N. A., & Borys, S. V. (1982). Further studies of the Tower of Hanoi problem solving performance of retarded young adults and nonretarded children. *Developmental Psychology, 18,* 922–930.

Stephens, W. B., Mahaney, E. J., & McLaughlin, J. A. (1972). Mental ages for achievement of Piagetian reasoning assessments. *Education and Training of the Mentally Retarded, 7,* 124–128.

Stephens, W. B., McLaughlin, J. A., Miller, C. K., & Glass, G. V. (1972). Factorial structure of selected psycho-educational measures and Piagetian reasoning assessments. *Developmental Psychology, 6,* 343–348.

Vernon, P. E. (1965a). Environmental handicaps and intellectual development: Part I. *British Journal of Educational Psychology, 35,* 9–20.

Vernon, P. E. (1965b). Environmental handicaps and intellectual development: Part II. *British Journal of Educational Psychology, 35,* 117–126.

Webb, R. A. (1974). Concrete and formal operations in very bright 6- to 11-year-olds. *Human Development, 17,* 292–300.

Weisz, J. R., & Yeates, K. O. (1981). Cognitive development in retarded and nonretarded persons: Piagetian tests of the similar structure hypothesis. *Psychological Bulletin, 90,* 153–178.

Wilton, K. M., & Boersma, F. J. (1974). Conservation research with the mentally retarded. In N. R. Ellis (Ed.), *International review of research in mental retardation* (Vol. 7). New York: Academic Press.

Zeaman, D., & House, B. J. (1967). The relation of IQ and learning. In R. M. Gagné (Ed.), *Learning and individual differences. Columbus, OH: Charles E. Merrill.*

7 On the Relationship Between Cognitive Styles and Cognitive Structures

David M. Brodzinsky
Rutgers University

For nearly six decades Jean Piaget and his co-workers have investigated the general patterns of structural development underlying children's thought and behavior (Piaget, 1970). Toward this end Piaget has focused on the constancy or universality of behavior found across individuals and situations. Moreover, he has attempted to explain this constancy in terms of a formal logico-mathematical model representing the development of intellectual competence.

Although Piaget's contributions to our understanding of the developmental process have been widely acknowledged, his theory nevertheless has been criticized for a number of reasons, not the least of which is that as a theory of competence, it has not proven to be very useful for explaining the behavioral variability that is so evident among individuals of the same age level (Case, 1974; Flavell, 1982; Overton & Newman, 1982). Indeed, within the Piagetian perspective individual differences have received little attention, except as a means of "explaining away" differences in rate and terminal level of development (Piaget, 1971a, 1972).

The lack of interest shown by Piaget for individual difference factors is now seen as a serious limitation of the theory even by sympathetic supporters of this perspective (Flavell, 1977, 1982; Flavell & Wohlwill, 1969; Neimark, 1981; Overton & Newman, 1982). Although the structures described by Piaget may be necessary for explaining thought and behavior — and some believe this too is a debatable point (Brainerd, 1978) — it is now clear that they are not sufficient for fulfilling this goal. In particular, a focus on structure, per se, does not offer an adequate explanation for the differences in rate and terminal level of development that are commonly observed; nor does it explain the differential accessibility to, and utilization of, competence across individuals and situations.

In the past 10-15 years an increasing number of researchers has begun to focus on the array of organismic and situational factors that moderate the development and expression of children's cognitive competence. Some of the more important of these factors are represented in this volume: intelligence, education, and culture. What I focus on in the present chapter is an individual difference factor that has received somewhat less systematic attention, at least within the context of Piagetian theory — namely, children's cognitive style.

I begin with a discussion of the nature and definition of cognitive style, followed by a brief description of previous theoretical and empirical attempts to link styles and operative structures. Finally, I present a new model for understanding the interrelationship between these two constructs. I caution the reader ahead of time that this model is speculative and offered for heuristic purposes only. The research in this area generally has not gone beyond the level of describing co-variances between certain styles and components of operative development. Consequently, one can only speculate at the present time on the causal linkages between these two factors and on the developmental antecedents of their relationships.

NATURE AND DEFINITION OF COGNITIVE STYLE

As Kagan and Kogan (1970) have noted, the current interest in cognitive styles can be traced, historically, to the writings of psychoanalytic ego psychologists such as Klein, Gardner, and Holtzman, and to theorists whose primary concern centered on issues of differentiation and integration of psychological functions, namely, Lewin and Werner. From these early theoretical foundations a voluminous body of research emerged on individual differences in cognitive controls and cognitive processes. This research emphasized the distinction between one's *ability* to solve a task and the *way* in which one goes about solving it. It is the latter characteristic that has come to be known as *cognitive style*.

The cognitive style construct has been defined in a variety of ways by researchers. Cutting across the many definitions, however, are a number of common features. Traditionally, cognitive style is conceptualized as a dispositional variable mediating the way in which the individual processes information. It is also assumed that this disposition represents a stable, self-consistent mode of adaptation linking cognitive and personal-affective domains of functioning (Goldstein & Blackman, 1978; Sigel & Brodzinsky, 1977; Witkin & Goodenough, 1981). In addition, as I have just noted, the emphasis is on ways of performing, not the capacity to perform. With respect to this last point, Kogan (1971) has offered possibly the best description of cognitive styles when he defined them as "individual modes of perceiving, remembering, and thinking, or as distinctive ways of apprehending, storing, transforming, and utilizing information" (p. 244). In the same article, Kogan went on to note that abilities also involve these properties although, importantly, they differ from cognitive styles in that "abilities concern level of skill—the more or less of performance—whereas cognitive styles give greater weight to the manner and *form* of cognition" (p. 244). Finally, one additional way of differentiating abilities and styles is to note that abilities are product oriented, whereas styles are process oriented. In other words, cognitive styles represent various ways of organizing and regulating behavior in the course of arriving at some product (Sigel & Brodzinsky, 1977).

The traditional description of cognitive style that has been presented raises several points that need to be addressed, if only briefly. First, defining cognitive style as a dispositional variable tends to elevate this construct to the status of a trait, and implies that individuals are characterized by one dimension or polar end of a style but not another. This view of cognitive style is unnecessarily restrictive. Instead, I prefer a view, similar to the one recently espoused by Messer and Schacht (in press) and Witkin and Goodenough (1981), which suggests that style represents a relative balance in the various means by which individuals process information, and not the presence versus absence or the absolute amount of these means. Thus, to use as an example the style of reflection-impulsivity, which I elaborate on more fully later, a reflective child is not one who exclusively employs specific information-processing strategies at the expense of alternative strategies, but one who uses a relative preponderance of particular strategies in comparison to others.

This view of cognitive style emphasizes the point that, at least theoretically, people have the capacity for expressing different dimensions of a style; that is, a child can manifest a reflective mode of adaptation at one time, and an impulsive mode at another time. But having the capacity to express a variety of processing styles or strategies does not guarantee that all of them will be utilized, or that they will be utilized with equal ease or frequency. Children clearly show preferences for certain modes of adapting as opposed to others. Moreover, their preferences are relatively stable across time and contexts (Kagan & Kogan, 1970; Kogan, 1973, 1976; Sigel & Brodzinsky, 1977; Witkin & Goodenough, 1981). This fact raises a central question about the basis for these relatively stable preferences. Why is it that some children typically adopt one style of information processing, whereas other children adopt a different style? To date, no definitive answer can be given to this question, although certainly a wide variety of explanations has been offered, including such factors as genetic determinants (Buss & Plomin, 1975; Plomin & Willerman, 1975), temperament (Kagan, 1971; Kagan, Lapidus, & Moore, 1978), maturationally based differences in hemispheric specialization

(Waber, 1977), motivation (Kagan & Messer, 1975; Messer, 1970), and differential socialization patterns (Witkin & Goodenough, 1981).

Finally, one may legitimately ask whether the distinction between cognitive style and ability is as clear cut as described earlier. Not surprisingly the answer is no. In the first place, a number of studies have reported low to moderate significant correlations between IQ or other ability measures and various types of cognitive styles (see Kogan, 1976; Messer, 1976; Messer & Schacht, in press; Sigel & Brodzinsky, 1977; Witkin & Goodenough, 1981, for reviews and discussion of the IQ-style relationship). As Messer and Schacht (in press) have pointed out, however, these correlations can be attributed, in part, to the way in which IQ is measured. Composite IQ scores, which typically tap a variety of abilities, skills, strategies, preferences, and motives, are likely to share some variance with almost any cognitive dimension, including cognitive style, simply because of their sheer diversity. In addition, Kogan (1973, 1976) has noted that certain styles such as field dependence-independence and reflection-impulsivity, which he calls Type I, are much more likely to be linked to ability level than other styles, simply because of the way they are operationalized; that is, in terms of performance that can be considered more or less veridical.

In summary, cognitive styles represent preferential modes or strategies of adapting in a problem-solving situation. The specific mode manifested by an individual at any one time, however, is likely to be influenced by a variety of organismic and situational factors, one of which may be ability level. Yet even if this is the case, it is apparent that style cannot be explained fully in terms of ability. As I suggest later in this chapter, what we normally refer to as ability in a Piagetian sense—that is, operative level—is as likely to be influenced by cognitive style as style is to be influenced by ability.

TYPES OF COGNITIVE STYLES

So far I have described cognitive styles only in a general sense, and in so doing have emphasized the commonality found among various style dimensions. In point of fact, however, researchers have typically focused not on those features that cut across diverse cognitive styles, but rather on those features that uniquely identify specific stylistic modes of adapting.

At times it appears as if the number of cognitive styles manifested by humans is limited only by the number of investigators of them. Messick (1976), for example, has identified 19 separate approaches to the study of cognitive styles. Of these only five—field dependence-independence, reflection-impulsivity, styles of conceptualization, breadth of categorization, and locus of control—have received serious attention by developmental researchers. And of these five, only the first two—field dependence-independence and reflection-impulsivity—have been studied in relation to the emergence and expression of operative thought. For this reason the present chapter focuses exclusively on the cognitive styles of field dependence-independence and reflection-impulsivity.

Field Dependence-Independence

A little more than 30 years ago Herman Witkin and his colleagues introduced the cognitive style of field dependence-independence into the psychological literature. Although this construct was originally linked quite specifically to individual differences in perception of the upright, field dependence-independence later was conceptualized in terms of the more general construct of psychological differentiation (Witkin, Dyk, Faterson, Goodenough, & Karp, 1962).

Witkin, like Werner (1948), assumed that psychological systems become increasingly differentiated with development, as evidenced by greater articulated analysis and structuring of experience. In one of his last published papers, Witkin (Witkin, Goodenough, & Oltman, 1979) described three major areas of developmental differentiation: self-nonself segregation, which manifests itself primarily in terms of cognitive restructuring skills and interpersonal competencies; segregation of psychological functions, which manifests itself in terms of various controls and defenses; and segregation of neurophysiological functions, which results in varying degrees of hemispheric specialization. Of these three areas, self-nonself segregation was the one in which Witkin located the cognitive style of field dependence-independence.

Field dependence-independence is defined by Witkin and his associates as the degree to which one is connected to versus independent of referents external to oneself. Field dependence, for example, is reflected in limited self-nonself segregation. That is, the field-dependent individual is likely to show a high degree of connectedness with other persons and with the environment in general. Field independence, on the other hand, is reflected in more complete self-nonself segregation. In other words, the field-independent person is likely to manifest a high degree of autonomy in relation to the social and nonsocial world.

The measures most frequently used to operationalize this individual difference dimension are the Embedded Figures Task (EFT) and the Rod and Frame Task (RFT). The Embedded Figures Task requires the subject to locate a simple figure embedded within a more complex geometric pattern. The Rod and Frame Task, on the other hand, requires the subject to adjust a luminous rod to true vertical when it is suspended within a tilted luminous frame in a darkened room. Subjects who are better able to overcome the field effects in these tasks so as to identify the simple figure in the EFT or align the rod to true vertical with greater accuracy in the RFT are said to be field independent. Conversely, subjects who have difficulty disembedding geometric figures from a complex background or who are less able to align the rod to true vertical within the tilted frame are said to be field dependent.

Although it is not my goal to review the empirical literature on field dependence-independence (cf. Goodenough, 1976; Kogan, 1976; Witkin & Goodenough, 1977, 1981 for recent reviews), at least two points are worth mentioning here. First, research suggests that although a subject's relative standing with respect to his peer group remains constant over time, absolute level of field independence increases at least into the late teens to early adult period, after which there is little change in performance until middle to late adulthood, when a decrease in field independence generally is observed (Comalli, 1970; Schwartz & Karp, 1967; Witkin, Goodenough, & Karp, 1967). Second, although past research typically has emphasized the greater adaptive value of a field independent orientation, it now appears that both ends of this stylistic continuum are adaptive, albeit in different domains of functioning. Whereas field independence has greater adaptive value in cognitive/academic areas, field dependence has been associated with greater interpersonal adaptiveness (Witkin & Goodenough, 1981; Witkin et al., 1979).

Reflection-Impulsivity

Approximately 15 years after the publication of Witkin's original work on field dependence-independence, Jerome Kagan and his associates (Kagan, Rosman, Day, Albert, & Phillips, 1964) introduced another new cognitive style into the developmental literature: reflection-impulsivity (also known as conceptual tempo). This individual difference dimension assesses the tendency to pause and reflect upon alternative answers in problems involving moderate to high response uncertainty. The Matching Familiar Figures Test (MFFT) is typically used to measure this dimension. It is a match-to-standard task involving a standard figure and either four, six, or eight variants, only one of which exactly matches the standard. (The number of variants depends on whether the subjects are preschoolers, school-age children, or adolescents/adults, respectively.) Subjects are asked to select from among the variants the one that exactly matches the standard. Total number of errors across all test items for each subject and his/her mean latency to first response are the measures used for defining a subject's cognitive style.

On the basis of a double median split for errors and latency, four separate dimensions of conceptual tempo can be identified in any subject population. Reflectives are those individuals who score below the median for errors and above the median for latency, whereas impulsives are those individuals who score above the median for errors and below the median for latency. Together, these two groups generally constitute about two thirds of any subject sample. Subjects who score above the median for both errors and latency – slow-inaccurates – and those who score below the median for these two variables – fast-accurates – are studied less often than reflectives and impulsives.

Children's conceptual tempo, like field dependence-independence, remains relatively stable over time with respect to peer group standing, although absolute level of performance does change (Kogan, 1976; Messer, 1976; Sigel & Brodzinsky, 1977). Research suggests an increase in reflectivity during the childhood years, at least until early adolescence (Messer & Brodzinsky, 1981), at which time a shift toward greater cognitive efficiency typically is observed (Salkind & Nelson, 1980) – that is, adolescent subjects begin to respond quicker while maintaining a high level of accuracy. Adult developmental trends for reflection-impulsivity are unclear because of the paucity of research with this subject population. One recent cross-sectional study, however, suggests a decrease in cognitive efficiency from middle to late adulthood (Denny & List, 1979).

In addition, a low to moderate positive relationship has been established between reflection-impulsivity and field dependence-independence (Messer, 1976; Neimark, 1975). The magnitude of the relationship indicates, however, that although there is some overlap between the two cognitive styles, it is doubtful that they represent the same type of response tendency or strategy.

Finally, the vast majority of research suggests that reflective individuals are superior to impulsive individuals across a wide range of cognitive/ academic and personal-affective tasks (Messer, 1976; Messer & Schacht, in press). This finding contrasts with the literature on field dependence-independence, which indicates greater superiority for field-independent individuals in cognitive areas, but greater superiority for field-dependent individuals in interpersonal areas. Several points, however, are worth mentioning about the apparent differences in adaptive value for these two cognitive style dimensions. First, most of the studies showing greater social adaptiveness among field-dependent individuals have used adult populations. Whether this pattern would be found with the same consistency among children is still unknown. Second, virtually all the conceptual tempo research indicating that impulsivity is a maladaptive style has used children. Indeed, we do not have much information on the benefits and limitations of a reflective or impulsive style (as defined by MFFT performance) in adulthood. It is quite possible that impulsivity, although maladaptive in childhood, could become adaptive in selective (but as yet unidentified) areas of functioning in adulthood – much as the characteristics of a field-dependent orientation are of value in the development of adult interpersonal competencies. In any event, the one consistent finding in the cognitive style literature – and the one most important for the purpose of this chapter – is the superior performance by field-independent and reflective individuals across numerous cognitive domains, including those that have been the primary focus of Piagetian investigators (e.g., performance on concrete and formal operational tasks).

COGNITIVE STYLES AND COGNITIVE STRUCTURES: THEORY AND RESEARCH

Developmental theorists who adhere to a distinction between competence and performance do so in the belief that a complete theory of psychological functioning necessitates two distinct components or models (cf. Flavell & Wohlwill, 1969; Overton & Newman, 1982; Stone & Day, 1980). The competence component refers to an abstract, idealized representation of what the organism knows or is capable of doing. In other words, it is the form or structure of knowledge. Competence is generally represented in terms of rule systems, logico-mathematical systems, central processing systems, and so on. Note, however, that competence does not refer to the actual psychological processes underlying a specific cognitive action, but only to the more general and abstract set of cognitive potentialities or boundaries that characterize the capabilities of the individual (Stone & Day, 1980). The performance model, in contrast, is a characterization of the specific psychological process utilized in a problem-solving situation. In addition, this component includes a description of the task/contextual and organismic variables that determine how, and under what conditions, competence gets expressed in actual thought and behavior. Variables such as task familiarity, stimulus complexity and ambiguity, subject's learning history, motivation, and attentional and memory limitations are but a few of the situational and organismic factors said to account for the variations in behavior commonly observed among individuals at the same developmental level. To this list can be added children's cognitive style. (For a more comprehensive treatment of the competence-performance distinction the reader is referred to Flavell & Wohlwill, 1969, Overton & Newman, 1982, and Stone & Day, 1980.)

With respect to the conceptual relationship between cognitive style and operative development, I have argued elsewhere (Brodzinsky, 1980, 1982), as have Overton and Newman (1982), that the difference in task success among cognitive style groups is based not on a difference in competence per se, but on differential access to competence. In other words, children who adopt specific information-processing strategies as opposed to others are more likely to have access to the full range of their capabilities, and hence, to be in a better position to use them. For example, although reflective children frequently outperform impulsive children in school-related subjects, it is not necessarily true that the former children are brighter than the latter children. Reflective children by virtue of their more cautious and methodical response style may simply be more efficient in activating and utilizing the relevant knowledge base and rule systems that underlie the academic problems with which they are presented.

It is also assumed that differential accessibility to, and utilization of, competence among cognitive style groups is not to be expected in all tasks or situations. Indeed, one should only find group differences in tasks and situations characterized by stimulus/contextual features and/or response requirements that share some commonality with the defining properties of the specific cognitive style in question. For example, field-independent children should outperform field-dependent children only when stimulus/field distinctions are ambiguous such as in embedded figures tasks and in the Rorschach, or when articulated analysis and cognitive restructuring are essential for task success such as in perspective-taking problems. Similarly, reflective children should be more successful than impulsive children primarily in situations that call for a cautious, analytic, and planful problem-solving approach.

Finally, it has also been suggested that the nature of the relationship between cognitive style and operative level is likely to change with development (Brodzinsky, 1980, 1982; Overton & Newman, 1982). That is, cognitive style differences in task performance are expected to be more readily apparent during transitional periods, and to some extent, during periods of structural consolidation than during periods prior to the development of operational competencies or after the competencies are fully stabilized. I have more to say about this assumption a little later.

Closely related to the set of theoretical asssumptions just described is the recent position taken by Neimark (1981) on the relationship between cognitive style factors and the development and expression of formal operations. Briefly, Neimark has argued that the relatively low success rate on formal operational tasks exhibited by many adolescents and adults is explained more parsimoniously in terms of a performance decrement related, at least in part, to subjects' cognitive style rather than to a widespread failure to develop formal operations. Specifically, field-dependent individuals are viewed by Neimark as being at a distinct disadvantage simply because of the way formal operations are usually measured. As a number of investigators have noted, the traditional Inhelder tasks of formal thought are relatively ambiguous and unstructured. They are also characterized by salient, but potentially misleading, perceptual cues. These stimulus conditions, Neimark argues, are the very ones that should produce a high rate of failure among field-dependent people. Because the latter group of subjects are likely to constitute a relatively large percentage of any population drawn at random, it is understandable that researchers have found a low success rate on formal operational tasks. Neimark suggests that the reported incidence of formal thought among adolescents and adults would increase substantially if we could find less ambiguous and less biased ways of measuring this ability (cf. Day & Stone, 1982).

To date, the most comprehensive, systematic, and productive attempt to link cognitive style factors and operative development is represented by the more general neo-Piagetian theory of constructive operators put forth by Pascual-Leone (1969, 1976, 1980; Pascual-Leone, Goodman, Ammon, & Subelman, 1980) and Case (1974, 1978a, 1978b). According to these investigators, children's actual behavior on a task is determined by the interplay between figurative, operative, and executive schemes (competence component) in interaction with a number of organismic and situational factors termed "silent operators" (performance component). These include such factors as the child's previous learning history, affective and personality factors, M-power (the maximum number of schemes a subject is capable of activating at any one time), and perceptual field effects. The last two factors—M-power and perceptual field effects—are particularly relevant for our purpose because of their theoretical link to children's cognitive style.

Both Pascual-Leone and Case have argued that field-dependent children are habitually low M-processors. That is, field-dependent children typically do not use as much effective M-power as they actually have. As a result, they are expected to fail more often on tasks requiring the coordination of multiple cognitive schemes than field-independent children. In addition, field-dependent children are also hypothesized to be more susceptible to the influence of salient perceptual cues within the stimulus field. When these cues are not only salient, but misleading as well, such as in a conservation of liquid quantity problem, field-dependent children are expected to perform at lower levels than field-independent children.

Finally, Pascual-Leone and Case not only have emphasized the role of cognitive styles in the utilization of cognitive structures, they have also argued that these individual difference factors influence the ease with which superordinate cognitive structures are actually constructed. In other words, performance differences among cognitive style groups, at times, may represent differential levels of competence, not just differences in access to, and utilization of, competence. The latter assumption, it should be noted, is at odds with the other conceptual positions I have outlined, including my own previous position on this issue. Without getting too much ahead of myself I should note that I now essentially agree with Pascual-Leone and Case, although I believe they have not gone far enough in describing when the cognitive style/operative development relationship is best understood in terms of a competence explanation and when it is best understood in terms of a performance explanation.

Empirical Findings

For all that has been written on the relationship between cognitive styles and operative development there actually has been relatively little systematic empirical work in this area. Fortunately, the research that has been done has yielded very promising results. For example, one of the most consistent findings reported in the literature is the positive relationship between field independence and knowledge of the concept of horizontality as measured by Piaget's water-level problem (Abravanel & Gingold, 1977; DeLisi, 1983; Liben, 1978; Neimark & Gomez, 1979; Pascual-Leone, 1969; Signorella & Jamison, 1978; St. Jean, 1976; Willemsen, Buchholz, Budrow, & Geannacopulos, 1973). This relationship has been observed in children, adolescents, and adults; and it has been observed even when spatial ability (Liben, 1978) or IQ (Abravanel & Gingold, 1977) have been controlled statistically. The explanation for this relationship generally has focused on the impact of perceptual field effects in the traditional water-level task. In fact, DeLisi (1983) has shown that reduction of misleading perceptual cues within the task substantially reduces the differences between field-independent and field-dependent children at the fifth-grade level. This finding was interpreted by the author as indicating that cognitive style differences in judgments of horizontality can be explained more parsimoniously in terms of performance factors than competence factors.

In addition to the horizontality problem, other spatial concepts also have been studied in relation to children's cognitive styles. Liben (1978), for example, found a positive relationship between field independence and children's knowledge of verticality. Furthermore, Satterly (1976) reported that field-dependent children were less successful than field-independent children on Piaget's haptic shape perception task (Piaget & Inhelder, 1956). A similar finding was reported by Kleinman (1977) for reflection-impulsivity. Specifically, reflective children, particularly those who were also conservers, were much more likely than impulsive children (regardless of conservation status) to exhibit logical haptic search strategies and, as a result, increased haptic matching accuracy.

Another spatial area linked to cognitive style factors is perspective taking. Measurement of this ability usually involves asking subjects to view a stimulus array and then to anticipate how the array would look if viewed from a position different from their own — as in Piaget and Inhelder's (1956) Three Mountain Task. Typically, subjects are asked to choose the correct perspective from a number of alternative pictures or drawings. Given the amount of response uncertainty and the impact of misleading perceptual cues in this type of task, it is quite understandable that research has indicated a positive correlation between field independence and perspective taking (Finley, Solla, & Cowan, 1977; Gough & Olton, 1972; McGilligan & Barclay, 1974; Okonji & Olagbaiye, 1975), as well as between reflectivity and perspective taking (Brodzinsky, 1980, 1982).

The relationship between children's cognitive styles and conservation behavior also has been examined. As the reader is undoubtedly aware, conservation is defined, in part, by the ability to overcome misleading perceptual cues such as the length or density of a row of objects in a number conservation task, or the unequal heights of liquid within contrasting beakers in a conservation of continuous quantity problem. Moreover, in conjunction with decentration, the child must be able to coordinate multiple stimulus cues simultaneously, and to engage in mental compensations and transformations. Given these task requirements, it should come as no surprise that studies have uncovered evidence of a positive relationship between field independence and conservation (Hill, 1980; Pascual-Leone, 1969), as well as between reflectivity and conservation (Ancillotti, 1982; Bartis & Ford, 1977; Brodzinsky, 1982; Cohen, Schleser, & Meyers, 1981).

The role of cognitive style in the expression of logical abilities also has been examined by Dillon (1980)—in this case with a population of hearing-impaired children ages 8–12 years. Dillon presented her subjects with a battery of Piagetian tasks consisting of multiple classification, order or appearance, and seriation items under one of several test conditions. The test conditions differed from one another in terms of specificity of feedback and degree of subject involvement. That is, in one condition subjects received only simple feedback as to whether their response was correct or not, whereas in another condition feedback consisted of actually pointing out to the child why a selected item was incorrect. In still another condition, subjects had to explain how they reached a specific solution. For some subjects this explanation was followed by specific feedback as well. Dillon found that children identified as impulsive on the basis of MFFT performance were less successful on the Piagetian battery than reflective children, but only under test conditions providing accuracy-inaccuracy feedback or when subjects had to provide elaborative explanations for their answers. In contrast, when subjects received no feedback, or when they received specific task-relevant feedback consisting of the reasons why a selected item was incorrect, performance on the Piagetian battery was unaffected by cognitive style. This pattern of findings supports the position that cognitive style groups are differentially affected by task and situational conditions and that differences in problem-solving behavior typically found among these groups are best explained in terms of performance factors.

In addition to the research on cognitive style differences on concrete operational tasks, other investigators have examined the role of these individual difference factors in the development and expression of formal operations. Case (1974), Linn (1978), Stone and Day (1980), and Day and Stone (1982), for example, have found a positive relationship between field independence and performance on a control of variables problem. Of interest, however, is the fact that the subjects in the Case study were actually within the age range typically asssociated with concrete operations, not formal operations. Case interpreted his result as suggesting that field independence may be linked to an earlier development of functional competence in the area of formal thought than is field dependence. In addition to the control of variables problem, investigators also have found significant differences between field-independent and field-dependent individuals on tasks measuring proportional reasoning (Linn & Swiney, 1981), diagnostic problem solving (Neimark, 1975), and permutations (Neimark, 1975). Significant positive relationships between reflectivity and measures of formal thought have also been reported (Neimark, 1975; Reibman & Overton, 1977).

Finally, a recent study by deRibaupierre and Pascual-Leone (1979) requires mention because it represents the first direct test of the theory of constructive operators in the area of formal thought. Working with 12- and 15-year-olds, and measuring formal thought in terms of a battery of tasks, these researchers found a clear positive relationship between field independence and formal operational reasoning. Of particular importance, however, was the fact that the relationship was not accounted for by field factors such as stimulus ambiguity as Neimark (1981) has previously suggested, but rather was due to the low effective M-power exhibited by the field dependent children. In other words, field-dependent children performed lower on the battery of formal operational tasks because of their propensity to underutilize their repertoire of executive planning schemes.

In general, the research to date, with but a few exceptions (e.g., Case, 1977; Vaidya & Chansky, 1980), indicates that cognitive style is a potent individual difference factor moderating children's, and even adults', performance on concrete and formal operational tasks. And yet despite this growing body of evidence we really do not understand very much about the nature the relationship between cognitive styles and operative development. One reason is that most studies have not examined the relationship developmentally, by means of either cross-sectional or longitudinal designs. Instead, researchers generally have utilized a single age level or have grouped children of varying ages together in attempting to establish correspondences between cognitive styles and components of operative thought. As a result, little is known about the developmental consistency of the cognitive style/operative development relationship. Do these factors show a similar pattern of relationship over time, or does the pattern change as each factor undergoes its own unique development? A second limitation of past research is that it has focused almost exclusively on children's correct operative responses. As Siegler (1981) recently pointed out, however, evidence of early or preliminary competence in a particular area is more likely to be found in the consistent use of strategies or rules leading to predictable patterns of errors rather than correct responses. In order to understand the role of cognitive styles in the development and expression of cognitive competence, particularly in the very early stages of transition, researchers must go beyond the traditional focus on task accuracy, to include systematic analyses of children's error patterns. Finally, most researchers, to date, have been satisfied with simply establishing correlational relationships between cognitive style factors and measures of operativity. Although this type of information is important, it does not answer critical questions pertaining to developmental causality. For example, although it is generally assumed that the emergence and expression of operative knowledge is facilitated by certain cognitive styles, it is just as plausible—in fact quite likely—that specific information-processing styles are facilitated by the development of logical operations.

What I am suggesting is that, in fact, we have barely scratched the surface of the relationship between cognitive styles and operative development. Most importantly, we need to go beyond the mere establishment of covariances between styles and structures, to examine the developmental or causal linkage between them. And we need to attack the critical question of whether cognitive style differences on operational tasks are best understood in terms of competence or ability factors, or whether these differences actually represent nothing more than differential access to, and utilization of, cognitive competence under specific task and situational conditions.

Reflection-Impulsivity and Perspective Taking: A Developmental Analysis

In the past few years I have begun to examine some of these questions through research focused on the relationship between reflection-impulsivity and children's spatial perspective taking. In this section I describe briefly three of the studies conducted as a way of calling attention to the type of designs and analyses that I believe are necessary to get us moving productively in this area.

In the first study (Brodzinsky, 1980), 4-, 6-, 8-, and 10-year-old children were administered the Matching Familiar Figures Test and a modified version of Piaget's Three Mountain Task. The relationship between reflection-impulsivity and children's spatial knowledge was examined both for task accuracy and for subjects' error pattern. As predicted, no relationship was found between cognitive style and perspective taking at 4 years of age, although at 6 years a clear relationship was established. The relationship, however, was not found for correct responses—subjects were still at chance levels on this measure—but rather was observed for children's error pattern. Specifically, impulsive children were more likely to make developmentally immature errors, such as choosing the response alternative representing their own view (an egocentric response), whereas reflective children were more likely to make developmentally mature errors, such as choosing a response alternative that represented a perspective 45° to either side of the correct response. At 8 years of age the relationship between cognitive style and perspective taking changed once again. Reflectives now made more correct responses than impulsives, whereas no differences were observed for pattern of errors. Finally, by 10 years, children in both groups were generally successful on the perspective task, thereby producing a ceiling effect.

These findings call attention to two important points. First, as noted earlier, the relationship between cognitive style and operative development is likely to change over time, with the greatest impact being observed during transitional periods. At the very least, therefore, investigators should include more than one age level in their research so that questions pertaining to the developmental consistency of the cognitive style/operativity relationship can be examined. Second, the data also point out the rather subtle way in which the relationship between cognitive style and operative knowledge changes as children actually move through the transition period. At first the relationship is found solely in terms of children's error pattern, and only later in the increasingly successful anticipation of the correct response. These results confirm the importance of going beyond the traditional emphasis on task success, to include a systematic examination of style differences in the pattern of errors manifested by children on various operative tasks (cf. Siegler, 1981).

Although the first study described had a number of methodological advantages over many other studies in this area—particularly the use of several age levels and the focus on both task accuracy and errors—it still was limited by its reliance on cross-sectional data. As Baltes, Reese, and Nesselroade (1977) have emphasized, cross-sectional designs tell us more about age differences than about developmental change. To examine the relationship between reflection-impulsivity and perspective taking developmentally, therefore, one must use a longitudinal design—a strategy that was adopted in the second study to be described (Brodzinsky, 1982). Besides its longitudinal focus, however, the study also examined the causal linkage among the variables by means of causal modeling analyses.

All 4- and 6-year-old children from the previous study were retested with the same measures 2 years later when they were 6 and 8 years of age. The first thing to note is that the pattern of results regarding the relationship between reflection-impulsivity and perspective taking at 6 and 8 years was remarkably similar across the two studies. In other words, both the cross-sectional and longitudinal data indicate that 6-year-old reflective children, although still performing at chance levels with respect to correct perspective-taking responses, were more likely to make developmentally mature errors and less likely to make immature errors, than 6-year-old impulsive children. In contrast, at 8 years of age the primary difference between reflective and impulsive children was found for correct responses, with the reflective children more likely to be accurate than the impulsive children.

The cross-lag correlations between cognitive style and perspective taking also were examined in this study. Generally, no relationship was found between reflection-impulsivity at 4 years and perspective taking at 6 years, or between perspective taking at 4 years and reflection-impulsivity at 6 years. In contrast, however, reflection-impulsivity at 6 years was significantly related to perspective taking at 8 years. Specifically, 6-year-old reflective children, in comparison to impulsive children, were more successful in coordinating spatial perspectives when they reached 8 years of age. No relationship was found, however, between perspective taking at 6 years and reflection-impulsivity at 8 years.

To test the causal connection between cognitive style and perspective taking at 6 and 8 years, the data were reanalyzed using a causal modeling procedure known as LISREL (Jöreskog & Sörbom, 1976). Figure 7.1 depicts the two models tested — the second of which is simply a more constrained version of the first. The figure shown uses a convention, fairly standard in the methodological literature, of representing causal relations by straight lines and correlational relations by curved lines. The numbers outside parentheses on straight lines are standardized regression coefficients, whereas those within parentheses are unstandardized regression coefficients. The numbers on curved lines are correlation coefficients.

Results of the structural modeling analysis suggested that impulsivity at 6 years is causally linked to performance on perspective taking at 8 years, whereas perspective taking at 6 years is unrelated to children's cognitive style at 8 years. Although these findings suggest a unidirectional causal linkage between cognitive styles and cognitive structures, this conclusion is certainly

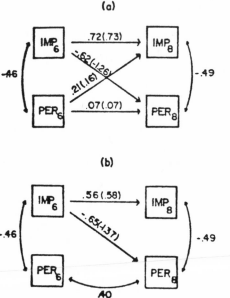

FIG. 7.1 Structural equation models relating impulsivity and spatial perspective taking at 6 and 8 years of age (from Brodzinsky, 1982).

premature, and probably too simplistic. In the first place, the study described examined only a narrow range of cognitive styles and operative skills. It is quite possible that a different, and more complex, picture would emerge if other cognitive styles and components of operativity were studied. Second, the causal linkage suggested by this study was based on nonexperimental data. A much stronger test of the causal model could be obtained through an experimental training study. For example, to the extent that cognitive styles are more likely to facilitate the emergence and/or expression of cognitive structures rather than vice versa, children trained in reflectivity should make better progress in the development of some targeted operative ability than children trained in operativity should make in the development of reflectivity. We plan to test this assumption shortly by means of a training study.

Finally, I would like to describe the results of an unpublished study conducted several years ago (Brodzinsky, 1978) because it touches upon an issue that I mentioned but did not discuss in any depth. As was noted earlier, cognitive style differences in task performance should not be expected beyond the time when the cognitive competencies underlying the task are reasonably well stabilized. Although at the theoretical, and even the intuitive, level this makes considerable sense, when one actually undertakes to test this assumption empirically one finds that it is a more complex and subtle assumption than it first appears to be. For example, by what age are the cognitive structures underlying the spatial coordinate system stabilized so as to preclude cognitive style differences in task performance? In the first study reported (Brodzinsky, 1980), no differences were found between reflectives and impulsives at 10 years of age. Does this mean that perspective-taking ability is stabilized by this age level? The answer appears to be no. In our unpublished study we gave 10- and 12-year-old reflective and impulsive children two versions of the perspective task. In one version (recognition task) subjects had to choose from a series of pictures the one that represented the other's viewpoint—this was the procedure used in our other research. In the second version (construction task), however, subjects actually had to construct the other person's view of the stimulus array using a set of materials identical to the standard stimuli. Although in the Brodzinsky (1980) study no cognitive style differences were found at 10 years of age, in this study 10-year-old impulsive children were clearly inferior to 10-year-old reflective children on the construction task. No differences were observed on the recognition task, however, nor were cognitive style differences found at 12 years of age. Thus, the question of the timing of structural stabilization, and its relationship to cognitive style differences in task performance, is difficult to answer. Clearly, as we increase the complexity of the task we are more likely to find evidence of structural instability—or more specifically, behavioral variability among subjects of the same age level. And we are also more likely to find evidence that cognitive styles account for a significant proportion of that variability—a point also made by Flavell (1982).

COGNITIVE STYLES AND COGNITIVE STRUCTURES: A DIFFERENTIATION MODEL

Up to this point I have described a number of general theoretical assumptions linking cognitive styles and operative structures, and have reviewed the existing empirical literature in this area. I would now like to sketch out a new conceptual model relating these two constructs. Before doing so, however, two important points must be made. First, this model is restricted to the developmental and interactional relationships between children's cognitive styles and operative thought. It is not intended to describe or explain the role of individual difference and situational factors as moderators of competence in a more general sense—as do the models offered by Pascual-Leone (1969, 1976, 1980) and Case (1974, 1978a, 1978b). Second, the current model must be considered speculative and most certainly incomplete at this time, given the paucity of research in this area. Yet even in its present form the model has heuristic value, and I hope it will generate increased interest in the role of cognitive styles in the development and expression of operative knowledge.

At the core of the model is the basic assumption that development is characterized by two dynamic processes—differentiation and integration. That is, development is viewed as proceeding from relatively global states comprising undifferentiated, isolated elements to states in which elements are increasingly articulated, differentiated, and integrated into coherent systems or frameworks. This assumption is tied quite closely, as the reader undoubtedly is aware, to Werner's (1948) orthogenetic principle, as well as to Piaget's (1970, 1971b) equilibration model. It is also linked to Witkin's (Witkin et al., 1979) differentiation theory of organismic functioning.

The processes of differentiation and integration, which are governed by sociocultural experience and maturation, are assumed to be manifested in all areas of the individual's life. For the present purpose, however, it is sufficient to distinguish between two broad sets of organismic functions: neurophysiological functions and psychological functions. As Fig. 7.2 denotes, differentiation/integration at the neurophysiological level is assumed to have a direct impact on psychological differentiation/integration. Although I do not deal with this aspect of the model in this chapter, it should be pointed out that there is a large empirical literature on the relationship between neurophysiological development, particularly brain lateralization, and the emergence and expression of various behaviors and cognitive skills (Bradshaw & Nettleton, 1981), including cognitive styles (Waber, 1977; Witkin & Goodenough, 1981). There has even been some speculation on the

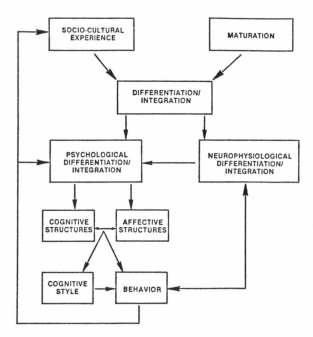

FIG. 7.2   A differentiation model of the developmental relationship between cognitive/ affective structures and cognitive styles.

role of cortical development as a basis for the type of cognitive changes described by Piaget (Gibson, 1977, 1978; Kraft, Mitchell, Langus, & Wheatley, 1980). Examination of the impact of maturational processes on psychological differentiation, particularly on the cognitive style/cognitive structure relationship, may therefore prove to be a productive avenue of research for future investigators.

Differentiation and integration of psychological functions are assumed to be manifested through the gradual emergence and transformation of cognitive and personal-affective structures. Cognitive structures, as was noted earlier, represent the form or organizational pattern underlying knowledge. Affective structures, however, are more difficult to characterize (cf. Mischel, 1971). On the one hand, they represent the energizing or motivating force behind thought and behavior. And yet they are much more than this. Affectivity also represents a "system of values" — the needs, interests, and valuations of the individual (Piaget, 1954, cited in Mischel, 1971).

Representation of cognitive and affective structures as separate entities in the diagrammed model is an oversimplification. These two organismic factors are assumed to interact continuously with one another (as represented by the double arrow) and, in fact, are viewed as inseparable and representing "correlative aspects of one and the same psychological phenomenon"

(Mischel, 1971, p. 322). Furthermore, it is in the context of this dynamic interplay between cognition and affect that cognitive styles are assumed to emerge. That is, cognitive styles are viewed as representing the interface between cognition and the person's system of needs, motives, interests, and valuations. It is further assumed that cognitive styles mediate task-oriented behavior, but only under specific conditions. As we previously suggested, style differences in task performance are expected primarily in situations characterized by stimulus/contextual features or response requirements that share some commonality with the defining properties of the specific cognitive style in question. In other situations – such as when tasks are unambiguous, low in complexity, and free of field effects – the impact of cognitive style factors is assumed to be minimal, thereby allowing for a more direct expression of cognitive/affective structures in behavior.

The model also posits a series of feedback loops between subject's behavior (this term is used in its broadest sense to include both action and thought) and both psychological and neurophysiological functions. This provision is part of the self-regulatory system of organismic functioning. As an example, consider the child who typically is thorough and systematic in deploying attention in problem-solving situations. Such a child is more likely to become aware of discrepancies between his/her existing beliefs or expectations and the realities of the specific problem situation than is the child who employs a more incomplete and haphazard attentional strategy. Recognition of, and need to resolve, such cognitive discrepancies is said to be a primary motivating force underlying the transition from lower order to higher order levels of cognitive organization (Mischel, 1971). Thus, the child's behavior – in this case in the form of more efficient attentional strategies – is the vehicle through which he/she is exposed to experiences that facilitate the development of increasingly more sophisticated cognitive/affective structures.

Finally, behavior is seen as impacting on the individual's sociocultural environment, and in so doing, providing a means for structuring the very experience that, in part, regulates the individual's development – as in the case of the child's behavior influencing the course of parental socialization practices (see Zimmerman, 1981, for a discussion of behavior as a vehicle through which the child constructs his/her world).

Having provided a general overview of the model, let me now focus more specifically on some of the important implications concerning the cognitive style/cognitive structure relationship derivable from this perspective, which I believe warrant close empirical scrutiny. First, the current model assumes that behavioral characteristics associated with specific cognitive styles are an influential factor in the *development* of cognitive/affective structures. Children who are cautious, planful, systematic in attention deployment and task analysis, more effective in activating multiple cognitive schemes simultaneously, and who are better able to overcome salient field effects—in other words, field-independent and reflective children—are expected to develop functional competence in specific cognitive areas earlier, and to move through transitional periods faster, than are field-dependent and impulsive children who are less likely to exhibit these self-regulatory and executive behaviors. Cognitive styles are also assumed to influence the *utilization* or *deployment* of competence once the abilities in question are reasonably well stabilized. In other words, a field-independent or reflective orientation is expected to facilitate access to, and subsequent expression of, operative knowledge, particularly in situations known to impede or inhibit successful task performance—for example, under conditions of high stimulus ambiguity or complexity, or when field effects are salient.

Thus, cognitive style effects are interpretable in terms of both a competence model and a performance model. Competence explanations, however, are assumed to be more useful for understanding the differences among cognitive style groups during the early transition to more advanced operative levels, whereas performance explanations are seen as being more parsimonious during periods of structural consolidation and stabilization.

How might we test the validity of these assumptions? By what means can we differentiate between cognitive style differences that are competence based and those that are performance based? Let me suggest some possibilities. First, to the extent that a cognitive style such as reflectivity actually influences the development of competence, then training preoperational children who are close to the transitional level for operativity in the type of self-regulatory and executive processes underlying the reflective style should result in significant gains in operative knowledge. Similarly, training children who already show some evidence of operativity to be more reflective should lead to a more generalized expression of operative thought in various knowledge domains. Moreover, to the extent that increased generalization of operative knowledge cannot be shown by means of simple task and procedural manipulations (such as reducing stimulus ambiguity and misleading perceptual cues, or using additional probes to uncover subject's knowledge), but is restricted to the training effect, then cognitive style differences in task performance are most readily understandable in terms of differential levels of competence.

On the other hand, there clearly are situations in which cognitive style differences in task performance can easily be reduced or eliminated simply by altering experimental procedures. Under such conditions competence explanations would seem to be inappropriate. Let me illustrate this point with a specific example from my own research. In two separate studies, school-age children from various conceptual tempo groups were asked to explain the meaning of verbal material containing either phonological, lexical, surface-structure, or deep-structure ambiguities. In one study (Brodzinsky, 1977) the stimuli were verbal jokes, whereas in the other study (Brodzinsky, Feuer, & Owens, 1977) they were simple declarative sentences with accompanying pictures. Two dependent variables were measured in each experiment: spontaneous comprehension and prompted comprehension. The prompted comprehension measure included all information generated by the subject spontaneously plus any additional information following a relatively nondirective probe by the experimenter (e.g., "Can you tell me more about why the joke is funny?" or "Can you tell me anything else that the sentence might mean?"). Results indicated that reflective children were more successful than impulsive children in explaining linguistically based incongruities both in jokes and in simple declarative sentences, but only for the spontaneous comprehension measure. The prompted comprehension measure, in contrast, indicated no difference between groups. This pattern of findings suggests that reflective and impulsive children, at least at the age levels tested and with this particular type of task, do not differ in their ability to uncover the meaning of linguistically ambiguous verbal material, but rather differ in their initial or spontaneous response to the problem situation. Reflectives are initially more cautious, more thorough in examining the stimulus, and probably are more effective in evaluating the quality of their response. Impulsives, on the other hand, initially respond quicker and are less likely to monitor their performance in terms of task requirements. And yet when impulsive children are encouraged by the experimenter to reconsider their response, and to evaluate the possibility of alternative or additional answers, their performance improves dramatically to the point that cognitive style differences are eliminated.

Generalizing from these findings to the area of operative development, it seems reasonable to expect that cognitive style differences in task success may, at times, reflect a similar *production deficiency* process — and hence be explainable in terms of performance differences rather than competence differences. This assumption can easily be tested by examining the relative impact of task and procedural manipulations on children varying in cognitive style and operative level.

To this point I have emphasized the role of cognitive style in the development and expression of cognitive structures. The current model, however, also assumes that cognitive structures influence the development of cognitive styles. That is, cognitive structures provide the form or organizational pattern that guides the emergence of specific stylistic modes of adapting. Operative thought, for example, which is characterized by logico-mathematical properties, is assumed to facilitate a more cautious, systematic, planful, and self-evaluative approach to problem solving than is preoperative thought. Operative knowledge is also assumed to facilitate cognitive restructuring and to reduce the impact of perceptual field effects. Simply put, the development of operativity is expected to promote a more reflective and field independent orientation.

The assumption that cognitive structures mediate the development of cognitive styles clearly is in line with Piaget's (1969) position on the relationship between cognition and perception (including the structuring of attentional deployment and perceptual search strategies). In fact, it is safe to say that had Piaget focused on the relationship between cognitive styles and cognitive structures he would have emphasized this aspect of their relationship — that is, the way in which operativity structures the emergence of information-processing styles, rather than vice versa. And yet the cognitive style literature virtually has ignored this problem. The only study on this issue is one of my own, which examined the developmental relationship between reflection-impulsivity and children's spatial perspective taking between 4 and 6 years and between 6 and 8 years (Brodzinsky, 1982). As the reader will remember, although reflectivity at 6 years was causally linked to successful perspective taking at 8 years, no causal relationship was found between perspective taking and cognitive style across any of the ages studied. Although these findings fail to support the assumption that cognitive structures facilitate the development of cognitive styles, it is far too early to reject this component of the model. In the first place, a very narrow range of operative skills and cognitive styles was included in the study. Future research needs to examine the causal linkage between other components of operative thought and information-processing styles. In addition, the use of a causal modeling approach, although an improvement over previous research strategies, may not have been sensitive enough to uncover the causal link between operative structures and cognitive styles. As I suggested earlier, the use of an experimental training study would provide a much stronger test of this assumption of the model. Thus, to the extent that operative structures do facilitate the emergence of specific information-processing styles, then children trained in operativity should also show gains in reflectivity and field independence.

CONCLUSION

The aim of this chapter has been to explore the relationship between children's cognitive styles and the development and expression of cognitive competence. That a relationship exists between these two factors is by now undeniable. The meaning or interpretation of this relationship, however, is less clear. Whether cognitive style differences in task-oriented behavior reflect differential levels of competence or simply differences in accessibility to, and utilization of, competence is still unknown. In fact, both explanations may be valid, although as I have suggested, for different aspects of the relationship. Furthermore, questions pertaining to the causal linkage between styles and structures remain unanswered. The model that I have offered suggests a dynamic reciprocal causal relationship between these two factors. And yet admittedly, the data needed to test this and other assumptions derivable from the model are not available. One hopes this will soon change.

In conclusion, the role of cognitive style factors in structural development promises to add a new and exciting dimension to Piagetian theory and research. At the very least, it will help us to understand individual differences in structural development and deployment. And it should prove invaluable for our understanding of the rules of structural transition—a most important but neglected topic in Piagetian theory.

REFERENCES

Abravanel, E., & Gingold, H. (1977). Perceiving and representing orientation: Effects of the spatial framework. *Merrill-Palmer Quarterly, 23,* 265–278.

Ancillotti, J. P. (1982). Dimension reflexive-impulsive de la personnalite et processus cognitifs chez l'enfant. *Cahiers de Psychologie Cognitive, 2,* 71–89.

Baltes, O. B., Reese, H. W., & Nesselroade, J. R. (1977). *Life-span developmental psychology: An introduction to research methods.* Monterey, CA: Brooks/Cole.

Bartis, S. W., & Ford, L. H. (1977). Reflection-impulsivity, conservation, and the development of the ability to control cognitive tempo. *Child Development, 48,* 953–959.

Bradshaw, J. L., & Nettleton, N. C. (1981). The nature of hemispheric specialization in man. *Behavioral and Brain Sciences, 4,* 51–91.

Brainerd, C. J. (1978). The stage question in cognitive-developmental theory. *Behavioral and Brain Sciences, 2,* 173–182.

Brodzinsky, D. M. (1977). Children's comprehension and appreciation of verbal jokes in relation to conceptual tempo. *Child Development, 48,* 960–967.

Brodzinsky, D. M. (1978). *Cognitive style effects in the recognition and construction of spatial perspectives.* Unpublished manuscript.

Brodzinsky, D. M. (1980). Cognitive style differences in children's spatial perspective taking. *Developmental Psychology, 16,* 151–152.

Brodzinsky, D. M. (1982). Relationship between cognitive style and cognitive development: A two-year longitudinal study. *Developmental Psychology, 18,* 617–626.

Brodzinsky, D. M., Feuer, V., & Owens, J. (1977). Detection of linguistic ambiguity by reflective, impulsive, fast-accurate, and slow-inaccurate children. *Journal of Educational Psychology, 69,* 237–243.

Buss, A., & Plomin, R. (1975). *A temperament theory of personality development.* New York: Wiley-Interscience.

Case, R. (1974). Structures and strictures: Some functional limitations on the course of cognitive growth. *Cognitive Psychology, 6,* 544–573.

Case, R. (1977). Responsiveness to conservation training as a function of induced subjective uncertainty, M-space, and cognitive style. *Canadian Journal of Behavioral Science, 9,* 12–25.

Case, R. (1978a). Intellectual development from birth to adolescence: A neo-Piagetian interpretation. In R. Siegler (Ed.), *Children's thinking: What develops?* Hillsdale, NJ: Lawrence Erlbaum Associates.

Case, R. (1978b). Piaget and beyond: Toward a developmentally based theory and technology of instruction. In R. Glaser (Ed.), *Advances in instructional psychology* (Vol. 1). Hillsdale, NJ: Lawrence Erlbaum Associates.

Cohen, R., Schleser, R., & Meyers, A. (1981). Self-instructions: Effects of cognitive level and active rehearsal. *Journal of Experimental Child Psychology, 32*, 65–76.

Comalli, P. E., Jr. (1970). Life-span changes in visual perception. In L. R. Goulet & P. B. Baltes (Eds.), *Life-span developmental psychology: Research and theory.* New York: Academic Press.

Day, M. C., & Stone, C. A. (1982). Developmental and individual differences in the use of the control-of-variables strategy. *Journal of Educational Psychology, 74*, 749–760.

De Lisi, R. (1983). Developmental and individual differences in children's representation of the horizontal coordinate. *Merrill-Palmer Quarterly, 29*, 179–196.

Denny, N. W., & List, J. A. (1979). Adult age differences in performance on the Matching Familiar Figures test. *Human Development, 22*, 137–144.

deRibaupierre, A., & Pascual-Leone, J. (1979). Formal operations and M-power: A neo-Piagetian investigation. In D. Kuhn (Ed.), *New directions in child psychology.* San Francisco: Jossey-Bass, Vol. 5.

Dillon, R. F. (1980). Cognitive style and elaboration of logical abilities in hearing-impaired children. *Journal of Experimental Child Psychology, 30*, 389–400.

Finley, G. E., Solla, J., & Cowan, P. A. (1977). Field dependence-independence, egocentricism, and conservation in young children. *Journal of Genetic Psychology, 131*, 155–156.

Flavell, J. H. (1977). *Cognitive development.* Englewood Cliffs, NJ: Prentice-Hall.

Flavell, J. H. (1982). On cognitive development. *Child Development, 53*, 1–10.

Flavell, J. H., & Wohlwill, J. F. (1969). Formal and functional aspects of cognitive development. In D. Elkind & J. H. Flavell (Eds.), *Studies in cognitive development: Essays in honor of Jean Piaget.* New York: Oxford University Press.

Gibson, K. R. (1977). Brain structure and intelligence in macaques and human infants from a Piagetian perspective. In S. Chevalier-Skolnikoff & F. E. Poirer (Eds.), *Primate bio-social development.* New York: Garland.

Gibson, K. R. (1978). Cortical maturation: An antecedent of Piaget's behavioral stages. *Behavioral and Brain Sciences, 2*, 188.

Goldstein, K. M., & Blackman, S. (1978). *Cognitive style: Five approaches and relevant research.* New York: Wiley-Interscience.

Goodenough, D. R. (1976). The role of individual differences in field dependence as a factor in learning and memory. *Psychological Bulletin, 83*, 675–694.

Gough, H. G., & Olton, R. M. (1972). Field independence as related to nonverbal measures of perceptual performance and cognitive ability. *Journal of Consulting and Clinical Psychology, 38*, 338–342.

Hill, D. (1980). Relation of field dependence to development of conservation. *Perceptual and Motor Skills, 50*, 1247–1250.

Jöreskog, K. G., & Sörbom, D. (1976). *LISREL III: Estimation of linear structural equation systems by maximum-likelihood methods.* Chicago: National Educational Resources.

Kagan, J. (1971). *Change and continuity in infancy.* New York: Wiley.

Kagan, J., & Kogan, N. (1970). Individual variation in cognitive processes. In P. H. Mussen (Ed.), *Carmichael's manual of child psychology* (Vol. 1). New York: Wiley.

Kagan, J., Lapidus, D. R., & Moore, M. (1978). Infant antecedents of cognitive functioning: A longitudinal study. *Child Development, 49*, 1005–1023.

Kagan, J., & Messer, S. B. (1975). A reply to "Some misgivings about the Matching Familiar Figures test as a measure of reflection-impulsivity." *Developmental Psychology, 11*, 244–248.

Kagan, J., Rosman, B. L., Day, D., Albert, J., & Phillips, W. (1964). Information processing in the child: Significance of analytic and reflective attitudes. *Psychological Monographs, 78* (1, Whole No. 578).

Kleinman, J. M. (1977). *Haptic perceptual search: Effects of conservation status, reflection-impulsivity, and systematic training.* Unpublished doctoral dissertation, Rutgers University.

Kogan, N. (1971). Educational implications of cognitive styles. In G. S. Lesser (Ed.), *Psychology and educational practice.* Glenview, IL: Scott, Foresman.

Kogan, N. (1973). Creativity and cognitive styles: A life span perspective. In P. Baltes & K. W. Schaie (Eds.), *Life span developmental psychology: Personality and socialization.* New York: Academic Press.

Kogan, N. (1976). *Cognitive styles in infancy and early childhood.* Hillsdale, NJ: Lawrence Erlbaum Associates.

Kraft, R. H., Mitchell, O. R., Langus, M. L., & Wheatley, G. H. (1980). Hemispheric asymmetries during six-to-eight-year-olds performance on Piagetian conservation and reading tasks. *Neuropsychologia, 18,* 637–643.

Liben, L. S. (1978). Performance on Piagetian spatial tasks as a function of sex, field dependence, and training. *Merrill-Palmer Quarterly, 24,* 97–100.

Linn, M. C. (1978). Influence of cognitive style and training on tasks requiring the separation of variables schema. *Child Development, 48,* 874–877.

Linn, M. C., & Swiney, J. F. (1981). Individual differences in formal thought: role of expectation and aptitudes. *Journal of Educational Psychology, 73,* 274–286.

McGilligan, R. P., & Barclay, A. G. (1974). Sex differences and spatial ability factors in Witkin's "Differentiation" construct. *Journal of Clinical Psychology, 30,* 528–532.

Messer, S. B. (1970). The effect of anxiety over intellectual performance on reflection-impulsivity in children. *Child Development, 41,* 723–735.

Messer, S. B. (1976). Reflection-impulsivity: A review. *Psychological Bulletin, 83,* 1026–1052.

Messer, S. B., & Brodzinsky, D. M. (1981). Three year stability of reflection-impulsivity in young adolescents. *Developmental Psychology, 17,* 848–850.

Messer, S. B., & Schacht, T. E. (in press). A cognitive-dynamic theory of reflection-impulsivity. In J. Masling (Ed.), *Empirical studies in psychoanalytic theory.* Hillsdale, NJ: Lawrence Erlbaum Associates.

Messick, S. (Ed.) (1976). *Individuality in learning.* San Francisco: Jossey-Bass.

Mischel, T. (1971). Piaget: Cognitive development and the motivation of thought. In T. Mischel (Ed.), *Cognitive development and epistemology.* New York: Academic Press.

Neimark, E. D. (1975). Longitudinal development of formal operations thought. *Genetic Psychology Monographs, 91,* 171–225.

Neimark, E. D. (1981). Confounding with cognitive style factors: An artifact explanation for the apparent nonuniversal incidence of formal operations. In I. Sigel, D. M. Brodzinsky, & R. Golinkoff (Eds.), *New directions in Piagetian theory and practice.* Hillsdale, NJ: Lawrence Erlbaum Associates.

Neimark, E. D., & Gomez, I. H. (1978, April). *Correlates of water level representation in college students: Academic ability, formal operations status, and field dependence/independence.* Paper presented at the meetings of the Eastern Psychological Association, Philadelphia.

Okonji, M. O., & Olagbaiye, O. O. (1975). Field dependence and the coordination of perspectives. *Developmental Psychology, 11,* 520.

Overton, W. F., & Newman, J. L. (1982). Cognitive development: A competence-activation/utilization approach. In T. Field et al. (Eds.), *Review of human development.* New York: Wiley.

Pascual-Leone, J. (1969). *Cognitive development and cognitive style: A general psychological integration.* Unpublished doctoral dissertation, University of Geneva.

Pascual-Leone, J. (1976). On learning and development, Piagetian style, II: A critical historical analysis of Geneva's research programme. *Canadian Psychological Review, 17,* 289–297.

Pascual-Leone, J. (1980). Constructive problems for constructive theories: The current relevance of Piaget's work and critique of information processing simulation psychology. In H.
Speda & P. Kluwe (Eds.), *Psychological models of thinking.* New York: Academic Press.

Pascual-Leone, J., Goodman, D., Ammon, P., & Subelman, I. (1980). Piagetian theory and
neo-Piagetian analysis as psychological guides in education. In J. Gallagher & J. Easley
(Eds.), *Knowledge and development: Vol. 2. Piaget and education.* New York: Plenum Press.

Piaget, J. (1954). *Les relations entre l'affectivité et l'intelligence dans le developpment mental de
l'enfant.* Paris: Centre de Documentation Univ.

Piaget, J. (1970). Piaget's theory. In P. H. Mussen (Ed.), *Carmichael's manual of child psychology* (Vol. I). New York: Wiley.

Piaget, J. (1971a). Theory of stages in cognitive development. In D. R. Green, M. P. Ford, & G.
B. Flamer (Eds.), *Measurement and Piaget.* New York: McGraw-Hill.

Piaget, J. (1971b). *Biology and knowledge.* Chicago: University of Chicago Press.

Piaget, J. (1972). Intellectual evolution from adolescence to adulthood. *Human Development,
15,* 1-12.

Piaget, J., & Inhelder, B. (1956). *The child's conception of space.* London: Routledge & Kegan
Paul.

Plomin, R., & Willerman, L. (1975). A co-twin control study and a twin study of reflection-
impulsivity in children. *Journal of Educational Psychology, 67,* 537-543.

Reibman, B., & Overton, W. F. (1977, March). *Reflection-impulsivity and the utilization of
formal operational thought.* Paper presented at the Society for Research in Child Development, New Orleans.

Salkind, N. J., & Nelson, C. F. (1980). A note on the developmental nature of reflection-
impulsivity. *Developmental Psychology, 16,* 237-238.

Satterly, D. J. (1976). Cognitive styles, spatial ability, and school achievement. *Journal of Educational Psychology, 68,* 36-42.

Schwartz, D. W., & Karp, S. A. (1967). Field dependence in a geriatric population. *Perceptual
and Motor Skills, 24,* 495-504.

Siegler, R. S. (1981). Developmental sequences within and between concepts. *Monographs of
the Society for Research in Child Development, 46* (2, Serial No. 189).

Sigel, I. E., & Brodzinsky, D. M. (1977). Individual differences: A perspective for understanding
intellectual development. In H. Hom & P. Robinson (Eds.), *Psychological processes in early
education.* New York: Academic Press.

Signorella, M. L., & Jamison, W. (1978). Sex differences in the correlations among field dependence, spatial ability, sex role orientation, and performance on Piaget's water-level task. *Developmental Psychology, 14,* 689-690.

St. Jean, D. (1976). *The water-level task as a measure of field dependence-independence.* Unpublished masters thesis, Rutgers University.

Stone, C. A., & Day, M. C. (1980). Competence and performance models and the characterization of formal operational skills. *Human Development, 23,* 323-353.

Vaidya, S., & Chansky, N. (1980). Cognitive development and cognitive style as factors in mathematics achievement. *Journal of Educational Psychology, 72,* 326-330.

Waber, D. P. (1977). Biological substrates of field dependence: Implications of the sex difference. *Psychological Bulletin, 84,* 1076-1087.

Werner, H. (1948). *Comparative psychology of mental development.* New York: International
Universities Press.

Willemsen, E., Buchholz, A., Budrow, M. S., & Geannacopulos, N. (1973). Relationship between Witkin's rod-and-frame task and Piaget's water-line task for college women. *Perceptual
and Motor Skills, 36,* 958.

Witkin, H. A., Dyk, R. B., Faterson, H. F., Goodenough, D. R., & Karp, S. A. (1962). *Psychological differentiation.* New York: Wiley.

Witkin, H. A., & Goodenough, D. R. (1977). Field dependence and interpersonal behavior. *Psychological Bulletin, 84,* 661–689.

Witkin, H. A., & Goodenough, D. R. (1981). Cognitive styles: Essence and origins. *Psychological Issues. Monograph 51.* New York: International Universities Press.

Witkin, H. A., Goodenough, D. R., & Karp, S. A. (1967). Stability of cognitive style from childhood to young adulthood. *Journal of Personality & Social Psychology, 7,* 291–300.

Witkin, H. A., Goodenough, D. R., & Oltman, P. K. (1979). Psychological differentiation: Current status. *Journal of Personality and Social Psychology, 37,* 1127–1145.

Zimmerman, B. J. (1981). Social learning theory and cognitive constructivism. In I. Sigel, D. M. Brodzinsky, & R. Golinkoff (Eds.), *New directions in Piagetian theory and practice.* Hillsdale, NJ: Lawrence Erlbaum Associates.

8 Cognitive Styles as Moderators of Competence: A Commentary

Nathan Kogan
Graduate Faculty, New School for Social Research

INTRODUCTION

Although intellectual ancestors of cognitive styles can be traced back to antiquity (see Vernon, 1973), it is largely within the last three decades that cognitive styles have emerged as a major topic of research in differential and developmental psychology. A contemporary view (possibly the prevalent view) locates cognitive styles in the interface between intellective abilities, on the one hand, and motivational and personality processes, on the other.

Consistent with this view, much of the past and current research in the area of cognitive styles has sought to explore their relationship to the ability and motivational-personality domains. It is the former relationship that constitutes the focus of David Brodzinsky's admirable chapter. Though that author acknowledges the role of "affective structures" in his proposed "differentiation" model, these structures do not receive the full-scale treatment that is given the cognitive structures presumed to account for variation in ability. This comment is not intended to fault Brodzinsky, for a thorough discussion of cognition-affect relations would require a separate chapter in its own right.

It is important to note that the typical approach to style-ability relationships is somewhat different from that discussed by Brodzinsky. Consider how most research on field dependence-independence (FDI) and reflection-impulsivity (R-I) has looked at the IQ construct. FDI is supposed to relate to abilities that are of an analytic nature—such as the Block Design subtest of the WISC—but is not expected to relate to performance on verbal subtests of the WISC (Witkin, Dyk, Faterson, Goodenough, & Karp, 1962).

In other words, a particular type of intelligence is actually assimilated within the cognitive style at issue. The reflection-impulsivity (R-I) construct, on the other hand, has typically been examined in relation to IQ from the standpoint of discriminant validity. The error component of the MFFT is consistently related to IQ, but the moderate magnitude of the correlations suggests that R-I cannot be reduced to IQ (see Messer, 1976). In sum, in the case of the two most heavily researched cognitive styles – (FDI and R-I), the exploration of style-ability relationships has been carried out within a predominantly individual-differences perspective.

It is to the credit of Brodzinsky that he has expanded upon that perspective in two important ways. Given that the conventional individual-differences approach – simultaneous assessment of the variables at issue – skirts the matter of causal priority, we are clearly indebted to Brodzinsky for a set of longitudinal data offering the possibility of teasing out causal sequences through the application of recently developed causal-modeling techniques. Of equal importance is the addition of the cognitive-developmental perspective. Choosing to assess Piagetian operations rather than strictly psychometric abilities, Brodzinsky has placed cognitive styles solidly within a dominant cognitive-developmental tradition. Of course, other developmentalists have had similar goals (and Brodzinsky offers an excellent review of their work), but none have gathered the sort of longitudinal data that Brodzinsky describes in his chapter.

As much as I value Brodzinsky's chapter, the role of commentator requires that I criticize as well as praise. This is no simple task, for Brodzinsky's presentation is well balanced and modest in the sense of recognizing the possibility of alternative interpretations to his own. He is well aware that the use of advanced quantitative techniques (such as causal modeling) with nonexperimental data does not necessarily guarantee the accuracy of inferences about causal direction. Other unlisted variables may in fact have causal priority over those actually employed in the research. Though formulated within the framework of the competence-performance distinction, the Brodzinsky chapter is even willing to acknowledge that alternative, possibly more adequate, formulations may be feasible. In short, the chapter's "openendedness" does not make it an easy target for criticism. Further, given my sympathy with the general goals of the chapter, it naturally follows that my critique will concern matters of emphasis. Brodzinsky's allegiance to the Piagetian enterprise is somewhat stronger than mine, and that is bound to make for some differences in opinion concerning what is of greater or lesser importance.

THE CONCEPTUALIZATION OF COGNITIVE STYLES

In his definition of cognitive styles, Brodzinsky is willing to acknowledge their dispositional nature but he is hesitant to label them traits for that would "imply that individuals are characterized by one dimension or polar end of a style but not another" (p. 149). A looser framework is preferred that allows for balance and flexibility. Witkin and Goodenough (1981) have coined the term "mobility of functions" to indicate that FI individuals may manifest FD behavior in certain contexts, and FD individuals may manifest FI behavior in other contexts.

The difficulty in the above formulation is its disdain for measurement constraints. There is good reason to believe that cognitive-style measures generate normal distributions. Children located at the extremes of the R-I dimension (assessed by latency and error performance) should be most consistent in their manifestation of a reflective or impulsive style. If this were not the case, the validity of the R-I dimension itself would have to be questioned. Of course, as one moves away from the extremes to the middle of the distribution, children will necessarily be less distinctively reflective or impulsive, and hence it would not be at all surprising to find these children employing both reflective and impulsive strategies contingent upon the situation.

Are we then not ascribing trait-like qualities to cognitive styles? To the degree that convergent and discriminant validity can be demonstrated, cognitive styles would fulfill trait-like criteria. On the convergent-validity side, the evidence (e.g., Witkin et al., 1962) is fairly impressive for the various indices of FDI (e.g., Embedded Figures Test, Rod-and-Frame Test, Body-Adjustment Test, WISC Block Design). Similarly in the initial R-I monograph (Kagan, Rosman, Day, Albert, & Philips, 1964) and in subsequent publications (see Kagan & Kogan, 1970), much evidence was brought to bear pointing to considerable generality across perceptual tasks distinguished by response uncertainty. On the side of discriminant validity with reference to diverse abilities, the evidence is more mixed. The search for such discriminant validity may be a misguided effort, however, if, in fact, cognitive styles are causally implicated in the development of abilities.

The point at issue, of course, is that one cannot have a meaningful dispositional variable (whether or not one chooses to call it a trait), and at the same time have complete mobility of functions. Brodzinsky is aware of this problem and attempts to resolve it by endowing children with "preferences for certain modes of adapting as opposed to others" (p. 149). In other words, children have a diversity of strategies in their repertoire, but have a systematic preference for the utilization of one of these strategies relative to possible others. This writer must confess to a certain unease in regard to the foregoing formulation. If one considers the criterial tasks for assessing FDI, they do not have the flavor of strategy selection. I seriously doubt whether the child reviews possible strategies for finding a simple figure embedded in a complex geometric form or for setting a rod to the true vertical, and then proceeds to utilize one of these strategies in preference to others. Similarly, in the R-I area, it appears unlikely that the child embarks upon the MFFT and other match-to-sample tasks with a multitude of strategies, and then deliberately chooses one of these when seeking the variant that is identical to the standard. In the case of both FDI and R-I, in other words, I suspect that there is little conscious deliberation on the part of children concerning the most appropriate strategy, but rather an immediate selection of a strategy consistent with children's dispositional tendencies.

The foregoing argument does not imply, of course, that new (more optimal) strategies for solving EFT and MFFT items cannot be taught. Connor and her colleagues (Connor, Schackman, & Serbin, 1977; Connor, Serbin, & Schackman, 1978) have had notable success in improving female children's performance on EFT items, and several investigators (e.g., Egeland, 1974; Meichenbaum & Goodman, 1971; Zelniker, Cochavi, & Yered, 1974) have succeeded in training impulsive children to adopt more reflective strategies on the MFFT. What remains unclear, however, is the extent to which these newly taught strategies represent a short-term effect, in which children revert back to their "natural" dispositional tendency after an interval of time. In this regard, Brodzinsky's proposal to examine training effects within a longitudinal context would offer an opportunity to assess the relative impact of dispositional tendencies and experimental modification efforts over an extended period of time. Such research would go a long way toward informing us of the value of experimental training programs in the cognitive-style domain.

Let us return for a moment to the issue of spontaneous strategy selection and use. The description offered by Brodzinsky may in fact be quite valid for what I have elsewhere (Kogan, 1973, 1976) called Type II and III cognitive styles. Consider styles of conceptualization, for example. On the Conceptual Styles Test (Kagan, Moss, & Sigel, 1963), a set of triads is offered that allows for three kinds of pairings—analytic, relational, and categorical. A variety of evidence (see Kagan & Kogan, 1970; Kogan, 1976) indicates that children by their early elementary-school years recognize the multiple possibilities of the Conceptual Styles Test and when asked for their preferred pairings, adopt a selection strategy leading to a solution perceived to be more elegant. For some children, the "elegant" solution might be the least obvious; for other children, the "elegant" solution might be the most imaginative. That children have multiple options available is demonstrated by the extreme ease with which they will switch from one strategy to another consistent with the modeling of one or another strategy by the experimenter (Denney, 1972). In short, the domain of conceptualization styles conforms to Brodzinsky's proposal of a preferential hierarchy of strategies, whereas his proposal appears less appropriate for the cognitive styles—FDI and R-I—with which the bulk of his chapter is concerned.

The emphasis on FDI and R-I, as noted by Brodzinsky, reflects the fact that these are the two styles that have been examined in relation to the emergence and expression of operative thought. On these grounds, styles of conceptualization and breadth of categorization have been excluded from consideration. Such exclusion is quite legitimate, of course, for neither of those topics has been examined in the context of "moderators of competence." It is only fair to point out, however, that the cognitive-developmental phenomena subsumed by conceptual styles and category breadth are highly germane to the Piagetian enterprise. Developmental shifts from complementarity to similarity in mode of classification and from perceptual to abstract bases for similarity judgment have preoccupied all of the major cognitive developmental theorists — Piagetian (e.g., Inhelder & Piaget, 1964) and non-Piagetian (Bruner, Olver, & Greenfield, 1966; Vygotsky, 1962; Werner, 1948). The bridges between these diverse traditions have been examined and discussed in detail elsewhere (Denney, 1975; Denney & Moulton, 1976; Kagan & Kogan, 1970; Kogan, 1976). The point at issue here is that certain styles may act as "moderators of competence," whereas other styles may represent a direct reflection of competence as such. It is not at all clear, however, how these latter styles relate to competence.

One possibility is that the more competent child has more classification options available. Some findings reported by Denney and Moulton (1976) may serve to illustrate the foregoing theme. For children ranging in age from 3 to 9, the developmental transition for similarity classifications proceeded from perceptual through functional and nominal bases for grouping. The earliest perceptual classifications were based on common color, and there is reason to believe that this may be the dominant basis for similarity grouping for most children in the early preschool years. By age 9, of course, color dramatically declined as a grouping strategy, but there is little doubt that it is available in the classification repertoire of these older children and could be called upon where circumstances require it. In other words, the less preferred strategy in the case of the older child might well be the only similarity option available to the younger preschool child.

An alternative possibility (as elaborated by Kogan, 1976) is that all of the styles of classification are available from a very early age, but increase in sophistication and quality in older children. Research reported by Nelson (1973) is illustrative of the theme. That investigator demonstrated that both perceptible and functional bases for grouping are accessible to 2-year-olds, a surprising outcome in the light of other findings suggesting a developmental shift from perceptual to functional classifications around 7 to 8 years of age (Bruner et al., 1966). As Nelson (1973) observed, however, there is no real disagreement; functional groupings become less concrete and more abstract, and perceptible groupings become less global and more analytic as the child develops across the age span in question. Within such a framework, competence would not necessarily be tied to the availability of multiple grouping options, but instead to the abstract or analytic character of concepts most preferred by the child.

SOME REFLECTIONS ON FIELD
DEPENDENCE-INDEPENDENCE

It is to Brodzinsky's credit that he has included a section on FDI in his chapter, despite his failure to include that style in his research program. There are limits, of course, to what any single investigator can do, but one can only regret the lost opportunity to collect longitudinal data linking FDI and Piagetian operations. The intriguing aspect of that linkage has to do with the conflicting predictions that derive from current formulations of FDI theory (e.g., Witkin, Goodenough, & Oltman, 1979). On the one hand, FI children are described as exhibiting greater autonomy in relation to both the social and nonsocial world, whereas FD children are presumed to be more connected to others in their environment. On the basis of these assertions, one might well expect FD children to excel (relative to their FI peers) on a perspective-taking task requiring that one infer what the world looks like through the eyes of another. On the other hand, the perspective-taking task employed by Brodzinsky (a modified version of Piaget's three-mountain task) is cast in a form that requires spatial visualization, a skill at which FI children have been shown to excel. Supportive evidence for the latter view is provided in Brodzinsky's chapter. Conceivably, FD children will be at an advantage only on perspective-taking tasks cast in verbal form (e.g., telling a story from the perspective of each of its characters in turn). It is also conceivable that perspective-taking tasks (regardless of spatial or verbal format) require that an analytic set be brought to bear, hence offering a general advantage to the FI child. These are some of the issues that, in hindsight, I wish that Brodzinsky had addressed in his research. From this writer's biased point of view, these issues are as interesting, possibly even more interesting, than the study of the relation between R-I and perspective taking.

Brodzinsky is clearly aware of the importance of FDI vis-à-vis Piagetian operations, but defends his choice to omit FDI on the grounds that R-I is a child-based construct, whereas FDI (particularly the interpersonal aspect linked to FD) has been largely adult centered. This writer is puzzled by the foregoing rationale in the light of a number of highly relevant FDI studies based on samples of preschoolers (see the review by Kogan, 1976) and older children (see the review by Kogan, 1983). Indeed, if the evidence for the greater social adaptiveness of FD individuals is in fact primarily adult based, as claimed by Brodzinsky, one might argue that the need for research on child populations is all the more warranted.

There are other aspects of Brodzinsky's discussion of FDI (and its comparison with R-I) that, in this writer's judgment, are slightly off target. Brodzinsky appears to accept in toto the revised version of FDI theory (e.g., Witkin & Goodenough, 1981) whereby both the FI and FD poles are presumed to have positive, though distinctive, value. The former is linked to restructuring skills, the latter to interpersonal competencies. Whereas the association between FI and restructuring engenders little controversy, there is considerable doubt whether the alleged interpersonal superiority of the FD person is reflective of genuine skill in the social sphere or is instead merely indicative of a social orientation.

Nakamura and Finck (1980) have shown how socially oriented children divided on the basis of their effectiveness (as indexed by self-reports of self-assurance) manifest behavioral differences in diverse situations. Further, a social orientation whether or not effective was associated with higher levels of FD. Within the FD category, in other words, it is apparently feasible to distinguish the socially oriented from the socially effective children.

As we have seen, there is an obvious social element in a perspective-taking task, yet the FI child (on the basis of the empirical evidence available thus far) is better at it when the task is spatial in character. As indicated earlier, we do not yet have enough evidence to judge whether this superiority generalizes to nonspatial perspective-taking tasks. What is clearly needed, then, is a better specification of the distinctive interpersonal competencies associated with FD and FI. The major obstacle at present to such further specification is the one-dimensional measurement constraint inherent to the FDI construct. Indexing a strength in the interpersonal area by means of a deficit in perception of the upright or in restructuring ability poses both conceptual and methodological difficulties (see Kogan, 1980). There may well be distinctive social sensitivities and competencies associated with FI and FD. The further delineation of these remains a task for the future.

The bipolar and purportedly value-free version of FDI theory contrasts with the dominant conceptualization of R-I in which an impulsive style is viewed as basically maladaptive. Though Brodzinsky acknowledges the possibility that an impulsive style might have as yet unspecified adaptive functions in adulthood, it is rather surprising that no mention is made of the efforts of Zelniker and Jeffrey (1976, 1979) to render R-I less value laden in childhood through the demonstration that reflectives are better at analysis of detail whereas impulsives are better at global analysis. The impact of the Zelniker and Jeffrey research for Piagetian operations is far from clear. Reflective children are at an advantage relative to their impulsive peers on both conservation and spatial perspective-taking tasks (Barstis & Ford, 1977; Brodzinsky, 1980, 1982). No one has raised the question of whether there are any Piagetian operations that might be facilitated by a global type of analysis. Conceivably, no such operations exist, the advantage for the impulsive child possibly lying in domains where more intuitive, holistic approaches are adaptive.

THE COMPETENCE-PERFORMANCE DISTINCTION

Since its introduction to the field of developmental psychology in the Flavell and Wohlwill (1969) essay, the idea in one form or another of a competence-performance distinction has gathered a number of adherents and continues as an active focus of theoretical and empirical inquiry to the present day. As Brodzinsky has noted, the competence-performance distinction bridges the philosophical perspectives of rationalism and empiricism, and this no doubt contributes to its considerable appeal. In its earlier application, the failure of competence to be reflected in performance was frequently attributed to interfering task factors (e.g., lack of familiarity, ambiguity). Special problems arise, however, when one invokes cognitive organismic factors to account for competence-performance discrepancies. In such cases, there may be a kind of formal equivalence between the interfering entity and the phenomenon to be explained. Thus, although cognitive styles and Piagetian operative structures derive from disparate theoretical traditions, the assessment instruments deriving from those traditions may be tapping quite similar psychological processes. Indeed, to carry the argument one step further, it is possible to apply the notion of a competence-performance distinction to cognitive styles in their own right.

As discussed elsewhere (Kogan, 1976), the geometric format of an embedded-figures test is presumed to make too great a demand on the attentional capacities of younger children, and hence embedded figures with meaningful content have been constructed to allow for a more adequate representation of children's "competence" in the FDI domain (Coates, 1972; Witkin, Oltman, Raskin, & Karp, 1971). A major point of contention, of course, focuses on the degree to which the new tests measure the same FDI construct as the original strictly geometric versions (Kojima, 1978). But the same kind of issue would surely arise if one were to modify Piagetian tasks of formal operations in an effort to eliminate their ambiguity and lack of structure, a suggestion recently put forth by Neimark (1981).

When task factors are cast in the role of "moderators of competence," there would very likely be some consensus on what to do to increase the familiarity or reduce the ambiguity of a task. It is relatively straightforward, for example, to increase familiarity through use of everyday materials in the construction of tasks, and to reduce ambiguities through the elimination of perceptually misleading cues. With cognitive styles in the role of moderator, however, the issue is considerably more complicated. There is the matter of which index to employ. Recent speculation by Witkin and Goodenough (1981), for example, suggests that the embedded-figures and rod-and-frame tests are tapping different components of FDI. Which should one select as a more reasonable moderator? Should one employ a "natural" index of FDI which is subject to performance decrements, or should one optimize the competence aspect of FDI by using a post-training measure. For example, Connor et al., (1978) observed that a brief training procedure not only raised FDI levels for young girls, but actually scrambled the girls' post-training relative to initial FDI rank ordering. Presumably, these post-training scores are more reflective of competence than the pre-training scores. R-I as well is subject to training effects wherein impulsive children adopt more efficient and/or reflective scanning strategies. All of the foregoing leads to the general question of how alleged moderators of competence shall be assessed. Regrettably, I have no answers at hand for these difficult questions, though they are the kinds of questions with which one will have to deal if cognitive styles are to be cast as moderators in the form spelled out in Brodzinsky's chapter.

Let me assume the devil's advocate role for a moment. The title of Brodzinsky's chapter refers to cognitive styles and cognitive structures, which carries the implication that these are distinct entities. It will be granted that stylistic and structural constructs have emerged from different theoretical traditions, but is it the nature of the theory or the intrinsic character of the instruments devised to test that theory that is the critical determinant of whether things are the same or different? Thus, if a task analysis should suggest that comparable cognitive processes are involved in the solution of formal-operations problems and embedded figures, how would it then be possible to maintain a distinction between styles and structures? There is in fact evidence indicating that FDI measures and various Piagetian operations load on common factors (e.g., Linn & Kyllonen, 1981; Linn & Swiney, 1981).

An obvious response to the foregoing argument is that the kinds of cognitive operations examined within the Piagetian tradition have an obvious end state. When conservation of weight, for example, is finally achieved, it assumes virtually the identical form in all children, and hence one can speak of universal cognitive structures that continue essentially intact over the remainder of the life span. Cognitive styles clearly do not lend themselves to a universal-achievement framework. They require the presence of individual variation at each "stage" of life, and, in fact, age-relevant instruments are constructed to ensure that such variation be maintained. Thus, in the FDI area, there are preschool, children's, and adult forms of the Embedded-Figures Test.

This contrast between universal achievement and lifelong individual variation clearly breaks down, however, when formal operational structures are at issue. It has been apparent for some time now that there is no universally achieved end state for formal operations, hence implying the presence of individual variation from early adolescence onward. Under these circumstances, distinctions between structures and styles (indeed, between competence and performance) become quite moot, and one can only wonder whether the issue reduces to the study of associations between performance on diverse kinds of problem-solving tasks. This represents the extreme psychometric position, of course. It is a position that Brodzinsky would almost surely reject, though he does endorse the views of Pascual-Leone and Case. These authors retain their adherence to a competence-performance contrast, but with considerable flexibility regarding the articulation of structures and styles with that contrast. This represents a middle ground between a strictly psychometric and a conventional competence-performance view, and I regret that the relative merits and liabilities of these three conceptualizations were not discussed more extensively in Brodzinsky's chapter.

One final point deserves consideration in the present context. Brodzinsky discusses unpublished research by De Lisi in the area of style-structure relationships that involves the attenuation of differences between FI and FD style groups on a Piagetian task (horizontality) through modification of some style-relevant aspect of that task. On the basis of such outcomes, De Lisi concluded that the observed differences are a reflection of performance rather than of competence. The task has become solvable by those initially unable to solve it. One can bring an alternative perspective to bear on the above phenomenon, however. When De Lisi removed misleading perceptual cues, there is good reason to believe that the problem became easier. This may simply reflect the fact that it was transformed into an easier problem. With particularly difficult problems, it is possible to offer a succession of hints that render such problems more accessible to progressively increasing numbers of individuals. One is simply lowering the hurdles or thresholds for problem solution. The critical question, of course, is whether the foregoing phenomenon makes better sense within a competence-performance framework or within a context of hierarchies of task difficulty. Is this devil's advocacy or an inherently reasonable alternative?

CAUSAL INFERENCES FROM LONGITUDINAL DATA

The unique aspect of Brodzinsky's chapter is the discussion of a set of longitudinal data analyzed from the perspective of causal sequencing. The reported outcomes appear to favor the view that a child's cognitive style at a particular age has a causal influence on his or her level of spatial perspective taking 2 years later. This is a finding of some importance, for the availability of longitudinal data sets has not inevitably led investigators to subject such data to causal-modeling analyses.

The ultimate issue, of course, concerns the degree of confidence that attaches to the outcomes reported. Brodzinsky's confidence cannot be especially high, given that he concludes his chapter allowing for the possibility that operative structures might influence the development of cognitive styles. Indeed, a quick glance at the differentiation model offered in Fig. 7.2 indicates a one-way causal sequence proceeding from cognitive structures to cognitive styles. It is difficult to know what to make of this discrepancy between an apparently unambiguous set of empirical findings and conclusions that are either equivocal or even in an opposing direction. Is it perhaps possible that Brodzinsky appreciates the feasibility of drawing causal inferences from nonexperimental data, while at the same time acknowledging that the analytic procedures employed cannot clarify the conceptual basis for the observed effects? We simply do not know *why* style, rather than structure, proved to be the causal agent in the present context. Given the present state of knowledge, then, it follows that one would not want to invest too much in a particular causal sequence. Another set of stylistic and structural variables might enter into a different kind of causal relationship. In sum, the application of causal modeling to the relation between style and structure has brought us to a state of limbo. It is evident that a considerable body of longitudinal data employing a multiplicity of stylistic and structural variables will have to be collected before the basis for directional effects can be effectively understood.

This commentary is clearly not the place for a technical discussion of structural equation models. Yet, this writer sorely missed some backstage information about the Jöreskog and Sörbom (1976) method. Within the psychological literature over the past decade, the cross-lagged panel method initially proposed by Campbell and Stanley (1963) has probably been the most popular technique for drawing causal inferences from longitudinal data. This technique has had its staunch proponents (e.g., Kenny, 1979) and its severe critics (e.g., Rogosa, 1980).

Certain psychometric assumptions regarding reliabilities and variable intercorrelations within and across time have to be met before the technique can be applied. Further, when examining possible causal relations between stylistic and structural variables, the variance problem must be of some concern. The trait-like quality of cognitive styles ensures that variances will remain reasonably constant across the childhood years. Piagetian structural operations, on the other hand, often imply a sequence proceeding from near-universal absence of the operation through a transitional acquisition period and terminating in complete mastery of the operation. Such a sequence must necessarily imply an inverted-U distribution of increasing and decreasing variances. Are such matters of no concern in the case of the Jöreskog and Sörbom (1976) methods? If the answer is no, then developmentalists have indeed been given a powerful tool. But, then, how is one to account for Brodzinsky's reservations? Although one would not expect a causal-modeling technique to prove that a particular directional effect is valid, one would at least hope that alternative outcomes could be discarded as unlikely to have truth value. In the absence of the latter, the point of causal modeling with longitudinal data is lost.

Much emphasis is given by Brodzinsky to the use of error-pattern analysis for teasing out developmental transitions. What remains less than clear, however, is the reason why style-structure relationships are reflected by error patterns at earlier ages and by sheer number correct at later ages. These interesting outcomes clearly are in need of an adequate theoretical explanation.

Perhaps, it would be useful to have such theorizing precede rather than follow the application of causal modeling.

TRAINING EFFECTS

As a preferred substitute to causal-modeling techniques with longitudinal data, Brodzinsky has proposed research in which styles or operative structures are taught with the aim of observing effects on operative structures or styles, respectively. If the directional effects should prove asymmetrical, inferences could be drawn regarding the causal directionality of the effect. In the present context, the demonstration that training for reflectivity enhanced spatial perspective taking would be consistent with the causal-modeling outcomes, if it were also shown that training in perspective taking did not increase reflectivity.

One can only admire the courage of Brodzinsky for undertaking research fraught with so many pitfalls. If an asymmetrical training effect should be obtained, how could one be sure that the results are not simply a reflection of the differential effectivenss of the training techniques employed. A large number of modification studies in the R-I domain (see Messer, 1976) have generated a set of procedures virtually guaranteed to reduce impulsivity (though not to the extent of rendering reflective and impulsive children indistinguishable). To the best of my knowledge, such powerful techniques for training spatial perspective taking have not been reported in the developmental literature, though the possibility of constructing effective training devices cannot be denied.

It is possible, of course, to examine the relative magnitude of the training effect within the style and structure domains. If such research should demonstrate the sticking power of the immediate post-training changes over a period of months (in comparison to changes observed in appropriate control groups), this would represent a set of findings of considerable significance for the present field of study. Only if such long-term effects are observed does it seem likely that transfer effects to a different class of tasks can be anticipated. It is difficult enough to obtain training effects within a domain such as match-to-sample tasks, let alone finding transfer to a different class of tasks. Further, the form of training best suited for obtaining within-domain effects may not be the most appropriate for producing cross-domain effects. Consider an example from the R-I area. Egeland (1974) was quite successful in teaching scanning strategies to reduce errors and increase latencies on the MFFT. The emphasis in the training was on decomposition of MFFT items—the standard and the variants—for the purpose of demonstrating the utility of feature matching. Such training would seem to be highly specific to match-to-sample procedures, and hence it is difficult to appreciate the benefit of such training for the domain of perspective taking.

In contrast, a training procedure such as reinforcement for delay and correct response (e.g., Briggs & Weinberg, 1973), though only partially successful in modifying R-I, might have a more generalized effect by virtue of enhancement of motivation to perform well on cognitive tasks. These are speculative conjectures, to be sure, but they do raise an important issue for any investigator searching for extended and cross-domain effects of a modification effort.

There is much to recommend the use of FDI measures (along with R-I) in the kind of training program envisioned. The inclusion of both styles, in fact, would permit one to examine the relative efficacy of task format and task content in promoting transfer-of-training effects. As indicated earlier, FDI and perspective taking share the property of spatial visualization. On the other hand, perspective taking as assessed by Brodzinsky (1982) requires the choice of one among a number of alternatives consistent with the format of the MFFT (though the latter offers a standard whereas the former does not). Both tasks, however, are distinguished by response uncertainty. Similarly, despite the shared spatial character of FDI measures and perspective taking, the former provide explicitly misleading cues, whereas the latter does not. Elsewhere (Kogan, 1983), I have discussed the paradoxical quality of training for FI in a purportedly value-free conceptual system. This issue is of tangential relevance, however, in a context where one is deliberately attempting to enhance children's performance in a context of spatial visualization.

CONCLUSIONS

For years, there has been much speculation about possible causal linkages between cognitive styles and abilities, but no genuine effort to explore the issue empirically. Brodzinsky has broken through the empirical barrier, and in the process has succeeded in bringing cognitive styles into the center of the cognitive-developmental arena. This is no small accomplishment, and must be kept in the foreground when contemplating the critical comments offered in the previous pages of this chapter. One cannot afford to forget that Brodzinsky's work represents an *initial* effort to derive causal inference in the present domain from nonexperimental longitudinal data. We may wish that the study had been more ambitious and that it included more of our favorite variables, but that burden will surely shift to others as causal modeling becomes more prevalent in the developmental area. This is not an invitation to join a bandwagon, of course, for, as I have tried to show, there are numerous pitfalls in the use of cognitive styles as "moderators of competence." There is also much promise, if theoretical options are not foreclosed. It is evident that there are diverse ways of conceptualizing the relation of cognitive styles to the competence-performance distinction; these deserve to be considered on a comparative basis with the aim of elucidating their merits and shortcomings.

In an extended discussion of styles in childhood and adolescence (Kogan, 1983), this author suggested that cognitive-style research may have peaked and entered a period of decline. Brodzinsky's chapter has sowed doubts in my mind as to the validity of the foregoing judgment. If any antidote is to be found, the direction taken by Brodzinsky in his chapter offers much hope for continued theoretical and empirical progress within the cognitive-style domain.

REFERENCES

Barstis, S. W., & Ford, L. H., Jr. (1977). Reflection-impulsivity, conservation, and the development of ability to control cognitive tempo. *Child Development, 48,* 953–959.

Briggs, C. H., & Weinberg, R. A. (1973). Effects of reinforcement in training children's conceptual tempo. *Journal of Educational Psychology, 65,* 383–394.

Brodzinsky, D. M. (1980). Cognitive style differences in children's spatial perspective taking. *Developmental Psychology, 16,* 151–152.

Brodzinsky, D. M. (1982). The relationship between cognitive style and cognitive development: A two-year longitudinal study. *Developmental Psychology, 18,* 617–626.

Bruner, J. S., Olver, R. R., & Greenfield, P. M. (1966). *Studies in cognitive growth.* New York: Wiley.

Campbell, D. T., & Stanley, J. C. (1963). *Experimental and quasi-experimental designs for research.* Chicago: Rand McNally.

Coates, S. (1972). *Preschool embedded figures test.* Palo Alto, CA: Consulting Psychologists Press.

Connor, J. M., Schackman, M., & Serbin, L. A. (1978). Sex-related differences in response to practice on a visual-spatial test and generalization to a related test. *Child Development, 49,* 24–29.

Connor, J. M., Serbin, L. A., & Schackman, M. (1977). Sex differences in children's response to training on a visual-spatial test. *Developmental Psychology, 13,* 293–294.

Denney, D. R. (1972). Modeling effects upon conceptual style and cognitive tempo. *Child Development, 43,* 105–119.

Denney, D. R. (1975). Developmental changes in concept utilization among normal and retarded children. *Developmental Psychology, 11,* 359–368.

Denney, D. R., & Moulton, P. A. (1976). Conceptual preferences among preschool children. *Developmental Psychology, 12,* 509–513.

Egeland, B. (1974). Training impulsive children in the use of more efficient scanning techniques. *Child Development, 45,* 165–171.

Flavell, J. H., & Wohlwill, J. F. (1969). Formal and functional aspects of cognitive development. In D. Elkind & J. H. Flavell (Eds.), *Studies in cognitive development.* New York: Oxford University Press.

Inhelder, B., & Piaget, J. (1964). *The early growth of logic in the child.* New York: Harper & Row.

Jöreskog, K. G., & Sörbom, D. (1976). *Lisrel III: Estimation of linear structural equation systems by maximum-likelihood methods.* Chicago: National Educational Resources.

Kagan, J., & Kogan, N. (1970). Individual variation in cognitive proesses. In P. H. Mussen (Ed.), *Carmichael's manual of child psychology* (Vol. 1). New York: Wiley.

Kagan, J., Moss, H. A., & Sigel, I. E. (1963). Psychological significance of styles of conceptualization. In J. C. Wright & J. Kagan (Eds.), *Basic cognitive processes in children. Monographs of the Society for Research in Child Development, 28* (2, Serial No. 86).

Kagan, J., Rosman, B. L., Day, D., Albert, J., & Philips, W. (1964). Information processing in the child: Significance of analytic and reflective attitudes. *Psychological Monographs, 78* (1, Whole No. 578).

Kenny, D. A. (1979). *Correlation and causality.* New York: Wiley.

Kogan, N. (1973). Creativity and cognitive style: A life-span perspective. In P. B. Baltes & K. W. Schaie (Eds.), *Life-span developmental psychology: Personality and socialization.* New York: Academic Press.

Kogan, N. (1976). *Cognitive styles in infancy and early childhood.* Hillsdale, NJ: Lawrence Erlbaum Associates.

Kogan, N. (1980). A style of life, a life of style. (A review of *Cognitive styles in personal and cultural adaptation* by H. A. Witkin). *Contemporary Psychology, 25,* 595–598.

Kogan, N. (1983). Stylistic variation in childhood and adolescence: Creativity, metaphor, and cognitive styles. In J. H. Flavell & E. M. Markman (Eds.), *Handbook of child psychology: Vol. 3. Cognitive development.* (P. H. Mussen, General Ed.) New York: Wiley.

Kojima, H. (1978). Assessment of field dependence in young children. *Perceptual and Motor Skills, 46,* 479–492.

Linn, M. C., & Kyllonen, P. (1981). The field dependence-independence construct: Some, one, or none. *Journal of Educational Psychology, 73,* 261–273.

Linn, M. C., & Swiney, J. F., Jr. (1981). Individual differences in formal thought: Role of expectations and aptitudes. *Journal of Educational Psychology, 73,* 274–286.

Meichenbaum, D. H., & Goodman, J. (1971). Training impulsive children to talk to themselves: A means of developing self-control. *Journal of Abnormal Psychology, 77,* 115–126.

Messer, S. (1976). Reflection-impulsivity: A review. *Psychological Bulletin, 83,* 1026–1053.

Nakamura, C. Y., & Finck, D. N. (1980). Relative effectiveness of socially-oriented and task-oriented children and predictability of their behaviors. *Monographs of the Society for Research in Child Development, 45,* (3–4, Serial No. 185).

Neimark, E. D. (1981). Confounding with cognitive style factors: An artifact explanation for the apparent nonuniversal incidence of formal operations. In I. Sigel, D. Brodzinsky, & R. Golinkoff (Eds.), *Piagetian theory and research: New directions and applications.* Hillsdale, NJ: Lawrence Erlbaum Associates.

Nelson, K. (1973). Some evidence for the cognitive primacy of categorization and its functional basis. *Merrill-Palmer Quarterly, 19,* 21–40.

Vernon, P. E. (1973). Multivariate approaches to the study of cognitive styles. In J. R. Royce (Ed.), *Multivariate analysis and psychological theory.* New York: Academic Press.

Vygotsky, L. S. (1962). *Thought and language.* Cambridge, MA: MIT Press.

Werner, H. (1948). *Comparative psychology of mental development.* Chicago: Follett.

Witkin, H. A., Dyk, R. B., Faterson, H. F., Goodenough, D. R., & Karp, S. A. (1962). *Psychological differentiation.* New York: Wiley.

Witkin, H. A., & Goodenough, D. R. (1981). *Cognitive styles: Essence and origins.* New York: International Universities Press.

Witkin, H. A., Goodenough, D. R., & Oltman, P. K. (1979). Psychological differentiation: Current status. *Journal of Personality and Social Psychology, 37,* 1127–1145.

Witkin, H. A., Oltman, P. K., Raskin, E., & Karp, S. A. (1971). *A manual for the children's embedded figures test.* Palo Alto, CA: Consulting Psychologists Press.

Zelniker, T., Cochavi, D., & Yered, J. (1974). The relationship between speed of performance and conceptual style: The effect of imposed modification of response latency. *Child Development, 45,* 779–784.

Zelniker, T., & Jeffrey, W. E. (1976). Reflective and impulsive children: Strategies of information processing underlying differences in problem solving. *Monographs of the Society for Research in Child Development, 41,* (5, Serial No. 168).

Zelniker, T., & Jeffrey, W. E. (1979). Attention and cognitive styles in children. In G. A. Hale & M. Lewis (Eds.), *Attention and cognitive development.* New York: Plenum Press.

9 Taking Charge of One's Cognitive Activity: A Moderator of Competence

Monique Lefebvre-Pinard
Adrien Pinard
University of Quebec at Montreal

After some preliminary considerations on the notion of moderators of competence and on the current distinction between competence and performance, the main part of this chapter consists in presenting an integrative model that describes the major components involved in an individual's taking charge of her cognitive functioning, and that shows in what way and how such a taking charge constitutes a crucial factor in the moderation of competence.

COMPETENCE, PERFORMANCE, AND THE MODERATION OF COMPETENCE

We have deliberately chosen to call moderators of intellectual competence the factors that influence not only the use or activation of competence, which is assumed to be already acquired, but also the very acquisition of this competence, accentuating more the "how" than the "what" of this acquisition. In this perspective, the classic distinction between competence and performance seems considerably less important than when just availability (i.e., what one *can* do) and accessibility (i.e., what one *does* do) are contrasted since most of the factors usually considered to influence performance also influence the acquisition of the corresponding competence.

We are all aware of the significance that this distinction between competence and performance has had in cognitive developmental psychology. It would be an interesting diversion, in fact, to trace its origin to the very old distinction certain philosophers in the Aristotelian tradition made among what they called *potentia pura* (the fundamental capacity to acquire an aptitude), *actus primus* (the acquisition of this aptitude), and *actus secundus* (the utilization of this aptitude). Be that as it may, however, it is Chomsky who made the competence/performance distinction famous in linguistics, and Flavell and Wohlwill (1969) who picked it up and tried to apply it to cognitive development.

Despite the commonsense appeal of this distinction (we do not always use an aptitude we possess), it raises serious problems of both a theoretical and an empirical nature; Flavell and Wohlwill (1969) were themselves conscious of these problems, as is Sternberg (this volume), who made this distinction the keystone of his model. To illustrate, first, the *theoretical* difficulty of this distinction, it may be useful to recall Chomsky's (1979) statement to the effect that "linguistic competence (the knowledge of the language) constitutes only one of the factors in performance" (p. 84) and that "there is, first of all, the question of how one is to obtain information about the speaker-hearer's competence, about his knowledge of the language" (1965, p. 18). Recall also the position of Premack (1979) who said he "always supposed that the aptitude for using a capacity was an integral part of that capacity" (p. 267). This led Jacques Monod (1979) to react immediately: "A man named Descartes already said the same thing" (p. 267), thus relating to what has been called the Cartesian dilemma, the problem of knowing in what way the use of a concept depends on having the concept.[1]

As to the difficulty of establishing *empirically* or operationally this theoretical (or "metatheoretical") distinction, the first problem stems from the fact that competence must be evaluated by performance itself, which remains, by definition, subject to the multiple contingencies affecting performance. It is not empirically obvious either that the failure to generalize to other fields the competence presumably acquired in a first field can be solely explained[2] by a simple failure of accessibility to the first competence without requiring the acquisition of a new competence.

Consider, for example, within the context of the conservation of volume, the Piagetian notion of *horizontal décalage*. Volume conservation is acquired much later than the conservation of substance or of weight and hinges on the child's ability to dissociate an object's surface area from its inner volume or capacity (Pinard & Chassé, 1977). Now, when one goes to the trouble of providing a sufficiently differentiated definition of horizontal décalage to account for the diversity of possible kinds (see, for example, Pinard, 1981; Pinard & Laurendeau, 1969) volume conservation is perhaps

---

[1]"Ce n'est pas assez d'avoir l'esprit bon, mais le principal est de l'appliquer bien" (Descartes).

[2]Obviously, purely peripheral factors like fatigue, distraction, etc. can also be responsible.

not to be explained—as, for example, Brown (1982) and Sternberg (this volume) have suggested—by later accessibility to a competence already acquired elsewhere, but by the *necessary* acquisition of a *new* competence.

In sum, it is difficult to overcome the impression that most of the so-called performance factors are in large part due to deficiencies of competence even though these factors ought, in principle, to mediate the utilization of competence. In other words, it is the availability of the processes that is missing and not only their accessibility. Thus, we are always faced with an inevitable contamination between competence and performance, precisely because of their theoretical and empirical interaction. This is perhaps what Cavanaugh and Perlmutter (1982) meant when they said: "one can never be certain whether impaired performance is due to faulty or absent use of well-articulated (memory) knowledge or 'efficient' use of inadequate knowledge" (p. 15). It is precisely this inevitable interaction that appears to us to raise what are probably unsolvable or, at the very least, still unsolved problems.

For all these reasons we simply prefer to forget this distinction between competence and performance or, at least, to view them on the same continuum as Goodnow has elegantly suggested (this volume). Thus, instead, we speak of moderators of competence, enlarging this notion to include the factors responsible both for the acquisition of competence, and for its use.

Among the numerous moderators of competence analyzed in this volume (e.g., schooling, cultural environment, etc.) we want to insist on one factor that seems to us quite crucial: the factor relating to the way in which an individual actually comes to take charge of her cognitive activities. It is not enough to learn to apply strategies or more efficient heuristics to attain objectives; it is also necessary to consciously get to know the strategies that are applied, in such a way as to be able to supervise their implantation and to evaluate if they, in fact, facilitate progress toward the objectives. This second aspect, having to do with the conscious knowledge and deliberate self-regulation of a cognitive enterprise, is essentially what this chapter is about.

This concern is far from being completely new. We could trace its origin to the pioneering work of Vygotsky (1934/1962). Indeed, Vygotsky was one of the first researchers in cognitive psychology to postulate a direct relationship between consciousness of one's cognitive processes and one's ability to control them, and to raise the problem of the conditions under which children eventually attain awareness and mastery of their own thoughts. This same concern has become more and more comprehensive and now shows up primarily in cognitive developmental psychology under the general heading of metacognition. Although a number of researchers (e.g., Baker & Brown, 1984; Flavell, 1981; Meichenbaum, 1981) are in agreement to include under this heading the knowledge that an individual can have of her cognitive functioning and the control that she can exert on her mode of cognitive functioning, others (e.g., Cavanaugh and Perlmutter, 1982) prefer to reserve the term for the knowledge that an individual has about her cognitive processes without including the executive processes that orchestrate cognition. We also found this concern in recent models of intelligence. For example, in the model of Sternberg (this volume), what he calls the metaprocesses or control strategies would be "the central intellectual competences of the human mind through which most, if not all, other competences come to be expressed." (p. 51). Similarly, Borkowski (in press), drawing on Campione and Brown's (1978) model, argues for the inclusion of metacognition in intelligence theory; given the close relationship existing between metacognition and the operation of control processes, the mature problem solver is assumed to integrate metacognitive knowledge with strategic behaviors (control processes) in solving problems.

In short, this ever-growing interest in metacognitive skills seems to us to again shed light on one of the capabilities of the human being that has been too long neglected by cognitive psychology: the capacity to take charge of the quality of one's own cognitive functioning and, in more general terms, to take charge of the development of one's own knowledge (Lefebvre-Pinard, 1980, 1983). The rest of this chapter is devoted to showing the crucial role of this factor as a moderator of intellectual competence.

TAKING CHARGE OF ONE'S COGNITIVE FUNCTIONING AS A MODERATOR OF COMPETENCE

After first presenting a sketch of an integrated model of what could be the essential components of an individual's taking charge of her own cognitive functioning, we show how these various components play a fundamental role as moderators of competence.

The components of the proposed model that are brought together draw upon different traditions that are more or less isolated from each other. First, the model draws upon the four components in Flavell's (1981) model of cognitive monitoring: cognitive goals, cognitive actions, metacognitive knowledge, and metacognitive experiences. It also borrows from the work of Brown and her colleagues (Baker & Brown, 1984; Brown, 1978) where the self-regulation of cognitive activities is emphasized, as are the executive processes at work while a cognitive enterprise is being carried out (see also Borkowski, in press, in this same vein). The model also takes account of two of the main aspects that have been highlighted by Meichenbaum's work (Meichenbaum, 1981; Meichenbaum & Asarnow, 1979; Meichenbaum, Burland, Gruson, & Cameron, in press) in a cognitive-behavioral perspective: the possibility of conscious access to cognitive and metacognitive activities and the interaction between cognition and emotion including the notion of the "internal dialogue" an individual engages in during the execution of a

task. Finally, the model accords an important place to Langer's work in social psychology (Chanowitz & Langer, 1980; Langer, 1978; Langer & Imber,
1980) where the essential distinction between mindfulness and mindlessness
seems to us to constitute a crucial component in taking charge of one's
cognition.

Figure 9.1 presents the general framework resulting from the integration
of these various components. In brief, the model proposes that an individual's taking charge of her cognitive functioning is based, first, on the *available
metacognitive knowledge* that she has about persons as cognitive agents,
sought-after objectives, cognitive and metacognitive strategies, and the nature of tasks. Taking charge also requires *on-line processes of self-regulation*
that take place during the execution of a particular task (learning, problem
solving, etc.). These self-regulatory processes (a) can be exercised according
to *a variable level of conscious cognitive attention,* (b) suppose *an activation*

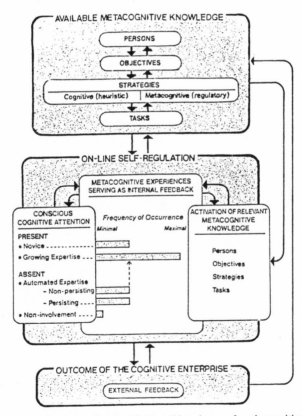

FIG. 9.1   The components involved in the taking charge of one's cognitive activity.

of metacognitive knowledge relevant to a given cognitive enterprise, and (c) are nourished by *metacognitive experiences that serve as internal feedback* to the individual and whose frequency of occurrence is in constant interaction with the activation of the relevant metacognitive knowledge and the level of conscious cognitive attention. Finally, it is *the outcome of a cognitive enterprise* that serves to validate, in the final analysis, the internal feedback that the individual gets from metacognitive experiences.

This is the general structure of the proposed model. It remains to be shown how the combined action and interaction of these various components can make the taking charge of cognition a crucial factor in the moderation of competence. We now examine the various components one by one.

Available Metacognitive Knowledge

The first component is the individual's available or existing metacognitive knowledge. It refers to the foundations on which her taking charge of a given cognitive enterprise is built. In a way, metacognitive knowledge constitutes the repertory of knowledge that an individual has accumulated on the different aspects of cognitive enterprises, and it can be called upon when needed. This is relatively stable knowledge that an individual is in possession of at a certain moment in her development, and it can be accessed even in the absence of a specific ongoing cognitive activity. This first component is largely borrowed from the notion of metacognitive knowledge developed by Flavell (1981). To the three variables (persons, strategies, tasks) involved in a cognitive task that, according to Flavell, can be the object of metacognitive knowledge, we believe that it is necessary to add a fourth variable bearing on the objectives that are being pursued in a cognitive enterprise.

First of all, the *persons* variable includes, according to Flavell, the knowledge an individual has accumulated about persons' (including her own) characteristics as cognitive agents. We believe that it is important to add a dimension that has been too often neglected by cognitive psychology: the awareness that an individual can come to have of the emotionally tainted internal dialogue she engages in while accomplishing a task and of the debilitating or facilitating effects that such a dialogue can have on her performance. The notion of an internal dialogue — discussed by Meichenbaum (1981) and that some members of his group have started to study experimentally (e.g., Henshaw, 1978) — seems to us crucial because it accounts for the expectations and attributions[3] that an individual expresses about her performance in a given task. The study of the impact that a person's knowledge about her cognitive resources exerts on the expression of competence in a given task,

---

[3]It is interesting to note that such expectations and attributions have been shown to be good predictors of performance in a variety of tasks (Bandura, 1977, 1980; Diener & Dweck, 1978).

therefore, appears to us incomplete if it does not include an evaluation of the individual's more or less explicit knowledge of the facilitating or debilitating aspects of the verbalizations that she makes to herself about her ability to succeed on a task.

In the second place, the *objectives* variable, which we have added to Flavell's three variables, refers to the explicit knowledge an individual may come to develop about the variety of objectives that may be in play in different cognitive enterprises and about the vital role they exercise on the planning and monitoring of a given cognitive enterprise. We believe that this form of metacognitive knowledge constitutes a particularly crucial moderator of competence: If an individual does not clearly identify in a given task which objective or series of objectives she chooses to pursue among all those that could be selected, she is scarcely in a position to apply the most appropriate cognitive strategies for making progress toward that objective nor the most effective strategies for monitoring her progress. As Brown (1982) has emphasized, the problem of selecting appropriate cognitive activities cannot be discussed without considering the question, "appropriate for what end?" An appropriate strategy must be one that is compatible with the desired end state. That is why it seems most essential that an individual comes to explicitly understand the importance of constantly keeping track of the end state she has in mind and of defining this desired end state relative to the specific uses to which the end product will subsequently be put. Such metacognitive knowledge must also be sufficiently differentiated for the individual to be able to recognize those cognitive enterprises for which there exists a clearly defined criterial task and those for which the objectives are not given in advance but instead require that she herself defines the desired end product as well as how hard she has to work on it. This last case frequently arises while reading a text, for example, when having to make the decision as to the degree and kind of understanding that is desirable to acquire and the use to which the knowledge acquired may eventually be put; this leads to setting criteria for comprehension that are either very demanding or simply satisfied by gleaning the gist of the text.

In the third place, *strategy* variables correspond to knowledge about the utility of cognitive and metacognitive strategies in one's repertoire and about how these strategies must be combined and sequenced in order to be able to carry out the given cognitive enterprise. It seems important to us to make a clear distinction between two components of metacognitive knowledge dealing with strategies, a distinction already suggested by Flavell himself (1981) but one which he does not seem to us to insist on enough. The most obvious component has to do with the knowledge about *cognitive* strategies; whether it is a matter of heuristics (e.g., Newell & Simon, 1972), of hierarchically organized conceptual rules (e.g., Gagné, 1968; Siegler, 1981) of lower order processes (Sternberg, this volume), or of schemata or procedures (Pascual-

Leone, 1980; Piaget, 1957), cognitives strategies always refer to the arsenal of means that a person has at her disposal while progressing toward the solution of a problem. These cognitive strategies are undoubtedly part of metacognitive knowledge but appear to us insufficient and of dubious efficiency unless they are seconded by a complementary metacognitive knowledge about *metacognitive* strategies whose function is to regulate progress toward the goal. For Brown (1978) such metacognitive or self-regulatory strategies include, for instance, checking the outcome of any attempt to solve a given problem, planning one's next move, monitoring the effectiveness of any attempted action, testing, revising, and reevaluating one's cognitive strategy, and so on. These metacognitive strategies are so general and transsituational that they are considered by Brown (e.g., Brown & Deloache, 1978) as prime candidates for what develops in cognitive development. Our concern in the present discussion, however, about available metacognitive knowledge is not with the specific realizations or applications of the metacognitive strategies, since this aspect is more directly related to the self-regulatory mechanisms that orchestrate cognition. The metacognitive knowledge base is exclusively concerned with knowledge about these strategies. What our model asserts is that to become an effective user of her cognitive system, an individual must come to know both the repertoire of "cognitive" strategies one has for making progress toward goals and the repertoire of "metacognitive" strategies one has available in order to monitor that progress before, during, and after an ongoing attempt to solve a given problem.

Finally, we have preserved in its entirety from Flavell's model (1981) the *tasks* variable of metacognitive knowledge. This variable refers to the knowledge an individual has accumulated on the differences that can exist from one task to another in terms of the quantity of information available and in terms of the implicit or explicit task demands and the impact that variations in task demands can have on the way to approach a given problem. What this definition brings out is that although each of these four types of variables is important in its own right, it is, in fact, rare that the metacognitive knowledge developed by an individual has to do with just one of these four variables; in the normal situation it has to do with the interaction among the "persons," "objectives," "strategies," and "tasks" variables for a given cognitive enterprise. It is probably by combining knowledge about several of these variables that an individual comes to develop differentiated knowledge of the compatibility between herself as an active cognitive agent and a given problem-solving situation.

What and how much an individual knows about particular aspects of cognitive enterprises seems to us to be a fundamental factor in the moderation of competence. As Brown (1982) has underlined, becoming an expert is largely the process of acquiring explicit knowledge about the rules, strategies, or goals needed for efficient performance. This topic is currently receiving a good deal of renewed attention in the literature. Prototypical of this type of research are studies using questionnaires and introspective interviews, whose main purpose is to find out how much children know about certain pertinent features of thinking, including themselves as thinkers, in such diverse areas as memory (Kreutzer, Leonard, & Flavell, 1975), reading comprehension (Myers & Paris, 1978; Kobasigawa, Ransom, & Holland, 1980), attentional processes (Miller & Bigi, 1979), or referential communication (Kurdek & Burt, 1981), and how this metacognitive knowledge may contribute to age-related improvements in cognitive performance (Cavanaugh & Borkowski, 1979, 1980; Salatas-Waters, 1982). Although it has been established that the amount of metacognitive knowledge increases with age, we still know very little about the origins of such knowledge, the ways in which the child acquires and organizes this knowledge, or the changes that come about with age in the characteristics and functions of this knowledge. Moreover, even for the adult, we lack basic information about the nature of individual differences related both to the content of metacognitive knowledge (this knowledge can be more or less complete, adequate, or differentiated) and to its structure (it can be loosely or well organized). More information is also needed on the problem of knowing in what way such variations can give rise to important differences in cognitive performance. That is why we believe that the content and structure of people's knowledge about their own cognitive processes deserve to be studied in their own right. As Cavanaugh and Perlmutter (1982) have recommended for the specific issue of metamemory, we believe that this study must be distinguished from the study of how effectively this knowledge is activated and translated into efficient self-regulation. To recognize explicitly the importance of studying metacognitive knowledge and its development seems particularly crucial for anybody interested in teaching both children and adults to become more effective users of their cognitive system. If we were able to identify and assess what aspects of metacognitive knowledge are needed to perform particular tasks in specific contexts, then it would be possible to help people acquire an explicit knowledge of the components and their interaction that affect their various cognitive enterprises.

On-line Self-Regulatory Processes

The second principal component of the model has to do with on-line self-regulatory processes. These processes appear to us to constitute an essential factor in the moderation of competence. The distinction between metacognitive knowledge, on the one hand, and self-regulatory processes that orchestrate cognition, on the other, is explicitly made by most of the researchers working in the field of metacognition (e.g., Baker & Brown, 1984; Flavell, 1981; Meichenbaum et al., in press). Although most of them agree that metacognitive knowledge can be derived from the use of executive processes and can contribute to their effectiveness, they nevertheless recognize two separate clusters of metacognitive abilities, which should be distinguished as such. Self-regulatory processes are concerned primarily with online executive mechanisms that orchestrate cognition during an ongoing attempt to learn or to solve problems. Self-regulatory processes, which have also been called executive mechanisms (Neisser, 1976), control processes (Borkowski, in press), or metaprocesses (Steinberg, this volume), are currently the object of considerable attention. A growing number of researchers working in the field of cognitive development now recognize that the growth of self-regulatory mechanisms underlies many of the behavioral changes that take place with development (Brown, 1978; Brown & Deloache, 1978; Flavell, 1981; Meichenbaum, 1981). This is not the place to describe once again the diversity of functions that the self-regulatory processes can exercise in the accomplishment of a given cognitive enterprise (see, however, Sternberg, this volume, for one of the most exhaustive lists yet drawn up on the nature and functions of the control strategies). Our purpose is elsewhere: We want less to insist on the nature and content of the self-regulatory processes than on their place and function among the other components intervening in an individual's taking charge of her own functioning. In other words, we want to try to show in what way and under what conditions an individual can engage in such self-regulation in order thereby to be able to take charge of her own cognitive enterprise.

According to our model, the self-regulatory processes are primarily nourished by *metacognitive experiences* that serve as internal feedback to the individual during a cognitive enterprise. The notion of metacognitive experiences is borrowed from Flavell (1981) who defined them as being conscious experiences (ideas, thoughts, feelings, "sensations") related to any aspect of the cognitive enterprise. In Flavell's definition, the metacognitive experience, an essential component of cognitive monitoring, refers sometimes to the portion of metacognitive knowledge consciously surfacing during a cognitive enterprise, and sometimes to the conscious experiences likely to occur when, for instance, an obstacle impedes progress toward the goal. We prefer, however, to consider the metacognitive experience as *conscious internal feedback* that the individual gives herself on her manner of managing her cognitive enterprise: it lets her know the progress that she thinks she has made or is able to make toward the sought-after objective. These metacognitive experiences have a varying probability of occurrence that is jointly determined by two factors: a variable level of conscious cognitive attention and a more or less efficient activation of the metacognitive knowledge relevant to the cognitive enterprise at hand.

A. Level of Conscious Cognitive Attention.   The notion of the level of conscious cognitive attention derives from the crucial distinction introduced

duced by Langer (1978) between mindfulness and mindlessness. It seems to us essential to integrate this distinction into a functional description of self-regulation because it facilitates understanding of the conditions under which an individual can have better access to some of her cognitive processes and can thus exercise a more strict control over her cognitive functioning. According to Langer's theory of the dual way in which people may behave, *mindlessness* is the absence of active ongoing information processing, where even complex actions unfold automatically, without conscious attention, on the basis of general "scripts" rather than on the basis of new incoming information. As a result, a person may be in a position of knowing that she can perform some task, without any longer knowing how she performs it, i.e., without knowing the intermediate cognitive steps that make up the performance. Several of Langer's experiments (Chanowitz & Langer, 1980; Langer, 1978; Langer & Imber, 1980) have shown that in some situations mindlessness and, in particular, "mindlessness of ostensibly thoughtful actions" may be quite maladaptive and may result in poor cognitive performance. Since the individual, when mindless, is by definition not aware of being in this state, she does not feel the necessity of examining more closely the particulars of the ongoing situation and thus cannot evaluate if her usual mode of response is, in fact, the most appropriate one to the requirements of the present situation.

On the other hand, *mindfulness* is a cognitively active state in which a person cognitively reconstructs a situation rather than calling up a structure already constructed for it. Langer's work has shown that such an active way of processing information has numerous advantages, at least two appearing to us closely related to the processes of self-regulation. First, when mindful, the individual is able to perceive during instead of after the task, that a situation presents an element that is new or different from the ones habitually encountered; as a consequence of this, she is able to reorient the rest of her actions toward the sought-after objective (Chanowitz & Langer, 1980). Second, when mindful, the individual is in principle more able to give an adequate retrospective report about the kind of cognitive rules she applied in solving a particular problem (Langer & Imber, 1980).

As can be seen by referring to Fig. 9.1, what our model underscores first is that the level of conscious cognitive attention determines, to a large extent, the probability of occurrence of metacognitive experiences. This ties in, moreover, with the position of Flavell (1981) for whom metacognitive experiences are more likely to occur if the individual engages in a conscious form of cognition. Second, an individual's level of conscious cognitive attention at the moment she undertakes a given task seems to us largely a function of the degree of expertise that she wields in this task. Although the level of cognitive attention for a given task can be modified during the execution of that task, it seems to us important to indicate how this level can vary at the very outset. Based on Langer's work it can be assumed, first, that an individual will be mindful when she undertakes a new task in which she as yet has acquired no expertise, provided that the task is sufficiently different from those that she is used to doing so that she is not able to apply a routine sequence of behaviors. Mindfulness will also characterize the individual who already has a certain expertise in a given task but who approaches this one with the intention of improving or optimizing her performance (growing expertise). In this case, the individual is concerned with constructing more differentiated and refined behavioral categories rather than simply falling into predetermined ones (Chanowitz & Langer, 1980).

These two kinds of cognitive presence at the outset of a task each favor in varying degrees the occurrence of metacognitive experiences. This is indicated by the relative length of the bars in Fig. 9.1, which represent the probability of the occurrence of metacognitive experiences in the two cases where conscious cognitive attention is present. Note that the frequency of metacognitive experiences is likely to be lower for non-expertise than for growing expertise because, in the first case, the individual's cognitive attention is almost exclusively centered on the features and demands of the new task. This hypothesis is in agreement with Markman's (1981) analysis of the mechanisms of comprehension monitoring, where she shows that the lack of systematization and organization of information, which is typical of non-expertise in any field, makes it very difficult for a novice to generate criteria that she can use to supervise her comprehension.

The proposed model also distinguishes two cases where conscious cognitive attention is absent: automated expertise and non-involvement. The case of cognitive non-involvement, which we take up first, is more primitive and likely to arise when an individual is cognitively or affectively overloaded; but it can also simply reflect an attitude of indifference or of "I don't give a damn" when faced with a task lacking in interest or thought to be too difficult. This form of mindlessness is particularly serious because the actual self-regulation in which the individual engages is then minimal, not to say nonexistent, with the consequence that the frequency of metacognitive experiences is practically nil.

The case of automated expertise is more sophisticated and is likely to occur when an individual finds her behavior directed by a kind of "automatic pilot," which provides very little conscious internal feedback. This form of mindlessness, which is very efficient and economical in countless cognitive enterprises, in no way excludes the possibility that an individual engages in some kind of self-regulation on her cognitive functioning. Such self-regulation takes place, however, without conscious attention and makes use of cognitive and metacognitive strategies that are overlearned and predetermined rather than of strategies that are (re)constructed and (re)evaluated as the cognitive enterprise unfolds. This kind of self-regulation thus draws directly on the metacognitive knowledge accumulated by the individual without the relevant portion of the metacognitive knowledge thus activated being made conscious. Such automated regulation, if it persists throughout the cognitive enterprise, can naturally permit an individual to perform adequately in numerous situations, especially when the characteristics of the situation mirror those that she has previously encountered; but in our opinion, it cannot permit her to improve or optimize her performance by getting the most out of what is novel in the current situation. For improvement to occur it is necessary that a conscious metacognitive experience signal the individual, during or after the task, that something is wrong, for example, in her cognitive enterprise; this compels her to disconnect, so to speak, from the "automatic pilot." Self-regulation thus becomes deliberate and is exercised in a more mindful way, a feature of growing expertise. That is why the model allows for the possibility that the level of conscious cognitive attention present at the beginning of a task can be modified during or even after the execution of the task, especially in the case where the individual passes from a form of automated expertise to a form of growing expertise (indicated in Fig. 9.1 by the broken vertical arrow). It goes without saying that when the cognitive enterprise turns out to be easier or duller than anticipated, the individual can also pass from a form of growing to a form of automated expertise, or even to a form of non-involvement in the task, with a concomitant decline in the probability of occurrence of metacognitive experiences.

B. Activation of Metacognitive Knowledge.   If the level of conscious cognitive attention depends on the more or less subtle and discriminating way in which an individual orchestrates, monitors, and checks her cognitive activities, it is nevertheless the activation of the metacognitive knowledge that provides the essential knowledge base without which the self-regulatory process would only be an empty shell and in no way able to moderate competence. The operation of self-regulatory processes is fueled by information generated from existing metacognitive knowledge. During the course of a specific cognitive enterprise, relevant portions of the individual's metacognitive knowledge are activated and can serve to produce metacognitive experiences. The activation of relevant metacognitive knowledge is distinguished from the bank of available metacognitive knowledge, however, in that the former intervenes during the execution of a particular task and is limited to just that knowledge about cognition that the individual brings to bear while performing this particular task. For example, the individual can activate that portion of metacognitive knowledge concerned with the cognitive goals that she can reasonably set herself in accordance with the nature of the task demands, the end product she has in mind, and the self-knowledge she has about her own cognitive competence on this type of task. She can also activate the knowledge she has about the effect the selection of a particular goal will exercise on the decisions to be taken, about the resources to be marshalled for the task, and the metacognitive and cognitive strategies to be employed.

In the process of on-line self-regulation where an individual constantly keeps an eye on the smooth running of her cognitive enterprise, the activation of metacognitive strategies plays a crucial role. Indeed, an individual may often deliberately choose to apply metacognitive strategies with the express purpose of obtaining more accurate feedback on the working of her cognitive system. In other words, these metacognitive strategies enable the self-regulatory process to "find out" how successfully each of the strategic behaviors has been executed and to what extent the chosen strategic repertoire is compatible with the desired end product. However, effective problem solvers probably know that metacognitive strategies are not the only ones capable of supplying such feedback. Indeed, such internal feedback can also arise as a by-product of the application of cognitive strategies designed to attain the goal at hand. As Markman (1981) has pointed out in discussing comprehension monitoring, it is not always necessary to have an explicit question "Do I understand?" in order to obtain information about one's own understanding. In the process of actively attempting to understand, one can also obtain invaluable information about how well one does understand.

The crucial role that the activation of the relevant portion of existing metacognitive knowledge appears to us to exert on effective self-regulation is still in need of careful experimental support. The only empirical evidence we have to date stems from research on the relationship between the knowledge of memory strategies (metamemory) with, on the one hand, the spontaneous use of these strategies in an actual memory task (e.g., Cavanaugh & Borkowski, 1980; Moynahan, 1973; Salatas & Flavell, 1976) and, on the other hand, with the maintenance of a trained mnemonic strategy (e.g., Cavanaugh & Borkowski, 1979). Although some of these studies have yielded low to moderate correlations between metamemory and memory, others (e.g., Paris, Newman, & McVey, 1981; Salatas-Waters, 1982; Wimmer & Tornquist, 1980) have suggested that metamemory is related to the acquisition of new cognitive skills as well as to the effective use of already existing ones. Also, these studies have just been done with elementary age children, and recent research (Salatas-Waters, 1982) seems to indicate that the relationship between metamemory and memory is much stronger in later school years. Future research on the conditions under which existing metacognitive knowledge can be optimally activated for improved self-regulation and performance should thus take into account the importance of developmental level.

To sum up, the activation of relevant metacognitive knowledge in some sense supplies content to the process of self-regulation. The number of metacognitive experiences depends on the richness and degree of organization of the activated metacognitive knowledge as well as on the adequacy and depth of the activation itself. These experiences provide the individual with differentially valid and informative internal feedback and are capable in turn of leading her to activate new portions of relevant metacognitive knowledge. These metacognitive experiences thus constitute a fundamental factor in the process of self-regulation and are just as much in dynamic interaction with the individual's level of cognitive attention as with her activation of the metacognitive knowledge relevant to the task. Metacognitive experience — whether it is actively elicited by the individual's application of appropriate cognitive or metacognitive strategies or whether it results from a "triggering event" that alerts her to a failure of comprehension — is a kind of monitoring mechanism that renders conscious what Anderson (1980) has called in a reading task "the clicks of comprehension and clunks of comprehension failure" (p. 496). Metacognitive experience also permits an individual to have conscious access, at least in part, to the on-line self-regulatory processes. It provides information on a regular basis about her progress on the cognitive enterprise and her chances of attaining the sought-after objective in such a way that she can eventually decide to alter the degree of conscious cognitive attention she gives the task, decide to activate and use some debugging or compensatory strategies if required, or even decide to redefine the initially sought-after objectives.

Outcome of the Cognitive Enterprise

Finally, metacognitive experience fulfills a function that appears to us particularly fundamental by permitting an individual to improve her cognitive functioning from one cognitive enterprise to another. The fact that an individual can have access to internal feedback that supplies information, bit by bit, on her way of managing a cognitive enterprise permits her to compare this internal feedback with the external feedback furnished by the outcome or final result of the enterprise. Whether this external feedback is furnished by the result on a critical task given to the individual (e.g., verbatim recall in a poetry examination) or generated by the individual herself (e.g., success in raising a bonsai plant after having read an article on the subject), it obviously constitutes the final control on the efficiency of a cognitive enterprise (if one wants to avoid an infinite regression). The external feedback points up whether the cognitive actions used to attain the sought-after goal have ended in failure or have instead resulted in a minimally adequate or even outright optimal performance. In confronting this external feedback with the internal feedback picked up while working on the task, the individual can also, in some sense, validate her internal feedback and learn to discriminate what kind of internal feedback provides the most exact information on her chances of achieving the sought-after objective. Besides, if the individual is mindful enough to take note of the type of co-occurrence between the two sources of feedback, she is then able to enrich her metacognitive knowledge with new information concerning, for example, the conditions under which a particular strategy is more or less adapted to a task, given the sought-after objectives and the characteristics of the persons involved. As illustrated in the model of Fig. 9.1, there is a reverse effect from the on-line self-regulation to the available metacognitive knowledge; this enables the individual to enrich her knowledge with the information that she has extracted from the internal and external feedback by increasing her knowledge of the positive and negative factors that mediate the acquisition and utilization of her intellectual competence.

One last remark of a more general nature on the model as a whole that has just been presented. Although our description of the way in which and the conditions under which an individual can engage in self-regulation of her cognitive functioning accords an important place to conscious forms of cognition, we are not necessarily claiming that all aspects of self-regulatory processes should always be executed in a deliberate and conscious manner. Without pretending to provide a definite response to this complex issue, we find it necessary to make a distinction between deliberate conscious intervention of self-regulatory processes and self-regulatory processes that go on below the level of consciousness. As Brown (1981) has emphasized, the on-line application of control processes such as monitoring, selecting, inferring, and so forth, seldom gives rise to a conscious experience, particularly when the problem solving proceeds smoothly. The automated forms of cognitive monitoring (that might have required conscious cognitive attention when first acquired, a possibility which could be verified in developmental studies) must, however, be de-automated in numerous situations where the usual response modes turn out to be insufficient to deal adequately or optimally with the problems encountered or the objectives pursued. Metacognitive experience thus permits the individual to have conscious access to a part of her on-line self-regulatory processes and obtain feedback on the operation of her cognitive system. What our model mainly emphasizes is that the individual has a variety of deliberate tactics at her disposal that she must learn to take advantage of in order to exercise planned-out control of her cognitive enterprises and to manage the development of cognitive competence. She can thereby deliberately increase the probability of occurrence of metacognitive experiences if, instead of simply waiting for some impediment that will block her progress, she actively creates these experiences either by giving conscious attention to the distinctive characteristics of the situation or by deliberately applying strategies that she knows will yield an internal feedback. In the same fashion, the knowledge about cognition that the individual brings to bear while performing a given task, even though it can be activated automatically without entering consciousness, can also be made conscious by the individual when required. The individual can also learn to make more and more explicit and statable the knowledge she has on the positive and negative factors that effect her performance and deliberately increase this knowledge from one cognitive enterprise to another.

Whether or not one requires explicit knowledge about the rules, strategies, or goals required for efficient performance thus appears to us to be an extremely powerful moderator of competence. As Brown (1982) has emphasized, people who are not aware of their own limitations or strengths or of their own strategic repertoire can hardly be expected to apply strategies flexibly or to capitalize on the resources available to them. We are inclined to think that in the course of development, an individual comes to gain, bit by bit, more conscious access to her metacognitive knowledge, that is, comes to understand more explicitly aspects of the self-regulatory processes she already uses implicitly. This hypothesis agrees perfectly with one of the laws of cognitive development formulated a long time ago by Vygotsky (1934/1962), according to which consciousness and control of the intellectual functions appear only at a late stage in development after these functions have been used and practiced unconsciously and spontaneously. According to Vygotsky, the development of knowledge would thus be marked by gradual increases in conscious control and deliberate exploitation of that knowledge. We believe, however, that such a development can be furthered by teaching both children and adults to get to know the mechanisms of self-regulation that they have at their disposal and the ways that they can deliberately intervene in their cognitive functioning. If we could help them to acquire an explicit knowledge of the components (and their interaction) that affect their cognitive enterprises, they would then become more capable of taking advantage of, controlling, and augmenting their intellectual resources.

CONCLUSION

In conclusion, we would like to say that the proposed model, which we are the first to recognize is still very sketchy and highly speculative, seems to us, nevertheless, to have a certain heuristic value in suggesting directions that research could take in the field.

It is obvious, first of all, that this model must be supplemented by research bearing directly on the developmental dimension of an individual's taking charge of her cognitive functioning. We freely acknowledge that in its current form this model seems to apply more to mature individuals and skilled problem solvers than to children or novices. We believe, however, that it can serve to generate new hypotheses on the way that metacognitive knowledge develops and is organized as well as on the origins and evolution of the processes of self-regulation from childhood to adulthood; but before being able to trace the steps marking the development of an individual's taking charge, it seemed to us necessary to try first to establish the essential components of the model on a more solid empirical basis. This led us to undertake our first studies on adults, where one can at least assume that they already possess the cognitive resources necessary to take charge of their cognitive functioning. The establishment of what might be called an "adult norm," which seems to us a pre-requisite to the study of the growth process itself, already raises a great many problems of a theoretical and technical nature that still require much research.

First, as to the metacognitive knowledge, we have started to study, with adults, certain technical and methodological problems such as the structure and content of questionnaires bearing on this knowledge, the analysis and categorization of cognitive and metacognitive strategies evoked by subjects during text comprehension, and so forth. Among the theoretical problems that we have begun to attack, suffice it to mention here the main ones: the conditions under which the metacognitive knowledge relevant to a given task may best be activated and may result in increased self-regulation and per-formance; the combined influence exerted on the utilization of one or an-other cognitive or metacognitive strategy by the objective that an individual sets herself and by the level of explicitness of the criterial task that is given to her; the influence exerted by the type of cognitive or metacognitive strategies that an individual knows and can explicitly identify on the kind of strategies that she activates and actually applies in a given task, and so on.

Second, as to the processes of on-line self-regulation, some of the prob-lems raised by the choice of methods to study these processes appear to us to deserve particular attention: the validity of the concurrent reports of subjects on the strategies employed, the relation between the content of these reports and the strategies actually used by subjects, the methods applied to the analy-sis of these reports and to the analysis of the strategies employed, and so forth. The fundamental theoretical questions that need to be studied in order to try to empirically validate the proposed model of self-regulatory processes seem to us as numerous as they are varied. For example, there is the study of the relations between self-regulation and performance by experimental ma-nipulation of the components' "conscious cognitive presence" and "activa-tion of relevant knowledge"; there is the operationalization of the notion of metacognitive experience; there is the analysis of the relations between the nature and the occurrence of metacognitive experiences, the level of cognitive presence, and the type of activation of metacognitive knowledge; there is the study of the relation between the internal feedback supplied by metacognitive experience and the external feedback furnished by the outcome of the cogni-tive enterprise; there is the identification of the conditions under which a cog-nitive enterprise, in order to be more or less adequate or optimal, can be exe-cuted on automatic pilot or must be accompanied by conscious cognitive attention; and so forth.

Once research provides at least elements of a response to these questions on the nature and functioning of an individual's taking charge of her cogni-tive activities, it will then be possible to tackle the crucial question of the de-velopment of this taking charge and, to determine, for example, the origins, the primitive forms (see, for example, the recent analysis proposed by Kopp, 1982, on the antecedents of self-regulation in early infancy), and the changes it undergoes in the course of evolution, and so on. It will then also be possible in a more applied domain to use these data as guidelines in the conception and eventual implantation of a systematic training program of metacognitive skills from elementary school through university. This project (which has also been suggested by Flavell, 1981, and Meichenbaum, 1980) is ambitious, but it is worthwhile to envision if we hope one day to check the current tendency in education to settle for the acquisition of minimal skills rather than resolutely to pursue the quest for the "outer limits of educability" (Fletcher, 1978).

ACKNOWLEDGMENTS

Preparation of this manuscript was supported in part by a team grant to the authors from the Ministère de l'Education of the Province de Québec (FCAC). Grateful aknowledgment goes to Dr. George Baylor who helped in the translation from French to English.

REFERENCES

Anderson, T. H. (1980). Study strategies and adjunct aids. In R. J. Spiro, B. C., Bruce, W. F. Brewer (Eds.), *Theoretical issues in reading comprehension*. Hillsdale, NJ: Lawrence Erlbaum Associates.

Baker, L., & Brown, A. L. (1984). Metacognitive skills and reading. In T. D. Pearson (Ed.), *Handbook of reading research*. New York: Longman.

Bandura, A. (1977). Self-efficacy: Toward a unifying theory of behavioral change. *Psychological Review, 84,* 191–215.

Bandura, A. (1980). Gauging the relationship between self-efficacy judgment and action. *Cognitive Therapy and Research, 4,* 263–268.

Borkowski, J. G. (in press). Signs of intelligence: strategy generalization and metacognition. In S. Yussen (Ed.), *Growth of insight*. New York: Academic Press.

Brown, A. L. (1978). Knowing when, where, and how to remember: A problem of metacognition. In R. Glaser (Ed.), *Advances in instructional psychology*. Hillsdale, NJ: Lawrence Erlbaum Associates.

Brown, A. L. (1981). Metacognitive development and reading. In R. J. Spiro, B. C. Bruce, W. F. Brewer (Eds.), *Theoretical issues in reading comprehension*. Hillsdale, NJ: Lawrence Erlbaum Associates.

Brown, A. L. (1982). Learning and development: The problems of compatibility, access and induction. *Human Development, 25,* 89–115.

Brown, A. L., & Deloache, J. S. (1978). Skills, plans and self-regulation. In R. S. Siegler (Ed.), *Children's thinking: What develops?* Hillsdale, NJ: Lawrence Erlbaum Associates.

Campione, J. C., & Brown, A. L. (1978). Toward a theory of intelligence: Contributions from research with retarded children. *Intelligence, 2,* 279–304.

Cavanaugh, J. C., & Borkowski, J. G. (1979). The metamemory-memory connection: Effects of strategy training and maintenance. *The Journal of General Psychology, 101,* 161–174.

Cavanaugh, J. C., & Borkowski, J. G. (1980). Searching for metamemory-memory connections: A developmental study. *Developmental Psychology, 16,* 441–453.

Cavanaugh, J. C., & Perlmutter, M. (1982). Metamemory: A critical examination. *Child Development, 53,* 11–28.

Chanowitz, B., & Langer, E. (1980). Knowing more (or less) than you can show: Understanding control through the mindlessness-mindfulness distinction. In J. Garber & M. E. P. Seligman (Eds.), *Human helplessness: Theory and application.* New York: Academic Press.

Chomsky, N. (1965). *Aspects of the theory of syntax.* Cambridge, MA: MIT Press.

Chomsky, N. (1979). A propos des structures cognitives et de leur développement. In M. Piatelli-Palmarini (Ed.), *Théories du langage, théories de l'apprentissage (le débat entre Piaget et Chomsky).* Paris: Editions du Seuil.

Diener, C. I., & Dweck, C. S. (1978). An analysis of learned helplessness: Continuous changes in performance, strategy, and achievement cognitions following failure. *Journal of Personality and Social Psychology, 36,* 451–462.

Flavell, J. H. (1981). Cognitive monitoring. In W. P. Dickson (Ed.), *Children's oral communication skills.* New York: Academic Press.

Flavell, J. H., & Wohlwill, J. F. (1969). Formal and functional aspects of cognitive development. In D. Elkind & J. H. Flavell (Eds.), *Studies in cognitive development.* New York: Oxford University Press.

Fletcher, J. L. (1978). The outer limits of human educability: A proposed research program. *Educational Researcher,* 13–18.

Gagne, R. M. (1968). Contributions of learning to human development. *Psychological Review, 75,* 177–191.

Henshaw, D. (1978). *A cognitive analysis of creative problem solving.* Unpublished doctoral dissertation, University of Waterloo, Ontario.

Kobasigawa, A., Ransom, C., & Holland, C. J. (1980). Children's knowledge about skimming. *Alberta Journal of Educational Research, 26,* 169–182.

Kopp, C. B. (1982). Antecedents of self-regulation: A developmental perspective. *Developmental Psychology, 18,* 199–214.

Kreutzer, M. A., Leonard, C., & Flavell, J. H. (1975). An interview study of children's knowledge about memory. *Monographs of the Society for Research in Child Development, 40,* serial no. 159.

Kurdek, L. A., & Burt, C. W. (1981). First-through sixth-grade children's metacognitive skills: Generality and cognitive correlates. *Merrill-Palmer Quarterly, 27,* 287–305.

Langer, E. J. (1978). Rethinking the role of thought in social interaction. In J. H. Harvey, W. J. Ickes, & R. F. Kiddo (Eds.), *New directions in attributional research* (Vol. 2). Hillsdale, NJ: Lawrence Erlbaum Associates.

Langer, E. J., & Imber, L. G. (1980). When practice makes imperfect: Debilitating effects of overlearning. *Journal of Personality and Social Psychology, 37,* 2014–2024.

Lefebvre-Pinard, M. (1980). Existe-t-il des changements cognitifs chez l'adulte? *Revue québécoise de Psychologie, 2,* 58–69.

Lefebvre-Pinard, M. (1983). Understanding and auto-control of cognitive function: Implications for the relationship between cognition and behavior. *International Journal of Behavioral Development, 6,* 15–35.

Markman, E. (1981). Comprehension monitoring. In W. P. Dickson (Ed.), *Children's oral communication skills.* New York: Academic Press.

Meichenbaum, D. (1980, October). *Teaching thinking: A cognitive-behavioural perspective.* Paper presented at the NIE-LRDC Conference on Thinking and learning skills, Pittsburgh.

Meichenbaum, D. (1981). A cognitive-behavioral perspective of intelligence. *Intelligence, 4,* 271–284.

Meichenbaum, D., & Asarnow, J. (1979). Cognitive behavior modification and metacognitive development: Implications for the classroom. In P. Kendall & S. Hollon (Eds.), *Cognitive-*

behavior interventions: Theory, research and procedures. New York: Academic Press.

Meichenbaum, D., Burland, S., Gruson, L., & Cameron, R. (in press). Metacognitive assessment. In S. Yussen (Ed.), *Growth of insight.* New York: Academic Press.

Miller, P. H., & Bigi, L. (1979). The development of children's understanding of attention. *Merrill-Palmer Quarterly, 25,* 235–250.

Monod, J. (1979). Intervention dans la discussion ayant suivi la présentation de J. Piaget: Schèmes d'action et apprentissage du langage. In M. Piatelli-Palmarini (Ed.), *Théories du langage, théories de l'apprentissage (le débat entre Piaget et Chomsky).* Paris: Editions du Seuil.

Moynahan, E. D. (1973). The development of knowledge concerning the effect of categorization upon free recall. *Child Development, 44,* 238–246.

Myers, M., & Paris, S. G. (1978). Children's metacognitive knowledge about reading. *Journal of Educational Psychology, 70,* 680–690.

Neisser, U. (1967). *Cognitive psychology.* New York: Appleton-Century-Crofts.

Newell, A., & Simon, H. A. (1972). *Human problem solving.* Englewood Cliffs, NJ: Prentice-Hall.

Paris, S. G., Newman, R. S., McVey, K. A. (1981, April). *Learning the functional significance of mnemonic actions.* Paper presented at the biennial meeting of the Society for Research in Child Development. Boston.

Pascual-Leone, J. (1980). Constructive problems for constructive theories: The current relevance of Piaget's work and a critique of information-processing simulation psychology. In H. Spada & K. Kluwe (Eds.), *Developmental models of thinking.* New York: Academic Press.

Piaget, J. (1957). Logique et équilibre dans les comportements du sujet. In L. Apostel, B. Mandelbrot, & J. Piaget (Eds.), *Etudes d'épistémologie génétique: Vol. 2. Logique et équilibre.* Paris: Presses Universitaires de France.

Pinard, A. (1981). *The conservation of conservation.* Chicago: University of Chicago Press.

Pinard, A., & Chasse, G. (1977). Pseudoconservation of the volume and surface of a solid object. *Child Development, 48,* 1559–1566.

Pinard, A., & Laurendeau, M. (1969). "Stage" in Piaget's cognitive development theory: Exegesis of a concept. In D. Elkind & J. H. Flavell (Eds.), *Studies in cognitive development.* New York: Oxford University Press.

Premack, D. (1979). Intervention dans la discussion ayant suivi la présentation de J. Piaget: Schèmes d'action et apprentissage du langage. In M. Piatelli-Palmarini (Ed.), *Théories du langage, théories de l'apprentissage (le débat entre Piaget et Chomsky).* Paris: Editions du Seuil.

Salatas, H., & Flavell, J. H. (1976). Behavioral and metamnemonic indicators of strategic behaviors under remember instructions in first grade. *Child Development, 47,* 81–89.

Salatas-Waters, H. (1982). Memory development in adolescence: Relationships between metamemory, strategy use, and performance. *Journal of Experimental Child Psychology, 33,* 183–195.

Siegler, R. S. (1981). Developmental sequences within and between concepts. *Monographs of the Society for Research in Child Development, 46* (serial no. 2).

Simon, H. A. (1980). Problem solving and education. In D. T. Tuma & F. Reif (Eds.), *Problem solving and education: Issues in teaching and research.* Hillsdale, NJ: Lawrence Erlbaum Associates.

Vygotsky, L. S. (1962). *Thought and language* (E. Hanfman & G. Vakar, Eds. and Trans.). Cambridge, MA: MIT Press. (Originally published, 1934)

Wimmer, H., & Tornquist, K. (1980). The role of metamemory and metamemory activation in the development of mnemonic performance. *International Journal of Behavioral Development, 3,* 71–81.

Author Index

Page numbers in *italics* show where complete bibliographic references are given.

Subject Index

DATE DUE